To
ELAYNE
with very sincere

friendship,

Hazel Kleffin.

12. February 1984.

CULTURE OF COMPASSION

The Spirit of Polish Jewry
from Hasidism to the Holocaust

CULTURE OF COMPASSION

The Spirit of Polish Jewry
from Hasidism to the Holocaust

By

HESZEL KLEPFISZ

Translated from the Yiddish
with an Introduction by

CURT LEVIANT

KTAV PUBLISHING HOUSE, INC.
NEW YORK

Library of Congress Cataloging in Publication Data

Klépfisz, Hészel.
  Culture of compassion.

  1. Hasidism—History—Addresses, essays, lectures.
2. Judaism—Poland—History—Addresses, essays,
lectures. I. Title.
BM198.K58 1983   296'.09438   83-13626
ISBN 0-88125-037-6

Manufactured in the United States of America

To the memory of
my father, mother,
brother, sister, and wife,
who perished in the Holocaust

Table of Contents

Introduction

Heszel Klepfisz, rabbi, author, university professor, and communal leader, exemplifies—very much akin to his medieval Spanish Jewish predecessors—the itinerant Jewish scholar in history. Like his spiritual forebears, who through the exigencies of fate were plucked from their native land and went into exile, he too has carried on his work undaunted. And with the leading personalities of the Golden Age of Spanish Jewry and the equally Golden Age of Polish Jewry, Professor Klepfisz is a Renaissance man of Jewish scholarship, combining a mastery of the secular and religious traditions. At home in the culture of the West, and nurtured by millennia of Jewish learning, he fuses these traditions and mirrors one in the frame of the other.

It is perhaps a curio of destiny that the author, a Yiddish-speaking Jew from Poland, found haven in a Spanish-speaking land in Central America. Professor Klepfisz has lived in Panama for much of the post–World War II period, and has been instrumental in bringing Jewish education and knowledge to both Jews and non-Jews in that land as professor at the university, director of a Jewish institute of learning, and leader of his community. But creating a book whose scope covers Holocaust and Hasidism, Polish Jewry and European culture and politics, the Jewish luminaries of Spain, and the shapers of the modern Yiddish and Hebrew belletristic tradition, could only have been accomplished by an individual whose cultural arena was formed at a particular time and in a particular place.

Such a scope, with its at-homeness with Marx and Dostoevsky as well as the gamut of Jewish thought, could only have come from a Polish Jew raised in a home where the light of secular studies was not muted at the expense of religious training. For we know very well that in Jewish pietist circles any learning not directly related to Torah/Talmud study is forbidden.

Heszel Klepfisz, however, was fortunate—and we in turn stand in his debt—that in his home (see the essay "My Father") all learning was welcome, and from an early age he absorbed and shared his erudition with others. His ability to integrate, to conceptualize, and, ultimately, to enlighten us, is a direct result of this early training and openness to the manifold cultures of Jewish Poland and gentile Europe. Aside from Poland or Russia in the early twentieth century, I doubt that there has ever been a place (certainly it doesn't hold true either in New York or Jerusalem of today) where one could have been the scion of rabbis, received a yeshiva education, and concomitantly read Haskalah Hebrew writings and secular European literature, an enviable three-pronged system of learning. Such is the cultural arena I have referred to of particular time and place.

The contents of *Culture of Compassion* are variegated, the styles diverse. Nevertheless, a single thread, a common theme, runs through the essays, which first appeared in various Yiddish journals. The opening piece, a philosophical dialogue with overtones of fiction and drama, reveals the intricacies of a sensitive and creative mind. In an imaginative leap, the author fuses the tragedy of Hasdai Crescas, who lost his son in a murderous pogrom in 1391 in Spain, with his own anguish some 550 years later. In this imagined encounter between a fourteenth-century Sephardic thinker and a twentieth-century Ashkenazic thinker, the author conjures up Crescas as a living, breathing human being. But this philosophical dialogue is not merely a simplistic comparison of suffering. Woven into the personal reminiscences are citations from Crescas's works and troubling questions, heavy with Akedah overtone. The author leaves us puzzling over justification of the divine decree in the annihilation of European Jewry, including his own beloved family, lost in the murderous German fury.

In *Culture of Compassion* are articles on Spanish Jewry, studies of various Hasidic courts, essays on aspects of Yiddishkeyt, and intimate portraits of a town and individuals. The diverse styles reflect the contents—objective and formal, imaginative and daring, and intimate, personal, and loving.

With diverse content and its corollary, diverse style, comes the theme that informs the entire work: the Jewish way throughout the ages, whether in medieval Spain or eighteenth-to twentieth-century Poland, inextricably linked with Jewish learning, culture, and compassion—indeed the culture of compassion of the title. For no matter how far removed the Middle Ages are from modern times, and no matter how wide the gap may be between Spanish Jewry of the Golden Age and the Jews of Poland, the essential Yiddishkeyt that radiated out of all of these Jewries is the common light that shines from this book. If Hasidism may be chosen as representative, one notes that this gap may be more apparent than real. That Hasidism is steeped in the kabbalistic thought propounded by the Sephardic mystics is but one of the links that binds Spain and Ashkenaz.

Nearly one-third of *Culture of Compassion* is devoted to various aspects of Hasidism and the specific nuances of each court or subgroup within it. With the popularization of this seminal movement, many people have received a kind of kindergarten tutelage in the subject. In fact, ask anyone and they will gladly sum up Hasidism while standing on one leg: joy in prayer, dancing and singing. Here, however, the interested reader will discover the true, the authentic spirit of Hasidism; he will discover the subtle soul difference between one Hasidic school of thought and another, between one rebbe and another. In tackling the spirit of Ger, Kotzk, and Pshishkhe, Professor Klepfisz has probed some of the most difficult and intriguing teachings and teachers of Hasidism.

The essay "The Spiritual Culture of Polish Jewry" can be considered a paradigm for the author's entire attempt and accomplishment. This all-encompassing evaluation is really a miniature history of Polish Jewry. Here again only a master of both the secular and the religious culture could have written the study and made it one seamless entity. A Talmud scholar might have been able to trace the development of talmudic and religious thought and commentaries; a secular cultural historian could have written about Yiddish and Hebrew literature and the arts. But only a man of deep-rooted Jewish letters, in the broadest sense of the term, could have written about the overall history of the Jews, their Torah study and mysticism and religious movements on the one hand, and Haskalah and modern Hebrew and Yiddish literature on the other. Professor Klepfisz has an extraordinary grasp of the inner dynamics and rhythms of Polish Jewish culture, for he was part of it. With specific examples, he shows us how this age-old Jewish civilization shaped the thoughts and creativity of those who moved thousands of miles away but never really left their spiritual home (among others he cites the noted Yiddish novelist and short-story writer, Joseph Opatoshu).

From the broad canvas of Polish Jewry presented in one rich, intense essay, Professor Klepfisz moves to an intimate portrait, a miniature one might say, in his loving tribute to the late, great scholar and professor of Jewish studies at Brandeis University, Simon Rawidowicz. With the verisimilitude of a fictionist—the same qualities evident in "Rabbi Hasdai Crescas in Conversation with a Polish Jew"—Klepfisz depicts his friendship with Rawidowicz, offers a memoirist's portrait of the man, and at the same time succinctly presents Rawidowicz's views of Jewish history and civilization.

A similar depiction, combining the personal with a broader and more objective sweep, may be seen in the remembrance "Zhirardov: A Jewish Shtetl in Central Poland," a cultural canvas of Professor Heszel Klepfisz's hometown. The same intimacy juxtaposed with a sociohistoric approach is evident. The author recreates for us (and this essay should be read in conjunction with "My Father") a period of history, an ambience that is no more. Note the various personalities that make up the town, the conflicting ideologies, the influence of the big city. Once again the sure touch of a creative writer's ability to vividly depict a certain time and place comes to the fore.

In "Zhirardov: A Jewish Shtetl in Central Poland" Heszel Klepfisz states that he has prayed in many shuls since he left the shtetl, "but I was never permeated with the holy shudder of great expectation as I was in that half-dark, ecstatic Ger *shtiebl* [prayer-room] in Zhirardov with its many wax-dripping candles that gaze down at me from a misty Yom Kippur of my childhood." A fellow countryman of Professor Klepfisz, a man who also left his native land and made his fame in another land, and another culture, a writer named Joseph Conrad, wrote in the preface to one of his great novels that the prime mission of the artist is to "make you see." With his multi-hued essays, thoughts, and remembrances, Dr. Heszel Klepfisz indeed makes us see—a world that the Hamans of this earth succeeded in destroying physically, but one whose spirit is indestructible. Just how ineffable and indestructible this spirit is may be seen again and again in this volume. Thanks to Heszel Klepfisz the life of that spirit has been renewed in *Culture of Compassion*.

1

Rabbi Hasdai Crescas in Conversation with a Polish Jew

I

I AM FREQUENTLY visited by figures from the distant past of Spanish Jewry—perhaps because I have lived in a Spanish-speaking country for the last few decades, and perhaps because my desk is strewn with books dealing with Jewish creativity in medieval Spain. Sometimes these personages say nothing; they just stand there, observing me silently as I turn the pages of their books, attempting to analyze their philosophic systems or study stanzas of their poetry.

On occasion, however, they engage me in conversation. I have become so accustomed to these visits that I consider them quite real. I am afraid to admit that often they are more real to me than the daily reality in which I am usually enmeshed. The borderline between fantasy and reality has been eradicated, and I recognize my visitors as soon as they slip into my room.

Few pictures exist of our prominent personalities of the Spanish-Jewish past; nevertheless, I have no difficulty in recognizing them. Their faces seem remarkably familiar, and there is no need at all for them to introduce themselves. I know them by the expression on their faces and by the look in their eyes. I recognize Abraham ibn Ezra by the touching, clever little spark that flashes in one eye while the other is half-closed; and I know that Rabbi Moses ben Nachman (Nachmanides) is before

1

me when I'm encompassed by a glance that seems to come
from far away. The face of Don Isaac Abarbanel is furrowed
with deep lines reminiscent of old parchment.

But sunrays surround me when I see the figure of Samuel ha-
Nagid, who bubbles with so much natural joy of life. Judah al-
Harizi always comes to me with a mocking smile. And Moses
de Leon dashes in with a quick, impulsive, stormy melody
which shakes one's soul and then melts into a dreamy religious
ecstasy. Recently, when I asked Moses de Leon about the
source of that transition in the melody which flows out of his
soul, that transition from tempest to tenderness, he answered
curtly: "From the Temple of Mystery."

I can even recognize my visitors by the sound of their voices.
For instance, I have learned to distinguish between the con-
sumptively hoarse voice of Solomon ibn Gabirol and the soft,
lyrical voice of Moses ibn Ezra.

Lately, I've had the opportunity of talking with Rabbi Hasdai
Crescas. On that day I just happened to pick up his book, *The
Light of God*. I had also been reading an appreciation of Crescas
by Joseph Jabez, a contemporary who lived at the end of the
fifteenth century who was also a refugee of the Expulsion from
Spain.

"The intellect of Rabbi Hasdai," writes Joseph Jabez, "surpassed that of all the philosophers of his time. He outstripped
the philosophers of Edom and Ishmael—that is to say, the
Christian and Moslem philosophers—and he was surely head
and shoulders above his fellow Jewish thinkers." I had also
read in Israel Zinberg's *History of Jewish Literature* the comments
of Solomon Dafiera, a fellow townsman of Rabbi Hasdai,
concerning Crescas's personality: "The anointed angel!" he
writes. "The Holy Ark with the Ten Commandments!"

Crescas and I began to talk about our respective hometowns.
He recalled Saragossa with an abundance of feeling. He spoke
of the distinguished lineage of the Jewish community which
flourished in that city. Jewish Saragossa had a plethora of
Jewish initiative and overflowed with Torah and wisdom. Jews
there climbed the ladder of success in various fields. They

developed commerce and also devoted themselves to matters of the spirit. Three hundred years before Crescas, Rabbi Bachya ibn Pakuda lived and preached there. In Saragossa Bachya wrote his book, *The Duties of the Heart,* which continuously inspired later generations with its moving challenge to reawaken noble Jewish virtures. Jews felt so well integrated in Saragossa, Crescas added, that the wealthy head of the community, Benveniste de la Caballeria, would put his signature on the national bank notes in Hebrew.

I spoke to him about Warsaw, where I grew up. I told him that no matter how amazed I was at the flourishing community in Saragossa, Jewish life pulsated and sparkled even more in Warsaw. There one could actually feel Jewishness. Not only was the home Jewish, but the street as well. A popular, mass Jewishness throbbed in Warsaw, the like of which surely could not have been seen in Saragossa. I told him about the Warsaw periodicals issued in Yiddish, Hebrew, and Polish. There people drank with unquenchable thirst from the fountains of the Jewish spirit.

If the remark of Judah Halevi, "Do not be seduced by the un-Jewish Greek philosophy, for it has only flowers but no fruit," was valid anywhere, it was applicable to Polish Jewry. The vast majority of Jews in Poland sought to nourish themselves with Jewishness at a time when a feverish unrest tore at the viscera of Poland.

"Perhaps," I admitted, "the Jews of Warsaw did not have the enchanting and external majestic splendor that marked the Jewish community of Saragossa. But once more I'll refer to a verse of Judah Halevi, the poet of Toledo, whom you no doubt feel close to: 'Let us look to the heart and not to the eye.' The special attributes of the Warsaw Jews did not reveal themselves to the eye. But they were revealed to the heart. Warsaw Jews could assert what the Jewish scholar declared to the king of the Khazars in Judah Halevi's *Kuzari*: 'Although we comprise scattered bones, our spirit has remained alive.' "

Rabbi Hasdai Crescas listened with interest. I continued:

"More than any other community in Jewish history, we in

Poland held that tradition had, and must have, a very important and indeed crucial place in the life of the individual and
the community at large. And this major point is convincingly
developed in the *Kuzari*. Tradition is the path that leads from
man to man; it also leads to oneself. Tradition is an ethical
experience, the product of a long historical development. It is
therefore a national experience. We Jews became what we are
because of the tradition transmitted from generation to generation. A millennium-long tradition, remarkably rich and multi-
hued, lived and breathed among Polish Jewry with magnificent intensity. I dare say that it was in the daily hustle and
bustle of the Polish Jews and in their magnificent Sabbaths and
holidays that the religious tradition became versatile and deep
and assumed those wonderful aspects which Judah Halevi
described in his poetic-philosophic vision."

II

THEN WE BOTH began to reminisce. Hasdai Crescas told me
about his young son who died in the bloody anti-Jewish riots.
"It happened in 1391, before we moved to Saragossa," he said
with a broken voice. "My family and I then lived in Barcelona.
Actually, the incitement against the Jews flared up in Seville,
but the wild flames spread quickly to town and village. In
Barcelona we witnessed a horrible slaughter. My son was
scarcely twenty years old. In the letter I sent to the Jewish
community in Avignon, I indited the lament of a father who
had to mourn for his son," Crescas sighed.

For a long while he remained silent, as though he had
descended to the abyss of his grief. His anguish seemed to be
outlined on his gray beard. Then he continued: "This is what I
wrote to our brethren in Avignon: 'Many people sanctified
God's name, among them my young only son, who was
engaged to be married. . . He was a sacrifice that I brought.
And I will justify the heavenly decree.' "

"Did you say justify, Rabbi Hasdai?" I interrupted.

I strained to meet his glance—but in vain. He stared off into
space. "The Jewish path throughout the generations," he said,

"began with the Binding of Isaac. Open the Bible to Genesis. Abraham received the divine call and was prepared to do the deed which later in our history was termed *Kiddush Hashem*— Santification of God's Holy Name. However, the truth is that on Mount Moriah the Binding remained but a trial, a test. Nevertheless, it pointed the way. I say 'way' and not 'fate.' Take a look at my book here and you can read once more my views about this matter."

At that moment he apparently felt strongly that he had to convince me. Both of us turned the pages. It seemed to me that our fingers fused.

"Look!" He guided my hand over the text. "Consider what's being said here. I believe in the conscious path of the individual and the community. These things don't happen because of ostensible predetermination. It is *we* who make the decision. If we want to be honest with ourselves, we must admit that we wanted that ancient trial to shape our national personality. It was *our* desire that we shape ourselves in this fashion and not in any other. So, then, there can be no room for bitterness or protest."

But I refuted his contention, saying, "Your assertion is only partially correct. Side by side with the Hebrew word *Hineini*— 'Here I am, Lord, ready to do your bidding'—which generations of Jews said when they, like Abraham, were face to face with the drama of anguish, there was triggered the 'why,' and the great complaint rose up like a storm. Jewish history, in effect, is unraveled between the *Hineini* and the 'why.' In the Second Psalm we already pose this demanding question: 'Why are the nations in an uproar?' Why do they rage against us? . . . When the Romans beset us with their evil decrees, not only the teachers of Judaism but also, according to the Talmud, the metaphysical forces of the universe shook heaven and earth with their despairing cry: 'Is this the reward for preserving the Torah? O God, is this the way you repay your faithful?'

"East European Jewry did not produce Marranos, as did Spanish Jewry. But still, we did not want to justify the bitter decree under any circumstances. And not only in my time.

During the Massacres of 1648 Jews also asked awesome questions. The anger between man and God intensified with the teachers of Hasidism. Reb Levi Yitzchok of Berditchev did not want to justify spilled Jewish blood. He summoned God to a *din Torah*, a rabbinic judgment. In the midst of the Day of Judgment he brought God to court. And on Tisha B'Av, the Ninth of Av, when we commemorate the destruction of the Temple in 70 C.E., Rabbi Pinchas of Koretz threatened heaven from the pulpit. Later they were reconciled, but they never ceased to rage.

"It's particularly hard for me to swallow your justification, Rabbi Hasdai. I am going to read to you the remarks of Don Isaac Abarbanel describing the tragic final path of the Jews of Saragossa and Toledo, of Malaga and Granada: 'I saw the children of Israel in despair and hopelessness. I saw them scattered over the mountains.' Can you justify this?

"Terrible questions reverberated in the death camps, where my parents perished to the notes of *Ani Ma'amin*, 'I Believe.' There, at the outbreak of grief and wrath, the poet Isaac Katzenelson asked: 'Why has my people been tortured?' In my youth, Rabbi Hasdai, I was very much influenced by the Russian writer Dostoevsky, who propounded a view which affected me deeply: 'The mathematical law that two times two is inexorably four is an insult. An insult to life. A prelude to death.'

"We should not accept any statement as decisive. Even a decree can be revoked. On the way to Moriah there also must be a stopping place. I don't even know when and in which valley of horror my parents, my brother and sister, and my wife breathed their last breath. I don't even know when to light the Yahrzeit candle."

Rabbi Hasdai Crescas listened grimly. We both felt exhausted. Finally he broke the silence.

"You mentioned Judah Halevi's philosophic system. We are a people with an ancient tradition. It can be said of us not only that the tradition lives in us, but that we live in the tradition. Jewish martyrdom is tradition too. Long ago, by the shores of the river Chebar in Babylonia, beneath heavens that were opened, the prophet Ezekiel—himself a refugee of our first great national catastrophe—taught us: 'In thy blood, live.' Blood and life—what a bizarre twosome! What an astonishing bond! But only Ezekiel, in whose visions the heavenly chariot moved, could achieve such a fusion. And only he, as he tells us in the third chapter of his book could have taken into his mouth 'the scroll of lament, weeping, and mourning' and fill his stomach with that scroll."

Our eyes wandered over the verses of the Book of Ezekiel.

III

OUR CONVERSATION CONTINUED. I told Hasdai Crescas that although many centuries have passed since he wrote his book, *The Light of God*, the concepts he develops there are extraordinarily timely.

"Yes," he remarked, "I completed my work in the month of Iyar in 1410."

"Almost six hundred years ago," I continued. "Everyone then believed that the world was limited, that the universe was closed, and that neither space nor time existed in it. All of them, the scientists, the philosophers, the scholars of physics. You, Rabbi Hasdai, were the first to oppose this system founded by Aristotle. You gave the science of physics and philosophy a mighty thrust forward. Because of the revolution which you prompted in science, human thought took on a bold, new direction. Giordano Bruno, Pico del la Mirandola, Spinoza, and perhaps even Newton learned much from you. Albert Einstein, the physicist who discovered atomic energy, could not have developed his theories if you hadn't opened up new horizons with your teachings about the infinity of the universe."

"It's good that you touch upon this point." Hasdai Crescas looked up at me once more. "But let's not move away from the theme we were discussing earlier. It seems to me that both in my time and in yours many people deluded themselves into thinking that in the world and in life everything can be open and clear. Despite my sincere respect for the great intellectual acumen and extraordinary talmudic knowledge of Rabbi Moses ben Maimon, I still directed a sharp critique against him. Maimonides sought to explain everything with speculative thought. He wanted to explain God, man, and Jew by means of the rational faculty; he found himself in spiritual bondage to Aristotle. I demonstrated that we cannot analyze infinity and mystery. It is impossible. The Greek philosopher dimmed Maimonides' vision, and blinded his follower, Levi ben Gershon (Gersonides), even more."

"A modern-day writer," I interjected, "Arthur Koestler, titled one of his last books *Zero and Infinity*, by which he meant that man is zero, an absolute nothing, ashes and dust, as the Bible says, and at the same time he is—infinite . . ."

"But something else should be added," Hasdai continued, "which I accent in the chapters of my book. . ."

Rabbi Hasdai's voice suddenly turned cheerful. Hitherto, I often had to bend close to hear him. But now his remarks rang out with a youthful vigor, so in contrast to his old face and gray beard. "Man is continually renewing himself. He is reaching out farther and farther into boundless distances; there is no end to his longing and striving. I'm sure you have noticed that I continually use these concepts and terms in my book. Traumatic personal and national tragedies must be also regarded from this point of view, despite the anguish and the enormous difficulty. You are looking for logic, rationality, and answers in the mystery. God, Jews, the Binding are all in another sphere. They, like the universe, are wrapped in thick mist. Loneliness is infinite, but longing is infinite too."

I felt that I was being crushed in the vise of Hasdai Crescas's words and feelings. Nevertheless, I struggled. I did not want to give in.

"You were a great influence on the philosopher Baruch Spinoza," I said. "And he advised, 'Do not yell, do not weep, only understand.' "

Rabbi Hasdai did not answer immediately. He gazed at the books scattered on the table. He opened one book, closed it, and finally said: "Mystery does not function according to reason but with thunder and lightning. I felt these thunders and lightnings upon the altar of my murdered son in Barcelona. Perhaps they rolled them down from Sinai. Perhaps they came from Moriah."

I did not stop struggling with him. I did not retreat in my desire to refute him.

"I still cannot justify what happened," I tried to subdue my shout. "I don't understand the horrible destruction of millions of Jews in the German death camps. I was left an orphan, a widower. The very same thing happened to mankind too. I wander around with a great rent in my heart. The same rage encompasses me which encompassed Job when his friends came to console him after his tragedy. The same rage oppresses me which oppressed the philosopher Kierkegaard when he returned to the theme of the Binding. Upon learning that someone had cited Job and Abraham in attempting to console an unfortunate mother who had lost her son, Kierkegaard stormed: 'There is no consolation; there is no place for, or possibility of, consolation.' "

We fell silent. Rabbi Hasdai slowly slunk out of the room, then soon returned. Standing by the door he said:

"But justification of the decree does not mean being numbed into silence. The universe is in a continual process of becoming. Man and Jew are far from being completed. Every generation has its pain but also its hope. The concept of continuing renewal works in us too. We are constantly renewing ourselves. The shock of the tragedy does not interrupt our creativity. Nor is our striving ever broken. The creativity of God and of man never ceases. The primordial forces of life constantly make themselves felt, even in our mourning. From the Jewish grief of generations emerges the fervor of renewed faith and the miracle of newborn creativity.

"Indeed, I wrote *The Light of God* at a time when a gloomy twilight had settled over Spanish Jewry. I wrote it with the express purpose of stirring my people with the will to live and create. I wanted to guide them through the storm and over the clouds of the mystery. And let me tell you that it was no accident that you immersed yourself in these chapters nearly six-hundred years later, when you were oppressed by the horror of the destruction of Polish Jewry. You feel that my concepts and ideas can pull you out of the valley of despair and bitterness into which you have fallen."

When the shadow of Rabbi Hasdai Crescas vanished, *The Light of God* was open at the page where he discusses the universe and God, man and Jew, and the process of constant renewal which they undergo. A heavy pall of strain and exertion hung over the room. I was left alone with painful memories of my parents and other close kin who perished somewhere in Auschwitz or Treblinka, in Maidanek or the Ghetto of Warsaw, and for whose souls I don't even know when to light a Yahrzeit candle.

2

Hasidism: The Movement that Developed Among Polish Jewry

IN OUR ERA—one of trauma and transformation, of wanderings and loss—is it worth turning our attention to a movement that developed two hundred and fifty years ago in the midst of Polish Jewry? Nevertheless, for a variety of reasons, this backward glance is—now more than ever before—vital for our generation. Perhaps too because in the extraordinarily rich Hasidic literature of the past two hundred and fifty years, the essential and important nature of Hasidic methodology has been blurred.

On the one hand, exaltation precluded a proper historical perspective and accented the element of miracle, as though wonder-working were crucial to the path and idea formulated by the creators of Hasidism. On the other hand, dry analysis marred the essence of a movement that sprouted from the heart and was built upon heart. In the long run, both the miracle element—so characteristic of the Hasidic book, *In Praise of the Baal Shem Tov*—and the ice-cold approach of many scholars of Hasidism are responsible for the inaccurate conception that exists concerning one of the most fascinating movements that have sprung up in modern Jewish history.

11

This look backward is also important for another reason: those who consider themselves followers of Hasidism cannot always be regarded as the proper spiritual heirs of its ideology.

I must admit that the legend is a very tempting form with which to begin the essay: Once upon a time . . .

Once upon a time there was a man who sought God. He did not find Him in quite the manner that he felt and intuited Him in his environment. He felt that the mystery of God had not penetrated the spirit of the people he dealt with. Where people recited their prayers he could not find God. So he went out to the field, to the forest, to the riverbanks. Day and night he prayed in solitude. He bent over the branches, over the flowers. He listened to birds singing, leaves rustling, wind whispering, bees humming. He climbed the tops of the mountains and was swept along in the current of the waters. He searched for God, the God of Creation. The God of kindness and love, the God of Israel. And he felt the breath of infinity. He had found God.

And when he found God, he also found himself. He had discovered his own soul. He sensed the reason why he had come into this world.

And then he returned to the place whence he came; to the people he had left behind. He returned with the sun in his eyes, with the light of discovery in his face, with the freshness of nature in his word. And he said to the people:

"Open your eyes. The world is full of secrets, of wonderful, radiant secrets. Come with me. I will help you find God and the way to yourself."

But the masses were tired and dejected. Immersed though they were in their workaday bustling, his clear word nevertheless penetrated deeply into their spirit. They believed. They were drawn to him. From town and village they streamed to hear his word. And their numbers continually increased. . .

My essay seems to want to proceed in this fashion, in the form of a legend, from beginning to end. But the man under discussion—Reb Israel Baal Shem Tov—was not a concocted legendary figure. He was a real person. And real people live in a given time, in a given place. The times and the environment put their stamp on a person—and that is the theme I will address first: the time and the place in which the Baal Shem Tov lived.

II

The time: 1700, the year of his birth. The place: Ukop, a small village in the Polish province of Podolia. This was a dramatic time in the history of Polish Jewry. Fifty-two years earlier, in 1648, an appalling misfortune had befallen the Jewish community of Poland; especially the Jewish community in the Ukraine, which at that time belonged to Poland.

In 1648, the wild bands of the brutal Cossack leader Bogdan Chmielnicki destroyed the flourishing Jewish community in Poland. Hundreds of communities were demolished. Many thousands of Jews were killed by fire and sword. Then the slaughters ceased, Polish Jewry began to bind its own wounds. The community attempted to rebuild the ruins and resume normal life. But it did not succeed. The wound was too deep.

In his chronicle of lament, *Deep Mire*, Rabbi Nathan Hanover bewailed the terrible ravage. In other laments and penitential prayers composed at the time, Jews moaned and wept over the destruction, which in Jewish history have been termed the Massacres of 1648 and 1649 (*Gzeiros Tach Vetat*).

The most tragic and bizarre questions surfaced. In "Scroll of Darkness," a poem of lament by the famous scholar Rabbi Shabbetai Cohen, the author cried out in fury: "Will You remain silent, O God? Will You permit all of this to happen, God of the heavens?"

In another stirring penitential prayer, Rabbi Samuel Halevi called out in rage and sorrow: "God, You have seen the suffering of Your children, and You did not look down from Your heights."

People began wondering if these were messianic times. Could these woes be the harbingers of the Messiah? Couldn't a Hebrew anagram be made of the first few letters of Chmielnicki's name pointing to the coming of the Messiah? Was the redeemer perhaps already knocking on the gates?

And a call was heard. It came from Smyrna, in Turkey,

whose empire then bordered upon Poland, including the province of Podolia. "I am your Messiah!" Shabbetai Zevi proclaimed. Ecstasy swept over a segment of Polish Jewry. Messianic hopes were kindled. People closed their stores. They
abandoned their little bit of poverty, and everyone—men,
women, and children—went to the ports, waiting for the
Messiah to transport the people of Israel to the Holy Land.

But their hopes were shattered. Shabbetai Zevi turned out to
be a false Messiah. Shabbetai Zevi donned the Arabic turban
and betrayed his people. He converted to Islam.

Polish Jewry wrung its hands in anguish. Was it possible that
all these awful sufferings were totally senseless? Could it be
that all these reckonings of salvation were completely baseless?
Was it possible that sanctification of the people would not
follow on the heels of this great *Kiddush Hashem*, this martyrdom? And after this fire of torment, would not the Jewish
people be made holy and uplifted?

Even after Shabbetai Zevi's apostasy circles of believing
mystics remained on Polish soil. A new messenger of tidings
appeared in southern Poland, declaring that he was a reincar-
nation of Shabbetai Zevi. His name: Jacob Frank. An adven-
turer and a charlatan, Frank was a man of debased morality.
Nevertheless, he had cast upon himself the mantle of the
redeemer. He quoted phrases from the Kabbalah. He said that
he had come to redeem the Shekhinah, the Divine Presence,
from its Exile. Jacob Frank claimed to be the earthly embodiment of the holy king of heaven.

In Jacob Frank's high-flown imagery, mystical fantasy was
entangled with the dream of renascent Jewish heroism. It won
believers among restless, ecstatic Polish Jews. Frank gained not
only adherents from the masses, but also several rabbis as well,
including the rabbis of Giline and Busk. Amid the mighty,
mystical fire which had encompassed Polish Jewry, the teaching of impurity won followers.

Jacob Frank and his followers were excommunicated. Black
candles were lit and extinguished. The shofar was blown. But
to no avail. Jacob Frank's movement grew from day to day. The
Jews experienced even greater disappointment and even

sharper pain. Frank and many of his followers converted to Catholicism. Not only did the wild charlatan decide to take revenge against those who had opposed his movement, but he concocted shameful accusations against the Jews of his own hometown. After Jacob Frank made an alliance with the Catholic clergy, he and the priests cast volumes of the Talmud on the bonfire in Kamenets-Podolsk. Polish Jewry writhed in anguish, humiliation, and deep chaos.

To make matters worse, the Jewish community was terribly split. The Polish kingdom was crumbling. Soon its thieving neighbors would divide up its land. The demoralized Polish rulers constantly made life more difficult for the Jews. They burdened the communities with enormous taxes. Powerful Jews, who did not distribute the tax burden equitably, began to ride roughshod over the community. Those close to the king or intimate with the local ruler squirmed out of their responsibility. The poor man who knew no one in high office and could wield no influence had to bear the entire yoke.

Tragic rifts now developed in the Jewish society. The scholar, who had the opportunity to spend many years learning in a yeshiva, looked with distain at the worker who had to do backbreaking labor. The scholar not only repulsed the ignorant man in this world—he blocked him from the world-to-come. Torah ceased to be what it was in truth: a source of life, religious inspiration, and lofty humanity. More and more the Torah was transformed into a collection of complex laws which the simple person could not comprehend. The Torah continually honed itself into a Torah of mind where there was no room for heart and feeling. In addition, the Musar books had widespread popularity; they made the Jewish spirit even more bleak and dreary.

Itinerant preachers traveled from town to town spreading the specter of fear; they warned that for the slightest sin Jews would be burned and roasted in the next world. And who was free of sins and transgressions? The Jewish heaven blazed with the flames of menacing hellfire. Not even a crumb of solace was to be found in the sea of terrible loneliness.

The existence of the Jewish people two hundred and fifty

years ago was in danger, for at that time Polish Jewry represented the Jewish people. Poland was the leading Jewish
spiritual center. And in its void hung—dreadful and tragic—
the question: Who would come to save? Who?

And then along came Reb Israel Baal Shem Tov.

III

The Baal Shem Tov came forth with his teaching in the same
region where Jacob Frank rose to ascendancy. Holiness was
born in the same place where impurity had gushed.

His biography, as attested to by historians, differs radically
from the biographies of the other rabbis and religious leaders of
that time. Upon reading the life story of a rabbi or spiritual
leader of that period, one discovers that at five the subject had
already displayed qualities of genius; at nine he had stunned
everyone with his piercing questions; and of course at thirteen,
when he was Bar Mitzvah, he had already thoroughly mas-
tered the entire Talmud and commentaries, and his fame was
spread all over the land.

It was entirely different with the Baal Shem Tov. Indeed,
during his childhood he was apparently no great scholar. A son
of poor parents named Eliezer and Sarah, he was orphaned at a
very early age. The community sent him to a cheder, but
according to his guardians he showed little zeal for learning at
school. He would disappear for days at a time. Later, he was
found alone in the forest, in the meadow, or by a riverbank.

The community despaired of making a respectable person
out of Israel ben Eliezer. He became a teacher's helper, carrry-
ing the young children to the cheder and singing prayers with
them as he accompanied them to school. But then he wandered
off to another village where he became an assistant shamesh
and displayed the same queer traits. Again Israel Baal Shem
Tov disappeared for several days in the forest. While others
slept, he studied. He was particularly drawn to the mysteries,
to the recondite elements of the Kabbalah texts. By immersing
himself in nature's secrets and in the secrets buried within him,
he achieved his spiritual maturity.

Once more the Baal Shem Tov wandered to another town, this time to Brody, where he married. His brother-in-law, the rabbi of Brody, Rabbi Gershon Kitever, was apparently ashamed of him. He thought of Israel as a common man, an ignoramus. The Baal Shem Tov had to leave Brody and settle in a part of the Carpathian Mountains between Kitev and Kosev.

He became a clay digger, digging for clay in the mountains and then transporting it to nearby towns and villages. Since he supported his family but meagerly, he also became a tutor, dragging himself from village to village studying with children. Still he was in dire need. His students later reported that the Baal Shem Tov was so poor that his naked toes would peek out of his torn sandals—he could not even afford a pair of shoes.

The Baal Shem Tov then became a wagon driver for his brother-in-law, the rabbi of Brody. Still later he turned to innkeeping, and even in this new endeavor he was no less strange and inscrutable. While the peasants were tippling and becoming drunk, he enjoyed standing by, listening to their songs.

From out of this fantastic fabric, the Baal Shem Tov's personality emerged, great in its remarkable simplicity. The people around him began whispering: Is he really such an ignoramus? Is he really as simple as he pretends to be? No, he is actually saturated with Torah. But his Torah is so different! It flows from the heart.

And furthermore: he could heal the sick. He knew the secrets of the grasses and herbs, which he applied against various ailments. He knew how to use the nectar of flowers. He was a wonder-worker and could perform miracles. He was a *baal shem*, a man who could perform miracles by using God's name. In those days, a person who could cure the sick with grasses and herbs, who could cast off the evil eye, write amulets, and give remedies in cases of need and want, was called a *baal shem*, a master of the Name.

But Israel ben Eliezer was also different and distinct from all the other name-masters who traveled from village to village. He could heal not only the body but also the soul. His words

were so clear and sweet. He was the good *baal shem*. The man
with the good name *(shem tov)*, the Baal Shem Tov, the Master
of the Good Name.

From near and far people began streaming to him in Mezhibuzh, where he lived at that time. They came for medicines,
hoping to become cured through him. They came even if they
suffered no ailments, for they craved to be close to him, to hear
his word, to watch his gestures and absorb his melody.

In fact, the Baal Shem Tov did not even wait for people to
come to him. He himself began traveling in the land, but he did
not behave like the other itinerant preachers. He did not
assemble the people in the synagogue; he did not preach
before crowds. He went to the people, to the marketplace
where Jews stood by their shops and stores, and engaged them
in conversation. He had such appealing fables, such beautiful,
enchanting stories. He opened up and discovered what was
flowering in everyone's heart.

In Praise of the Baal Shem Tov, the book later published by his
students, tells that one gray morning the Baal Shem Tov came
to Sharograd. That morning there was no minyan in the
synagogue. The well-known scholar, Rabbi Jacob Joseph, came
to the synagogue as usual, but only the shamesh was present.

"Where are all the Jews today? Why hasn't anyone come to
prayers?" the rabbi asked anxiously.

Frightened and shaken, the shamesh replied, "A stranger
came to town this morning. He stood in the middle of the
marketplace and began talking and telling stories. Nobody
wants to leave him."

"Who is this Jew?" the rabbi asked angrily.

"I—I don't know," the shamesh stammered. "He looks like a
farmer, like a village Jew with a walking-stick in his hand and a
pipe in his mouth."

"Bring him to me immediately," ordered the Sharograd
rabbi.

The shamesh returned at once with the village Jew.

"You disturbed public prayer today," the rabbi reproached
him, the Baal Shem Tov.

"I put a little bit of soul into the Jews today," the Baal Shem Tov replied with a smile. "There is no soul in your manner of studying and your way of praying."

A long discussion then ensued between the rabbi of Sharograd and the wandering village Jew. Israel Baal Shem Tov told one story, a second, a third. At first the rabbi listened with disdain, then with interest, and still later with ever growing attentiveness. At this point, something began to stir in Rabbi Jacob Joseph, the rabbi of Sharograd. He himself became a pupil of the Baal Shem Tov, one of his most respected disciples. Years later he wrote his book, *The Generations of Jacob Joseph*, an early classic of Hasidic literature.

The number of pupils and followers who gathered around Israel Baal Shem Tov constantly grew. The folk loved him. After all, he too was a child of poor people, hence he knew full well the soul of simple folk. But scholars and rabbis, seeking men of the spirit, the dissatisfied and those haunted by an inner restlessness, also came to him. He developed his thoughts with the help of fables and aphorisms, or by means of short explanations and comments on the Torah. These sayings, aphorisms, and apparently offhand remarks, which contained deep Jewish feeling and religious and ethical thought, were transformed by the Baal Shem Tov into a system with an original conception. This innovative doctrine was called Hasidism.

IV

WHAT WAS ITS message? It should be stated at the outset that Hasidism was a mystical teaching, of which a significant literature was already extant during the Baal Shem Tov's lifetime. Elements of mysticism are found even in the Bible. The prophet Ezekiel had a vision of heavenly wheels and a heavenly chariot. Motifs of mysticism appear in the Talmud and the Midrash. By the eighteenth century, the magnificent edifice of Jewish mysticism, the Kabbalah, was already well known. Its fundamental text, the *Zohar*, whose strands can be traced back to a Mishnah sage, Rabbi Simon bar Yochai, had already been written, widely disseminated, and honored in the Jewish world.

Hasidism, however, was a new mysticism. To be sure, it contains the ancient Jewish concept that God is omnipresent, that the entire world is replete wtih godliness, and that no place is devoid of God's presence. But in this new teaching, complex ideas and tenets were directed at the simple man; nevertheless, they were not simplified, and they lost nothing of their profundity.

In the Kabbalah, God was in the heavens, high in His celestial domain. It is difficult to comprehend Him. However, in Hasidism, God descended to earth. He is close by, with us, within us. We can feel His presence constantly, as expressed in the Hasidic folksong:

> Master of the world, I'm going to sing a song to You.
> You, You, You.
> Wherever I turn—You.
> Wherever I face—You. . .
> Time and again, You, only You.

God is to be found not only in the spirit but in the body. Not only in goodness but also in evil. Not only in holiness but also in impurity. Even in sin, in decadence, the divine sparks glow. One must only know how to find them and withdraw them. The Shekhinah, God's Divine Presence, suffers from having to drag itself to all places of transgression and human degradation. But the Shekhinah goes along, hoping that perhaps in the abyss of sin man will lift up his glance and notice God's presence. And God is certainly present in nature, where His wonders obviously manifest themselves. According to the Baal Shem Tov, the numerical value of the Hebrew letters for "God" and "nature" are identical: both add up to eighty-six.

But let no mistake be made. Hasidism is not pantheism. It is not Spinoza's philosophy, where nature and the divine are one and the same. In Hasidism, God reveals Himself in nature— but He remains above it. He is its Creator.

This new system centered not only upon God but also upon

man. The Musar books, which by then had inundated the Jewish community, asserted that man was full of sins. The phrase "iniquitous man of flesh and blood" floated in the air; it penetrated Jewish consciousness and oppressed the Jew. But the Baal Shem Tov stated: "Man is pure, pure as a baby. It is Satan who whispers into our ears that we are sinful. That's the trick that Satan plays on us. Man is good and the world is good."

The Baal Shem Tov once cried out: "*Oy vey*, the world is full of light, full of sun, but man's small hand covers his eyes and blocks out the sun." And then, as was his custom, he immediately told a parable: "A musician once played a wonderful melody which enchanted the listeners. Along came a deaf man and asked, 'What's delighting the people? What's all the enthusiasm about?' " The Baal Shem Tov concluded, "There are too many deaf people in the world, and they don't hear—they don't listen to the divine melody."

The existence of evil and the problem of evil perturbed the architect of this new teaching and gnawed at his conciousness. But according to the Baal Shem Tov there was meaning and purpose to evil. Evil helps us to assess and recognize the value of goodness—just as darkness teaches us to appreciate the meaning and value of light. The old verse from Genesis, "It was evening and it was morning, one day," was interpreted by the Baal Shem Tov in the following way: "The evening and the morning create the day. Without evening there is no morning."

In Hasidism's new teaching flowed waves of optimism and love of mankind. Not only was doing evil to one's fellow man forbidden, but one should even refrain from thinking evil. No man is obligated to judge another man. No one has the right to punish someone else. If a man is burning with pious zeal he should apply it to himself. But we must pray for one another, pray for our common spiritual and moral ascendancy. The Baal Shem Tov said, "Judges who judge and punish the people at a time of need and anguish, and offer them no consolation and look for no saving graces—such judges themselves deserve to be brought to judgment."

In Hasidism, joy was accented. One cannot serve God with

melancholy. One should go through life with joy, not with gloom; not with fear, but with assurance and happiness.

The Jewish man in the street was overwhelmed with fear of the punishment that awaited the sinner in the world-to-come. But the Baal Shem Tov never grew tired of opposing the preachers who spread this nightmare. "Stop lecturing the people," he told them. "Every Jew does something which can make the heavens shudder." And to his fellow Jews he called out: "Don't be afraid! Your soul will be uplifted. Whoever believes that he is a child of God cannot possibly be overcome by sorrow. One can look for God even in the abyss. One can return to God and repent even from a state of extreme sinfulness. Repentance can be achieved only with joy."

The mystical tradition created two hundred years earlier in Safed by Rabbi Isaac Luria stressed fasts and mortification of the flesh. Rabbi Isaac Luria, known in Jewish history as the Holy Ari, contended that by tormenting the body man helps to fight the forces of evil in the world and is instrumental in hastening the Redemption.

This ascetic approach, however, did not please the Baal Shem Tov. He declared that one can also serve God by eating and drinking and by enjoying God's world. Eating and drinking can be made more lofty, and they can ennoble. The Baal Shem Tov poked fun at those who added fast-days to the Jewish calendar. "Even in heaven they are laughed at," he said. "They think that their fasting improves the moral state of the universe and works who knows what kind of wonders. It does nothing of the sort."

The verse in Isaiah 58:7, "Do not ignore your fellow man" (lit. "your flesh"), was interpreted by the Baal Shem Tov literally. "Do not ignore your own flesh-and-blood body, because when your body is sick, the soul also loses its strength." When the Baal Shem Tov was informed that other masters of the Name were writing amulets only after a fast, he declared boldly: "And I write an amulet only after a meal."

During one Simchas Torah, according to *In Praise of the Baal Shem Tov*, his pupils were celebrating in his house. After they had had quite a few drinks, the Baal Shem Tov's wife came into the room and told him: "Almost all the wine is gone. There will be nothing left for Kiddush and Havdalah."

"So what if there won't be any wine left for Kiddush and Havdalah?" the Baal Shem Tov replied, "Jews have to be happy and not brood or worry."

The Baal Shem Tov once stated that the difference between him and those who order fasts was this: "Angry and embittered doctors prescribe bitter medicines. The good, friendly doctor prescribes medications as sweet as honey."

The Baal Shem Tov wanted to expel the melancholy that had settled over the Jewish community. The world is not a vale of tears, he said. Every man was born to benefit from good fortune and joy. Even in difficult times a Jew is forbidden to despair. God's mercies still hover over His people, Israel. One must not lose faith and hope.

The Baal Shem Tov knocked on every Jew's heart, saying: "Do you hear? Do not lose hope!" He gave new strength to masses of people who were tormented physically and exhausted spiritually. There is no more holy calling than to chase gloom from a Jew. Joy is a very lofty thing, but it becomes even loftier when transformed into ecstasy. The concept of ecstasy (*hislahavus*), with its Hebraic root, "to become inflamed" (*lahav*), originated in Hasidic literature. Don't serve God mechanically, and don't perform a favor for another man mechanically—but put your entire soul into it, your entire ecstasy. One must become inflamed.

Once, in a house where barrels of grain were stored, the Baal Shem Tov prayed to revoke a decree against the Jews. He became so inflamed in his prayer, and began to dance and jump with such ecstasy, that the barrels danced along with him. The Baal Shem Tov explained that God had rejected Cain's sacrifice and accepted Abel's because Abel brought *himself*—that is, he approached God with his entire being and with all his soul. Only when one brings oneself as a sacrifice does a sacrifice have any meaning.

The Baal Shem Tov, the poor orphan who grew up in

anguish and loneliness, carried within himself the sources of
unending joy. His teaching came from the heart. It is not true
that the Baal Shem Tov opposed Torah learning, for he himself
studied Torah. He merely protested against a one-sided expression of Jewishness. He criticized those Jews who were conceited because of their Torah learning and who looked with
disdain at others who had no opportunity of enriching their
Jewish knowledge.

"The evil impulse wants to come to the student and persuade him to stop learning," the Baal Shem Tov said ironically.
"But the evil impulse knows that the scholar won't listen
because Torah gives honor, importance, esteem. So then what
does the evil impulse do? He disguises himself as the good
impulse and encourages the scholar to study continuously so
that he has no time whatsoever to contemplate the true nature
of Judaism." Another time the Baal Shem Tov pointed to a
scholar and remarked, "He studies so much Torah that he has
actually forgotten that there is a God in this world."

The Baal Shem Tov's brother-in-law, the rabbi of Kitev,
wanted to poke some fun at him and asked, "Where did you
learn the laws of putting on tefillin?"

"In some Yiddish books," the Baal Shem Tov answered.

It is important to remember that the "learning" that could be
derived from these little Yiddish books (read mostly by un-
scholarly women) was held in utter disdain. But for the Baal
Shem Tov, faith was more important than learning; living an
honest Jewish life was more important than erecting a tower of
talmudic pilpul and hairsplitting arguments. The poor Jew who
toiled hard in order to provide for his family deserves no less
attention and love than the Torah scholar.

Once the Baal Shem Tov came to Anipol. He spoke with
several members of the Jewish community and finally pointed
to a poor stockingmaker. "He is the foundation stone of the
entire community."

In another village which the Baal Shem Tov visited, he found
working Jews in a depressed mood. "We are not studying
enough," they complained to him. "We are not praying
enough."

"A *Mincha* which a Jew manages to say in a hurry makes even the angels in heaven shudder," the Baal Shem Tov interrupted. And, as was his wont, he immediately told a little story. "Two Jews once lived in the same house. A Torah scholar and an ignorant worker, whom the scholar regarded with contempt. One hundred and twenty years later they came to the next world. There the Torah scholar was told: 'You cannot enter the Garden of Eden because you looked down at your neighbor.' And it was the worker, the ignoramus, who had the privilege of entering Paradise. A Psalm which a Jew recites with utter devotion, even if he does not understand the meaning of the words, rises higher than the pages of the Talmud which someone has learned. What counts is the intent and the ecstasy."

It is characteristic that this simple village rabbi attached importance to spirituality in prayer. When one prays; he said, one should not pray for material needs. One must cast away the "I" and not distress the Creator with trivial matters. While praying, the Jew's goal should be to strip himself of materiality. "If a man is satisfied with himself after having finished praying," the Baal Shem Tov said, "and if he hopes to get a reward for his prayer, it means that he has prayed to himself and for himself. Before you find God you must find yourself."

The Talmud says that the sage Elisha ben Abuya, who later became a heretic, did not repent because he heard a heavenly voice declaring that his repentance would not be accepted. This prompted the Baal Shem Tov to remark, "Oh, what an extraordinary opportunity Elisha ben Abuya missed! He could have served God solely out of love, knowing with confidence that he would receive no reward. And prayer itself can be different than is commonly assumed. The important thing is that it flow out of feeling. A melody, just a melody without words, can also be a prayer. Even a conversation with another Jew can be considered prayer. When taken in the proper light, weekday matters can often invigorate the soul. And who said that prophecies come down from the heavens? In the remarks of a simple man one can occasionally hear the call of God.

"And who said that one must pray in the synagogue? Wher-

ever Jews gather and pour out their hearts to the Master of the
Universe is a holy place. And who said that one must pray at
specified times? One cannot tell a child when he may speak to
his father. Limitations are valid only for slaves."

The following incident, so frequently retold in modern Yiddish literature, apparently happened to the Baal Shem Tov. It is
the story of a shepherd lad who did not know how to pray but
who nevertheless wanted to express his longing for God. So on
Yom Kippur the youngster took out a whistle in the synagogue
and began to blow it in the middle of the *Neilah* service. The
worshippers were shocked and angry. But the Baal Shem Tov
later said that the shepherd lad's whistle had opened the gates
of heaven.

V

Five hundred years prior to Rabbi Israel Baal Shem Tov,
Maimonides declared that the perfect man is one who rises
above the crowd. According to the Baal Shem Tov, no one can
rise above the crowd, nor should he. All men should seek
perfection, said the teacher who grew up among the Jewish
masses in the Ukraine. All of us, you and I, have the innate
power to ascend higher and higher. Everyone is like a ladder
whose feet are on the ground and whose top reaches the
heavens. Man must recognize the wonderful strengths and
potentials which he possesses.

"There are two kinds of people," said the Baal Shem Tov.
"An absolutely wicked man and the one who persuades himself that he's a saint. The wicked man can repent. But the man
who persuades himself that he's a saint—how can he find a
way to repentance?"

Along with the joy that poured out of his personality, remarks, and deeds, the Baal Shem Tov also taught the ideal of
modesty—a quintessential humility which is profoundly expressed in a synthesis of one's inferiority and one's self-
importance. This synthesis was later reflected in an astute
remark of Reb Bunim of Pshishkhe.

"Every man," stated Reb Bunim, "has to carry in one pocket

the verse, 'I am but dust and ashes,' and in the other pocket the phrase, 'Because of me the world was created.' For I am a child of God, and I was formed in His image. This is the only way of preventing man from considering himself higher and better than someone else. At the same time, the tasks before him will not lose their significance, and he remembers that he is chosen above all other creatures."

The Baal Shem Tov never wearied of instructing his followers how to climb uphill. Before his death, during his last moments of consciousness, he whispered, "Get away from me, foolish and vain pride. Even when I'm passing from this world you come to me and say, 'Look here, Israel, what a beautiful funeral you're going to have! Get away from me, foolish vanity. Do not pester me.' "

Hasidism also taught that a Jew in his loneliness must have someone to lean on. The Jew needs the Hasidic leader, the rebbe who is also called the *zaddik* ("saintly man"). The *zaddik* is no better than other Jews. He merely tries harder to bring himself closer to God and to feel for and empathize with his fellow man. And indeed, in the company of the rebbe, and with him, the striving for godliness and humanness can be strengthened in people's hearts. It is good that Jews are together and can strengthen each other together, that they long together and lift each other up together. That is how one person helps another and becomes united. People become brothers. Differences are erased. One sees that one is not alone in the world. And one gets an entirely new feeling. When one is with Hasidim and with the rebbe one is imbued with faith.

This new system also took a position regarding the questions and problems which had traumatized the Jewish people in the first half of the eighteenth century. The founder felt personally responsible for the fate of the people and warmly embraced all their strata with love. Even Shabbetai Zevi, the Baal Shem Tov argued, had a spark of holiness in him, but regrettably, impurity had consumed him.

The Baal Shem Tov's love of Israel is seen in his view of the degeneration represented by Jacob Frank, the false Messiah and charlatan, and his movement. He said, "Jacob Frank and his followers were overly persecuted and forcibly driven from the Jewish camp." When the Frankists converted to Christianity, the Baal Shem Tov wrung his hands in pain and sighed, "The Shekhinah is now weeping over its children who have lost their way. As long as they were part of their people, hope still smoldered—perhaps, maybe. But once the limb was severed there was no longer any chance of return. Every Jew is a limb of the Shekhinah, and in every Jew's soul there glow the sparks of godliness."

Hasidism was the name of this teaching, and the disciples of the Baal Shem Tov were called Hasidim. *Hasid* was actually an old word and embodied an ancient concept. In the Bible, *hasid* depicts a man who does deeds of lovingkindness. During the Hasmonean period a sect flourished whose adherents were called Hasidim. In the Middle Ages, a group in Germany called themselves Hasidim. A great and profound book called *Sefer Hasidim*, or *The Book of the Pious*, relevant in all generations for its ethicality and refined traits, was created by these noble thinkers.

But the Baal Shem Tov's movement had no connection with the Hasidim of thirteenth-century Germany. Before the Baal Shem Tov no such teaching and no such movement existed in Jewish history.

Naturally, this does not mean that the Baal Shem Tov's thoughts were all new. In the culture of a people that spans thousands of years and who since ancient times have been preoccupied with the problem of God and man, one can find the seeds of every movement. But this does not diminish Hasidism's originality. Moreover, Hasidism is not only a teaching. It is something more: it is a way of life, a civilization.

With staff in hand and pipe in mouth, the Baal Shem Tov wandered to towns and villages, teaching Hasidism and radiating warmth. Every community graced by his teaching was renewed, touched by the breeze of new meaning. The Baal Shem Tov did not write down his teachings; this was done later by his disciples. He himself was the embodiment and revelation of his own teaching.

Even during his lifetime legends began to be told about him. He did not bring tidings of a Messiah who had been born. That is why one can label as false the interpretation by Jewish and non-Jewish writers who, in their attempt to "modernize" the Hasidic movement, cast upon it a non-Jewish and even a Christian garb. Such a view cripples both the founder and the teaching of Hasidism. No, the Baal Shem Tov did not bring tidings of a new heaven-sent redeemer. He did not promise Jews a better economic state or an end to their poverty. That is why scholars who strain to interpret the flowering of Hasidism and the personality of the Baal Shem Tov in a purely Marxist fashion are also far from the truth. They have not the faintest notion of the remarkable aspects which are characteristic of the great Jew from Ukop and of his original movement.

The Baal Shem Tov opened up the wellsprings of inner joy and of happiness which overflow in man himself. He showed how essential and crucial it was for man to find his own inner, true, and intimate path to God, man, and Jew. It is not a path led by a heaven-sent redeemer or by an organized revolt. It is a path which man has the capacity to traverse on his own and which he can reach by his own will, faith, and warmth.

The Baal Shem Tov's will is one of the stirring documents in our religious and ethical literature. It is absolutely unimportant whether the will was written by the Baal Shem Tov or by one of his followers. Its value is not diminished by this. But his disciples' view that their rebbe spoke to future generations is important. In this will the Jew is shown with naive simplicity how he can climb higher to God, refine himself, and improve his character traits; he is taught how to dispel gloom and feel the joy of being a Jew.

Rabbi Israel Baal Shem Tov died in Mezhibuzh on the second day of Shavuos, in 1760. The teaching that originated at the foot of the Carpathian Mountains was spread by the Baal Shem Tov's disciples over the entire length and breadth of the Ukraine, Poland, and neighboring lands. It shook the Jewish world and won over significant parts of its population. Naturally, it also prompted bitter opposition. Against Hasidism there arose religious Jews—later called Misnagdim—who

feared that the movement would destroy the basis of Jewishness: studying Torah. Followers of the Haskalah, the Jewish
enlightenment, also came out against Hasidism, for they saw it
as a fortress of primitivism and prejudice. Hasidim, Misnagdim, Maskilim—these were the three great contending
movements in Jewish society in the generations that succeeded
the founding of Hasidism. The battles that they waged with
each other were frequently vitriolic.

But Hasidism possessed life force, dynamism, and great
charm. Often its truculent opponents became faithful followers. Frequently, outspoken Misnagdic rabbis made a complete about-face and became ardent Hasidim. Rabbi Shneur
Zalman of Liady, the great scholar and intellectual, was overwhelmed by the spiritual force of Mezhibuzh and built islands
of Hasidism in the land of the Misnagdim.

Leading Maskilim were often attracted by Hasidism's fervor
and became inflamed by its teachings. I. L. Peretz began his
literary career as a Maskil and ended it as the lyrical singer of
Hasidism in modern Yiddish literature. Hillel Zeitlin came to
modern Hebrew literature after being influenced by Nietzsche
and hearing in Haskalah circles the stormy call of Micah Joseph
Berditchevsky to reevaluate and reject the spiritual values of
Judaism. Later, however, Hillel Zeitlin purified himself in the
sanctity of Hasidism.

Martin Buber spread the light of Hasidism in the non-Jewish
world, and even though Buber's neo-Hasidism was not always
faithful to the Baal Shem Tov's original thought—nevertheless,
because of Buber many gentiles were dazzled by the spiritual
world of Hasidism and by the incomparable poetry concealed
in its treasures. The inner essence of the *oeuvre* of S. Y.
Agnon—just to mention one of our contemporaries—his
themes, his symbols, and even his style are all thoroughly
influenced by Hasidism. Agnon's works are a modern writer's
attempt to spin out the tradition of the old Hasidic books and to
convey the thought and style of olden times to the contemporary reader.

One ought not to fault Hasidism by saying that it has not

always possessed the authenticity and purity of its beginnings and that the institution of the zaddik and the belief in the rebbe have not always been so nice and lofty. We must remember that there is no movement which does not occasionally deviate into side paths. But this must not cast a shadow upon Hasidism or upon its creators.

Anyone who considers himself honest and serious concerning Jewish history and its development in the last two hundred and fifty years must admit that Hasidism brought enduring and constructive values into Jewish life which provided substance and stronghold in times of chaos and anarchy. Hasidism surely saved the Jewish people from menacing disintegration in an era of decline. And Hasidism has not lost its significance and value in our time, in contemporary Jewish culture, and in day-to-day Jewish life. Despite all the criticism that can be leveled at the conduct of certain Hasidic leaders, we cannot deny that Hasidism is still dynamic and creative and that its contributions to Judaism and Jewish values are enormous in historic scope.

The ideas of the Baal Shem Tov can still be a beacon to lead us out of our contemporary maze. Reb Nachman of Bratzlav's stories still contain elements that can lift the spirit. The brilliant Torah remarks of Reb Mendel of Kotzk still possess the deep Jewish thought that can sustain all generations. The life of Reb Levi Yitzchok of Berditchev still radiates with the great examples that a Jew is duty-bound to follow. And in the methods which were developed in Pshishkhe and Vurke, in Ger or in Alexander, there is still substance and stronghold for the Jewish spirit. But the teachers of Hasidism, true to the concept formulated by its founder, Reb Israel Baal Shem Tov, did not merely write their teachings of articulate thoughts; with their own lives they struggled to show that Hasidism is not merely a beautiful theory but a feasible way of life for the Jew.

Reb Itche Meir of Ger, the author of *Hidushey ha-Rim*, interpreted the letters that make up the name "Israel." If "Israel" is read as an acrostic, it yields the Hebrew phrase: "Sparks of fire, the flame of God." "This," Reb Itche added, "shows the Jew that he must be fiery in his ecstasy and carry the flame of God in his heart and soul."

In our time, when Jewishness has often been transformed into something frozen and cold, the deep meaning that Hasidism gave to Jewry and Jewishness is worth reviving and renewing.

3

Hasidism's Teaching of the Heart

I

IN THE SPIRITUAL culture of Jewry, as indeed in Jewish life altogether, man's relationship with his fellow man has always been imbued with great significance. It may be impossible to "nationalize" categories of feeling and couple them with the character and lifeways of a specific people or a particular ethnic group; but it is not farfetched to say that through the course of history compassion and empathy have become Jewish traits.

Plato did not set compassion at the center of his ideal republic. And Aristotle did not include empathy in the system that he elaborated for man and society. Even when the Jewish concept of a merciful God and the ideal of man who must follow the ways of a merciful God penetrated non-Jewish ideology through Christian teaching, compassion still remained a Jewish trait in its practical intent and daily usage.

Nietzsche probably did not know that "merciful sons of merciful fathers" is an age-old appellation for the Jewish people, and that we never intended to cast it off from our religious and national identity. Also, he probably did not know that kindness was primary among Abraham's qualities. We are certain that our first patriarch's life was deeply rooted in this trait. But even though Nietzsche might have been unfamiliar with these details, he understood full well that compassion is a thoroughly Jewish practice.

33

As it turns out, we never really cared what people said or thought about our views of kindliness. In the forty years that Israel wandered in the desert, whose raw and primitive nature faithfully mirrored the heartless and primitive human society during the period of idolatry, Moses did not waver in his determination to "soften" the hard hearts of those who were to build the Jewish tomorrow.

In that landscape and under those circumstances, it was not easy to sow the seeds of ethics and morality. But there, for the first time in history, the thought developed that one can and *must* cut open the heart that has become callous. "Cut away, therefore, the thickening about your hearts, and stiffen your necks no more" (Deuteronomy 10:16), and inspire waves of love for the suffering and the dejected. As they faced a merciless reality, it was natural that these new ideas could not immediately strike roots. But yet the doctrine of tenderness was promulgated among the hard boulders of the wilderness.

This was the teaching of the heart: Widows and orphans must be treated with care and concern. One must treat slaves and servants humanely. They must not be beaten even if they are foreign "Canaanites." The poor man must be sustained. At every opportunity—whether support or gift of grain is discussed—we are instructed how to share food with the needy.

Even if the poor man is in debt, he must not be treated cruelly. The garment he pledged against a loan must be returned to him before nightfall, lest he freeze during the cold night. The poor man is your kinsman ("Do not harden your heart and shut your hand against your needy kinsman," Deuteronomy 15:7). Surely it was not coincidental that the chapter of laws and statutes that follows the Revelation at Sinai is devoted to the human warmth one must show to slaves, who are a totally unprotected segment of society.

As previously mentioned, one could not expect these moving ideas to have an immediate impact on day-to-day Jewish conduct. People were enticed not only by foreign gods but by the foreign way of life—the all-encompassing heartlessness. But even at a time when people thought that it was absolutely impossible to inroot Jewish traits among Jews, the spark of compassion was not thoroughly extinguished. And the outside world took note of this. Naturally, we are not enchanted by all that happened in the Jewish land during the times of a king like Ahab. But even then the defeated soldiers of Aram preferred being taken prisoner by Jews. They said: "We have heard that the kings of the house of Israel are magnanimous kings" (I Kings 20:31).

Of course, love and kindness were the moral contribution of the prophets. For all the severity and rage that pours out of their prophecies, it is the stirring note of empathy that vibrates in their sorrow. They continued with various nuances to accent the demand to cut open the callous heart that was originally expressed during the desert wanderings. Here is the prophet Micah's ringingly clear response to the question: What is good for man? "He has told you, O man, what is good, and what the Lord requires of you: Only to do justice, and to love goodness, and to walk humbly with your God" (Micah 6:8). Isaiah declared, "Learn to do well" (Isaiah 1:17), and through various examples Ezekiel developed this concept by the rivers of Babylon: One must excise one's heart of stone, and let empathy and humanity throb there. "I will remove the heart of stone from your body and give you a heart of flesh" (Ezekiel 36:26).

This ideology is contained in all the books canonized in the Holy Scriptures. Sighing over the fate of those who suffer is not heard only in the Psalms. Elsewhere too one feels the deep yearning to bring joy into the gloomy existence of the lonely and forlorn. The introductory lines of Psalm 102, "A prayer of the afflicted, when he faints and pours out his complaint before the Lord," can serve as an opening for other, nonlyrical chapters in the Bible.

Job does not cry out alone. His tragedy prompts an echo in people's hearts; it tears at the heavens and even causes the heavens to split asunder and God Himself to describe the meaning of anguish. The pessimism of Ecclesiastes is connected not only with asking the point of the universe, of the rising and setting of the sun, and of the ceaseless coming and going of generations. The abyss of his inconsolable sorrow is found in "the tears of the oppressed" (Ecclesiastes 4:1). Skeptical as he is, and in whatever philosophical mood he may judge events, his spirit rages when he notes the injustices committed against the weak and unprotected. "I returned and considered all the oppressions that are done under the sun; and behold, the tears of the oppressed, and they had no comforter" (Ecclesiastes 4:1).

Those who point to the ramified talmudic literature or rabbinic interpretations, or to philosophic speculation and the responsa literature, as an expression of stern one-sided law, actually distort the significance of those works. We encounter in them not only a vigorous call to man and Jew to ascend the ladder of ethics but also laws that rigorously protect the powerless, those who daily face up to life's problems.

What is the best quality to which a man should cling, and what is the finest human attribute? This is the question that Rabbi Yochanan ben Zakkai, the teacher of Yavneh, asked his students. (It was Rabbi Yochanan who in a moment of menacing danger saved Yavneh and gave direction and orientation to the entire culture that was later concentrated in Halakhah [law] and Aggadah [folklore].) We are told exactly which of his students' answers won his enthusiastic approval: the finest attribute was "a good heart" (*Ethics of the Fathers* 2:13).

From among all the Torah's laws and statutes, Rabbi Akiba—who was also able to transform the great personal and national tragedies into a victory of ideals and feeling—considered the commandment "Love your fellow man as yourself" (Leviticus 19:18) as *the* great commandment. And on Yom Kippur, the day when man and God are engaged in earnest dialogue, it is the dialogue between man and man that remains decisive on the balance scales of good and evil. For when the problem of man's relationship with his fellow man becomes complicated, one cannot presume that the person who observes ritual will merit having his prayers ascend to where prayers are supposed to ascend.

It is true that the Talmud devotes attention to all the tendencies and shadings in man's nature. But clearly, the things that come from the heart and reach the heart are treated with special warmth. Charity, kind deeds, visiting the sick, and like traits that show profound human solidarity, assure all of us both worlds (the world-to-come and the world of here-and-now). The poor tithe—the help for the needy—is a permanent way of life. Going beyond the call of the law is more important than the law. Jerusalem was destroyed because its people followed a hard, inflexible principle. God demands of us the heart.

No wonder, then, that a civilization built upon such foundations always treasured these age-old, inspiring ideas, in different locales and under all kinds of circumstances. Love of fellow men, love of fellow Jews, did not simply remain theoretical concepts which one could choose to implement or not. They grew and fused into the Jewish people; they became part of the Jewish psyche. They became an inseparable part of the Jewish week and holiday. A Mishnah passage accenting the importance of a good, sympathetic heart has been incorporated into our daily prayers (*Peah* 1). And more: it serves as an introduction to the prayers. It is supposed to open the doors to the temple of the Siddur, the prayer book.

The obligation of every individual Jew and of every Jewish community to redeem captives, to make every effort to free Jewish prisoners or innocent victims who were unjustly incarcerated by a wicked regime, is a repeated leitmotif in all periods of our history and everywhere in the Diaspora.

The practice of *maos chittin*—giving money for a Passover fund—a voluntary and yet well-organized assistance which must be extended to all who cannot afford to prepare for the holiday, is part of our written and unwritten Code. It is obligatory upon all Jews, whether they follow Rabbi Joseph Caro's *Shulchan Aruch*, the glosses of Rabbi Moses Isserles, or those of Rabbi Isaac Luria (the Ari).

Throughout our history, many—and not only moralists—laid building blocks for the structure of attributes. The medieval Spanish-Jewish poet Moses ibn Ezra was influenced by

Moslem poetry. His essay on poetry focuses on the rules of rhyme and rhythm—yet this Jewish poet also deemed it necessary to add that every man's goal should be to improve his own traits and influence his fellow man to do likewise.

In twelfth-century Spain, Maimonides introduced the ideas of Aristotle into Jewish thinking. But he infused the Greek system of logic with Jewish ethicality. Needless to say, his magnum opus, the *Mishneh Torah*, begins with a call to observe with all one's soul and might the eternal values of Jewish morality. In his philosophical work, the *Guide to the Perplexed*, the thinker from Cordoba returns to this theme. Maimonides avers that society becomes perfected through our improving of our own traits—and that that is the most important thing in life (*Guide* 3:35).

We rightfully complain that we live at a time of the twilight of values. But it is incorrect to state that this has caused compassion and goodness to absolutely cease to be Jewish traits. The significant Jewish thinkers of the recent past were moralists. Their great concern was how to inspire men's hearts amid the raging, licentious winds, and how to prevent the Jewish heart from becoming blunted.

At a time when the Prussian school of thought had the upper hand in European philosophy and tenderness and empathy were held to be diametrically opposite to the goals of modern society and modern cities, Shmuel David Luzzatto retained his belief that compassion and goodness were absolute values. That is why they cannot be cast aside along with the caprices of fashion.

With different ways and approaches, Hermann Cohen, Franz Rosenzweig, and Martin Buber came to the same conclusion. They said that good and evil are not dependent upon outside factors, but stem from within us and our hearts' reactions. That is why our life has meaning only when we introduce the prophetic idea of God and man into the chaos of the world.

It is true that the communes of the Essenes, spurred by the desire to purify themselves in lofty Jewish traits, delved deeply into their thoughts two thousand years ago in their tents by the shores of the Dead Sea. But the pioneers who founded the kibbutzim in the Galilee at the beginning of our Return to Zion, albeit with changed lifestyles and with new terminology, strove in exactly the same fashion to tear the lonely, suffering individual out of his apathetic, cruel surroundings and to place the fallen crown of pure traits upon the head of man and Jew. There may be a huge gap of time between the Dead Sea Scrolls and the reflections of Aaron David Gordon, but both brim with determination to introduce—at a time of spiritual desolation— passion and vigor into ideals which can never become attenuated.

In our generation, we have not basked in the fire of *ahavas yisroel*—love for one's fellow Jew—as did Rabbi Israel Salanter. But this does not mean that we are a totally orphaned generation. For the authors of *Chofetz Chaim* and *Chazon Ish*, the field of law (*halakhah*, or "way") which they worked in had the practical meaning of walking in the proper way. It is a path that leads away from the egoistic "I" and lets one embrace one's fellow man with true love.

The Chofetz Chaim traveled the length and breadth of Russia and Poland in wagons and sleighs, distributing his book of the same name. In it he declared: Guard your tongue from speaking evil. Do not say evil things about anyone. Uproot jealousy and hatred from yourself. Implant love and goodness. And the Chazon Ish, the saintly scholar of Bnei-Brak, mirrored the Jewish outlook of compassion and kindliness.

Both men reflected the hopes and expectations of the individual and the community—indeed, eternal Jewish dreams— which are the higher reality and contain the quintessential meaning of our existence.

The eternal and monumental aspects of modern Jewish literature are actually a continuation of the generations-long Jewish call for a higher humanity. There are many examples, but one work that should be cited is S. Ansky's drama *The Dybbuk*, where elements of mysticism are used to bring feelings of justice and compassion into petrified hearts. We should also mention that the eternal beauty that radiates out of the folk stories of I. L. Peretz is part of the splendid Jewish traits described in them.

In Warsaw, where I grew up, every night amid the tumult and bustle of daily life, Jewish youngsters in a little *beis medresh*, a house of study, in the noisy neighborhood of Franciszkańska Street, set stringent demands upon themselves. These youngsters, known as Musarniks, demanded full devotion and honesty of their own conscience. They demanded feelings of compassion and purity of their hearts. Actually, this was the attitude that Jews and Judaism have demanded of themselves and of others ever since we began our march through history.

II

The purpose of this essay, then, is not to deny that improvement of behavior traits was always characteristic of the various movements, religious and secular, which arose in Jewish life and which expressed Jewish civilization in all its forms. Nevertheless, it is not superfluous to stress that in Hasidism the old Jewish traits of charity and compassion took on new fire. Indeed, good deeds were not the special monopoly of Hasidism and Hasidic masters; but the intent, the ecstasy, the passion which Hasidism put into its entire doctrine actually blazed into flames when it came to the concepts of *ahavas habrios* and *ahavas yisroel*—love of one's fellow man and love of fellow Jews.

Reb Simcha Bunim of Pshishkhe explained that we do not recite a blessing when we donate to charity because for that commandment one cannot and must not make any preparations, for meanwhile the needy person may die of hunger, God forbid. Reb Meir of Premishlan said that of the three foundation stones of the world—Torah, sacred service, and kind deeds—the last is most important. This remark was based upon the verse in the Psalms (99:3): "For I have said that kindness will build the world." Kindness is the foundation stone of the world.

The Kotzk rebbe, Reb Mendele, explained why the phrase

"holy shall ye be" appears in the plural in Hebrew (*kedoshim*). A person can rise to the level of holiness only when he stops thinking of himself as a separate individual and is not constantly wrapped up in himself and with his own needs, but feels that he is part of the community and cares for others. With a shift of letters, *sheker* ("falsehood") becomes the opposite of *kesher* ("link" or "connection"). The Jew who is not linked up heart and soul with the community at large is subjugated by falsehood.

Reb Pinchas of Koretz explained the biblical verse "the offerings of food due Me, as offerings by fire" (Numbers 28:2) as follows: Feeding fellow human beings is the sacrifice God wants of us. The above-mentioned Reb Meir of Premishlan had his own interpretation for the traditional order of the Passover Seder: *Kadesh* ("Sanctification," or "Recite the *Kiddush*"), *Ur-'chatz* ("Wash hands"), *Karpas* ("Eat greens"), *Yachatz* ("Break the matzah"). When the Jew proceeds to sanctify himself before God and wash away his sins, he must first of all share his bed and bread with a needy person. (In this interpretation, a play on words is made with *karpas* ["greens"] by breaking it up into two words: *kar* ["pillow" or "lodgings"] and *pas* [another word for "bread"].) And it was the view of Rabbi Jacob Isaac, the Seer of Lublin, that the improvement of behavior is *the* vision of man, and that sincere moral striving is the essence of life. In Hasidism, he stated, we want people of fine attributes to develop, people who master their own deeds, for we cannot understand how a Jew could lack such warm Jewish behavior traits.

Truth to say, even those who opposed Hasidism could not close their eyes to the special ecstasy which caused the old Jewish lifeways to perk up among Hasidim. People were amazed at the vibrant meaning given to such overused terms as "friendship" and "love of mankind," often empty of meaning.

The anti-Hasidic satire *Revealer of Secrets* by the Haskalah writer Joseph Perl was not sparing in its biting and bitter criticism. Nevertheless, when during the first decades of the nineteenth century masses of Jewish emigrants began to stream illegally from Russian-occupied regions to Galician-Austrian provinces and were imprisoned, Joseph Perl could not hide the fact that the Hasidim attempted to have them set free, assuring the authorities that these Jews "were born in Tarnopol." Exactly the same thing is shown in another anti-Hasidic satire written at that time, *Valley of Refaim* by Isaac Ber Levinson. He said that the Hasidic courtyard literally swarmed with beggars who got warmth and help there.

A contemporary historian, Dr. Raphael Mahler, who was far removed from the Hasidic outlook, states in his book *Hasidism and Haskalah* that the lofty humanitarian social elements which had become entrenched in the movement deserve earnest attention and appreciation. Even non-Jewish government officials stressed this fact. In a report sent by the Austrian police at the beginning of the nineteenth century we read: "that is why members of this sect are called Hasidim, for they perform acts of kindness for the suffering and needy."

It seems that in this ecstatic readiness to assist the poor and dejected we find—in a rather strong measure—the reason for the strong attraction that Hasidism had for the East European Jewish masses. Surely, the way was shown by Israel Baal Shem Tov, the teacher's assistant from Mezhibuzh, himself needy and hungry, a brother in want with others who were humiliated and exploited.

But those who came after him also gave heart and soul to eliminate the individual's and the community's sorrows. And even in a lifestyle where the cord of compassion for one's fellow man never ceased to vibrate, the Jewish spirit had to be stirred up by the waves of kindness and goodness which flowed with unrestrained vigor in Hasidism.

"Why do you think the Baal Shem Tov was called by that name?" Reb Pinchas of Koretz once asked his congregation. And he continued: "He was called Baal Shem because he called the Jewish soul by its name (*shem*). He awakened it and encouraged it to drink from the wellsprings of kindness and *ahavas yisroel*."

Jews were amazed by each of the teachers of Hasidism on account of their words and deeds, their lives and accomplishments. Take, for instance, Reb Leib Sarah's, a man whose life is a mixture of legend and fact. Yet we know that he constantly wandered through Jewish settlements and devoted his entire life to revoking decrees against Jews, redeeming captives, and feeding the hungry. He did not set out on a journey without a sack—so the Hasidic tale tells us—for in it he placed Jewish troubles. He put that sack under his head when he went to sleep, and its contents insinuated themselves into his sensibility and thoughts.

And we have Reb Wolf Zbarizher. Once, when his wife had an argument with the housemaid, she took the girl to the local rabbinic court for a judgment. Seeing Reb Wolf running after them, his wife told him that he need not trouble himself, for she was capable of presenting her side. Reb Wolf answered that he was not going to the courtroom for her sake, but to defend the maid, a poor orphan who unfortunately had no one to plead her cause. This same Reb Wolf Zbarizher declared everything he owned as abandoned every evening, so that if thieves entered at night, they would be free of the sin of robbery.

And we have Reb Menachem Mendel of Kosov, who knew how to couple moralizing with tenderness. He made Hasidim cry when he asked them why they were not doing more to ease the bitter fate of the poor and needy. And there is Reb Levi Yitzchok of Berditchev, who argued dramatically with God. With holy impudence he called the Creator to judgment—for when it concerns Jewish troubles even the Creator of the Universe is obliged to justify Himself. "What can I do?" Levi Yitzchok argued with God, "if Jewish sighs are constantly roaring in my heart and I cannot silence my demand that You should be what You are and should be: a merciful Father."

Here, in the history of Hasidism, there is no need to rummage and seek out the names of those who studied the Torah of the heart with all their heart and soul and fulfilled it down to the last detail. They surge forth in a current which cannot be stopped. We are actually inundated with oceans upon oceans of goodness. For instance, Reb Hirsh of Zhiditchev, who married off dozens of orphans. And each time there was a wedding in his own family, a wedding had to be arranged for a orphan, which he provided for. Charity, Reb Hirsh stated, is purity, and he who gives charity becomes pure.

And we have Reb Naftali of Ropshitz, who kept his Hanukah menorah pawned all year and distributed the sum realized among the poor. And there is Reb Uri of Strelisk. Whenever he spoke publicly he always stressed how important it is to make friends; to feel the sorrows of a fellow Jew as if they were your own. And we have the Seer of Lublin, who did not consider his day concluded until he had given to the needy every last penny in his possession.

And there is Reb David of Lelov. Upon seeing Jewish tenant farmers unjustly thrown into jail, he cried bitterly. It is told that when his son was ill, Hasidim came to visit him. "Why are you so solicitous about my son?" he said. "Do you show the same concern when other Jewish children are sick, God forbid?" With his anguish and love, he embraced the world and all its living creatures. He berated the wagoner for whipping his horse. One must ultimately give an accounting of oneself, Reb David said, even for mistreating animals.

When Hasidic teachings occasionally repeat themselves, and remarks made by one leader are also ascribed to another, it happens most often when the subject is the commandment "You shall love," which flows out of the ancient Jewish sources. Both commandments which begin with "You shall love" (one referring to God, the other to one's fellow man) are essentially one. One must love one's fellow man as one loves oneself. That means: with all his faults and defects.

Who offered this interpretation? One can read in the Hasidic books that many of the great Hasidic masters from the Ukraine, from Congress Poland, from Galicia explained the intent of these verses in this fashion. Reb Nachum of Tchernobil said that the Holy Temple will stand in every Jewish heart when a sacrifice is brought there for those who expect our help. He foreswore all repose throughout his life, but traveled through towns and villages to redeem those who suffered anguish on account of evil-minded Polish squires.

Reb Yechiel Mikhl of Zlotchev asserted that before he began his morning prayers he bound himself to all of Israel; and only when he felt that he was bound up with the entire community of Israel could he bind the straps of the tefillin to his arm. And Reb Moshe of Kobrin wanted the congregation to realize why Moses assembled the Jews on the morning after Yom Kippur. Moses did this because he wanted to teach us that one should express love not only on the holy day but also on the day after the fast has ended, as well as during the rest of the year.

Reb Yechiel Meir of Gostinin, who was called "The Psalms Jew," once flared up at the sexton. The sexton had asked a Jew who had arrived in the morning after a long journey whether he had recited his prayers. Reb Yechiel Meir told the sexton: "The first thing you should have asked him was whether he had eaten breakfast."

Reb Yechiel Meir left a list of twenty rules he had written for himself—rules that reminded him how to conduct himself. One of them states that he should not do things unthinkingly, and that every moment should be filled with love and compassion. When Reb Yechiel Meir was informed that one of his bitter opponents had fallen ill, he began to pray for him fervently.

"If he hates me, he evidently has a good reason for it," Reb Yechiel Meir said, "and hence the responsibility falls upon me to pray for him."

Reb Shmelke of Nikolsburg asserted that Jews are obliged to give to charity even if one deprives oneself of food. Once, a poor man came to him for a donation and he did not have a penny at home to offer him. He searched several drawers, found a gold ring, and gave it to the man. When Reb Shmelke's wife discovered what he had done, she reproached him.

"How could you do such a thing?" she said. "Giving away such a precious ring."

Reb Shmelke then ran after the poor man. "Mister," he

shouted, "it's a very valuable ring. Don't let them cheat you when you sell it!"

III

Let us now focus on Reb Moshe Leib of Sosev. Assessing who in the Hasidic world ascended the highest rungs of kindness is extremely difficult. But perhaps more evidence has been amassed about Reb Moshe Leib than about any of the others who, like him, transformed periods of anguish and dejection into dramas of human exaltation. The stories about Reb Moshe Leib in various Hasidic books testify as to what a wonderful phenomenon was the teaching of the heart in Hasidism. Reb Moshe Leib of Sosev was a student of the above-mentioned Reb Shmelke of Nikolsburg. It is from him that he learned Torah, Kabbalah, and most especially, *ahavas yisroel.*

Reb Moshe Leib of Sosev was the rabbi whom I. L. Peretz depicted so warmly in his famous short story "If Not Higher." The rabbi, dressed in peasant's clothing, went into a forest to chop wood and then went to the cottage of a poor, ill widow, where he heated her stove and brought sparks of belief and faith into her depressed spirit. However, Peretz changed the facts somewhat. He ascribed these deeds and events to the rebbe of Nemirov. Peretz also changed the time to the Penitential Days prior to Rosh Hashanah.

The Hasidic books state the facts as related by Reb Zvi Hirsh from Zhiditchev. The latter had heard controversial stories about Reb Moshe Leib's recitation of the Midnight service in commemoration of the destruction of Jerusalem. So on a cold winter night he slipped into the rebbe's prayer room. He saw Reb Moshe Leib rise, garb himself in peasant's clothing, go out into the snow-covered courtyard, bring up some wood from the cellar, bind it into a bundle, place the bundle on his shoulder, and begin to walk.

Reb Zvi Hirsh followed Reb Moshe Leib in the bitter cold of the winter night to the edge of town. Reb Moshe Leib stopped before a battered cottage. When he entered, the rebbe of Zhiditchev looked through the window and learned the true meaning of the Midnight Service.

In a bed lay a woman pressing to her heart a tiny infant. Reb Moshe Leib chatted with the woman in the peasants' language, heated the oven, and consoled her regarding her want. While he was chopping wood and lighting the fire, he recited the prayers of the Midnight Service.

Reb Zvi Hirsh said that he could hear Reb Moshe Leib humming with his usual, heartrending melody: "Shake the dust off yourself; arise, O Jerusalem. Have compassion, Master of the Universe, and let the walls of Jerusalem be rebuilt!"

In *Deeds of the Righteous* we read that Reb Moshe Leib once confided that he had learned the true meaning of love of fellow men from a simple village peasant. The gentile sat in a tavern with several friends; when he was a bit tipsy he asked his pal:

"Do you like me, or don't you like me?"

"Sure I like you," replied his friend.

"You say you like me," the peasant continued, "but you don't even know what I need. If you really like someone, you know what he needs and what he's missing."

And Reb Moshe Leib ended his story by saying: "It was only then that I first understood that loving people means sensing their needs, linking oneself with their pains, and feeling their troubles."

In various books we see how Reb Moshe Leib displayed his solicitude and fatherly devotion to sick children. With his own hands he would bind their wounds. With his own hands he rubbed salve on their scrofulous heads. And with his own mouth Moshe Leib sucked the pus out of their abscesses. "He who cannot persuade himself to suck the pus out of the abscesses of sick children's wounds," he said, "hasn't even reached the half measure of *ahavas yisroel.*"

Reb Moshe Leib was called the father of widows and orphans. Whatever he possessed he gave away to people who needed help, even though he and his family also lived in want. He had a woman neighbor whose children died at a young age, and she came to Reb Moshe Leib to complain. In her bitterness she blurted out:

"He is not a good God. A God who gives children and then takes them away is a cruel God."

"Don't say things like that," Reb Moshe Leib's wife shouted at her. "Rather say that God's ways cannot be understood and that everything He does is for the good."

But Reb Moshe Leib justified the mother. "Not everything must be accepted with love," he said. "And apparently even God must be reminded to be compassionate." According to the books the following incident, related in many different versions, happened to him. Once, on the night of *Kol Nidrei*, he was late coming to the synagogue. On his way Reb Moshe Leib heard a baby crying who had been left alone at home. He let the congregation wait until he had pacified the child.

Interestingly, in this moving teaching of the heart no difference was made between Jew and gentile. Jews suffered more and more intensely, and hence they needed empathy more. But every man is a part of God and deserves our goodwill. Once, when a drunken peasant knocked on Reb Moshe Leib's window in the middle of the night and asked him to admit him and provide a bed, the rebbe let him in and prepared a bed for him. When Moshe Leib was asked how he could share everyone's sorrow, he answered:

"Everyone's sorrow is my sorrow, so it's absurd to talk about sharing. Everyone's anguish is my anguish."

He would travel from fair to fair, where in those days one could meet Jews from various regions and listen to Jewish complaints and cries of woe. But, the story goes, he would also look after the horses and calves and bring them pails of water when they were thirsty.

It would be incorrect to assume that with such magnificent purity of heart there was no room for scholarship. Reb Moshe Leib wrote original interpretations of the Talmud, which were published posthumously by his students. He would also make remarks which displayed his profundity. "Everything was created with a purpose," he said. "Even bad traits came into the world not without reason. There is even a purpose in nonbelief. If a man comes up to you with an outstretched hand, do not send him away with the excuse that God will help him. *You* must help him, as if there were no one else in the world to ease his burden, and as if there were no God."

Rob Moshe Leib said that our path during our brief lifespan on this earth may be compared to the blade of a knife. On both sides lies an abyss, and in the middle is a thin, narrow path— sharp and lurking with danger. He also remarked that the poor man can readily have faith in God, for he cannot depend on anyone else. But the rich man, you see, is in an entirely different position. It is more difficult for him to have faith, for his wealth calls to him in a multitude of voices: "You can rely on your wealth! Your wealth gives you security!"

As soft and docile as he was, the rebbe of Sosev quarreled with the callous, heartless Polish landowners when it came to redeeming Jewish captives. He was unusually aggressive with them and demanded justice for the unjustly treated and humiliated Jewish tenant farmers. He put his life in jeopardy in order to save them from the claws of injustice.

The Hasidic books and the folk legends also tell tales about his departure from the world in 1807. The leitmotif is characteristic of his personality. Reb Moshe Leib of Sosev was always busy arranging marriages for orphans. He engaged bands of musicians, composed melodies and dances, and participated in the wedding dances. He made certain that people were merry at the weddings of the poor, as if they were celebrations of the wealthy. It goes without saying that he would later attend to the livelihood of the matched couples. And that is how, as the tales spun by the folk tell us, with bands of playing musicians, with the melodies which expressed his deepest feelings, Reb Moshe Leib was brought to his eternal rest.

IV

When Reb Bunim of Pshishkhe was asked if he knew a rebbe whose heart was broken and yet whole, he answered: "Yes, I knew one. It was Reb Moshe Leib of Sosev."

But the truth is that this rare combination of brokenness and wholeness, of sigh and song, which manifested itself in the life and works of Moshe Leib of Sosev, and which transforms him into a distinct representative of a culture and a way of life, is actually the great expression of Torah of the heart, an age-old teaching that was renewed with fire, vigor, and ecstasy among East European Jewry. There, the drabness of life was compensated by a pattern of behavior which—even to our generation that lived and breathed in those environs—seems awfully distant. There, the daily reality was replete with traits which seem unreal to us.

There, in that world that is no more, people who were strangers were brought home to the Sabbath table, having been spotted at the doorway of the synagogue or the Hasidic prayer-house at the end of the service. Even if their appearance was beggarly, they were given a place of honor at the table among the family—just because they were strangers and Sabbath guests. There, scholars, men of noble degree, and even simple folk considered it a moral duty to spend at least a couple of sleepless nights a week tending the ill, who often were neither relatives nor friends. There, provisions were made that Jews passing through a community would have a place to spend the night.

There, on a Saturday morning people went through every courtyard where Jews dwelled with the call, *"Gut shabbes, Jews!"* This was the sign to bring down challah and food to be distributed among the poor. Indeed, within a few minutes baskets were full of Sabbath gifts. There, Jewish families who themselves lived modestly on the fringes of poverty took yeshiva students into their homes and gave them meals. There, existed voluntary institutions whose names smacked of ancient times—"House of Bread" and "Supporters of the Poor"—and they provided needy families with all the necessities for a holiday.

There too, in tiny outlying communities, existed societies such as "The Shelter," "Visit the Sick," "Dower the Bride." This heartfelt display of humaneness was rendered quietly and without fanfare. There, on the eve of World War Two, when the brutal Germans expelled masses of Jews from their homes to the Polish border town of Zbonshin, organized help for the refugees sprang into being; it encompassed great and small, and all levels of the society worked together in this rescue mission; such assistance also blazed selflessly when portents in heaven and on earth pointed to the tragic decline of East European Jewry.

Of course not everyone was an angel there. But goodness was a way of life. Compassion was spontaneous and natural. Conduct that was out of line with kindliness was regarded as an impudent, spiteful act against God, Judaism, and the teaching that man is created in the divine image.

Acts of compassion and traits of kindness were surely not the monopoly of any special movement or sect within Judaism. Yiddishkeyt in all its forms was permeated with social fervor. The element of humaneness was expressed in all strands of Judaism. And throughout the ages man was supposed to hearken to the humanitarian call to realize his human potential.

But this teaching of the heart that developed in Hasidism surely made a great and historic contribution to the synthesis of brokenness and wholeness, and to the spontaneous culture of compassion that was characteristic of East European Jewry.

4

Reb Levi Yitzchok of Berditchev and the Auschwitz Generation

I

REB LEVI YITZCHOK of Berditchev's path was, naturally, the one of Hasidism—he followed the Baal Shem Tov's teaching that stressed heart and feeling. In the flowing sea of Jewish tribulations, this teaching welled up with wondrous joy and emotion—and in times of wrath and horror, it breathed enthusiasm and courage into a depressed Jewish spirit.

But when Reb Levi Yitzchok of Berditchev began to spread his teaching to his fellow Jews in Ukrainian and Polish towns and villages, the Baal Shem Tov was no longer alive. As interpreted by his disciples, the doctrine of the wandering village teacher of Mezhibuzh took on the most diverse forms. As might have been expected, these disciples introduced their own nuances into the simple and yet deeply mystical teaching that had been revealed in the Carpathian Mountains. Into this young, budding movement they placed the stamp of their own personalities.

Reb Dov Ber of Mezeritch, who is known as the "Maggid," enhanced Hasidism's spiritual heritage with a superb, incisive intellect. The Baal Shem Tov's son had cast his white kaftan on the Maggid's shoulders to indicate that the Maggid was worthy of being the follower of the founder of Hasidism. Hasidism, originally a teaching of the heart, was developed by the Maggid into a teaching of profound thought.

This is apparent in the Maggid's sermon collections pertaining to God and creation, man and life. Here he develops a world view that draws upon the Kabbalah and bathes in the light of the *Zohar*, a world view that dares to penetrate the secrets of the universe and of existence. The Maggid discusses the people of Israel's role in God's plans, and states that since everything in our life and striving is a mystery, it is impossible for us to penetrate the secretive veil spread over us and within us and plumb the why and wherefore of our sufferings and joys. We must find a perfect, exalted person to take us by the hand and show us the way which leads to God and to our own inner self.

Actually, this concept was stated hundreds of years earlier by Maimonides. In Reb Dov Ber's sermons, the figure of the perfect personality possessed neither the sophisticated culture nor the scholarly attributes so characteristic of Maimonides. In Reb Dov Ber's view, the perfect personality breathed with Polish-Jewish folksiness and even spoke with a Volhyn Yiddish accent. But neither Maimonides nor the Maggid of Mezeritch paid much attention to the daily needs and practical requirements of each and every one of us; both stated that for man's happiness and satisfaction the cosmic role to which he aspires is crucial.

Once, after returning from a visit to Mezeritch, Reb Aaron of Karlin was asked what he had learned there.

"Nothing," he replied.

"What do you mean nothing?" he was asked again.

To which Reb Aaron responded, "In Mezeritch I learned that I am absolutely nothing."

According to the testimony of others who also attempted to seek stronghold and substance in their proximity to the Maggid, Reb Dov Ber did not warm their hearts with parables and stories in the manner of the Baal Shem Tov. The Maggid inspired reverence. He awakened holy trembling. But the oppressed and tormented Jew who threw himself thirstily into the wellsprings of Hasidism actually craved and yearned for that refreshing strength which flowed so energetically from the

Baal Shem Tov and which could lead the Jew out of his gloomy despair and loneliness.

Similar warnings and admonitions were directed at the Jew by *The Generations of Jacob Joseph*, written by another of the Baal Shem Tov's great disciples. This book, by Rabbi Jacob Joseph of Polonoi, in the province of Volhyn, was doubtless extremely important for the growth of the new movement. Rabbi Jacob Joseph is surely one of the sharpest and most virulent polemicists in our entire literature. His castigating the manifestations of moral debasement that he decried in his book shook his readers.

The same sense of shock overwhelms us nowadays as we read his book nearly two hundred years after its publication. The rabbi of Polonoi criticizes, rebukes, preaches, and zealously attacks the dreadful wrongs committed by man against man. These are all the more painful and disgraceful when committed by those from whom one would have least expected it—rabbis, community figures, leaders of the people of Israel. In the storm of his fearless admonitions, none of these powerful personages are spared.

True: Rabbi Jacob Joseph's book earned its fame as one of the early classics of Hasidic literature. Still, questions remain. Were rebuke and the listing of sins, which surely would serve only to increase the individual Jew's guilt feelings and intensify the bitterness in the hearts of people who were already embittered, really the essense of the Baal Shem Tov's teaching? Didn't Reb Israel Baal Shem Tov come down from the Carpathian Mountains for the sole purpose of raising the fallen and placing balsam on their wounds? Shouldn't Hasidism, as developed by its teacher and founder, preach less to the people and preoccupy itself more with finding good attributes in Jews, even if they were rolling in the quagmire of sin?

The profound concepts that Reb Shneur Zalman of Liady introduced into Hasidic teaching sparked immense admiration for him and for his work, the *Tanya*. In this original study, Reb Shneur Zalman, the founder of the Lubavitch movement, makes his mark as a giant of Halakhah (Jewish law), a master of profound thought, and one of the keenest minds in the history of Jewish spirituality.

However, it should be said that this new and bold interpretation also prompted astonishment not only among the opponents of the Hasidic movement but also among its adherents and supporters. In the *Tanya*, the teaching of Baal Shem Tov has seemingly taken on a new form. It no longer overwhelms with its sincerity and simplicity but is transformed into a philosophical system and ascends the rungs of speculative intellect. In the dense language of Reb Shneur Zalman the teaching became wisdom, intelligence, understanding—and, in the final analysis, ceased to be accessible to the average man. Was this what Hasidism was supposed to be at the dawn of its history? In this new and unexpected garb, could Hasidism soothe the spirit and caress and console the pained Jewish soul?

In those days, followers of the Baal Shem Tov who did not achieve the glory of the Maggid of Mezeritch or the author of the *Tanya* also wandered about through the towns and villages of Volhyn and Podolia. Nevertheless, in their own form and manner they too spread and embodied the idea of Hasidism.

Reb Moshe Leib of Sosev focused on the Jew's needs and sufferings, his dreams and hopes. He devoted himself to healing the poor, mangy Jewish children. Reb Moshe Leib of Sosev used to put salve on the scabies-laden heads of children and bind their wounds, happy that he was destined to ease the torments of the little ones. With his own mouth he often sucked the pus out of the children's abscesses, and he did this with the full conciousness of a Jew who was fulfilling the mitzvah of *ahavas yisroel*, love for one's fellow Jew, with his entire heart and soul.

A Hasidic book, *The Deeds of the Righteous*, has a story about Reb Moshe Leib, which later appeared in various versions and in the course of time was ascribed to other zaddikim. Once, during the night of *Kol Nidrei*, while going to his synagogue, the rebbe of Sosev heard a baby crying in a house. He realized at once that the child had been left alone by his parents, who no doubt were at the synagogue. He entered and sat down, attempting to calm the sobbing child. Stopping the baby's crying was more important and more precious for Reb Moshe Leib than being with the congregation on the night of Yom Kippur.

In the well-known story by I. L. Peretz, "If Not Higher," no name is given to the Hasidic rebbe who on *Selichos* night would go into the forest and chop wood to heat the house of a poor widow. But I. L. Peretz based his story upon material he had read in *Deeds of the Righteous,* which identifies this remarkable rebbe as Moshe Leib of Sosev and adds that the rebbe of Zhiditchev was present, for he was visiting Reb Moshe Leib.

In those days Reb Meir of Premishlan returned to the original teachings of the heart developed by the Baal Shem Tov. He constantly repeated that nothing in man's life is more important than kindness and compassion—traits which are human and not necessarily Jewish. The rebbe of Premishlan laid particular stress on the prayer: "For You hearken to the prayers of all mankind."

From this list of exceptional personalities of that era one should not omit Reb Zev Wolf of Zvarish, who in his simple fashion called upon Jews to embrace people near and far with love and warmth. On a frosty winter night, when his wagoner stood outside guarding the horses, Zev Wolf of Zvarish chased the wagoner into the house and watched the horses himself, almost freezing to death because of the raging cold. This folk rabbi would always assert that the Jew in his daily hustle and bustle doesn't need punishment or preaching, but sincere empathy and consolation. Reb Menachem Mendel of Kosov followed a similar path to man and God. He saw love of our fellow Jew as our principal obligation; it is for this that his soul and all our souls have descended into this vale of tears.

All the colorful sparkle of Hasidism notwithstanding, the growing movement still lacked a teacher who would combine the moving human attributes of a Reb Moshe Leib of Sosev and the intellectual talents of a Reb Dov Ber of Mezeritch. Missing was a zaddik who would stamp the movement, which had serpentined along diverse paths and byways, with deep thought and glowing feeling, and who would be able to impress upon the people the charm of his personality. Lacking was the teacher who would embody the harsh reality of daily life and yet be woven of poetry and legend.

The times were difficult. It was a period of searching, of crisis and uncertainty. A majority of the Jewish people was then concentrated in Eastern Europe. The last decades of the eighteenth century and the dawn of the nineteenth cast a great fear and many difficult problems upon the people. The Polish kingdom fell apart, and with the crumbling political structure, the Jews were vulnerable and subject to the caprices of every temporary ruler.

The French Revolution, whose resounding echoes had also reached the Jewish centers, and the Napoleonic Wars that followed, increased the social and economic agitation and brought spiritual bewilderment. Everything seemed to be in a state of precariousness and shock. The Hasidic movement and its teachings, which one or two generations earlier seemed to be a stronghold for the Jew in a crumbling world, also stood at the parting of the ways.

II

Forty years after the destruction of millions of Jews in the gas chambers of Auschwitz and Treblinka, we marvel at the poise with which Reb Levi Yitzchok of Berditchev dealt with adversity. He handled his personal troubles and suffering, as well as the raging storm that seethed within him as he faced the anguish and woe that befell the community. He is etched into the memory of generations for his arguments and disputes with God and for his great defense of the Jewish people. Yet when it came to his personal life, the same Levi Yitzchok was also quiet and patient, literally a "Bontshe Shveig" (as in the memorable story of I. L. Peretz).

He is called Reb Levi Yitzchok of Berditchev, but he lived in Berditchev only the last twenty-five years of his life. Persecuted and driven out by communities where he attempted to settle,

he was forced to wander from place to place. A slice of Eastern
Europe's Jewish geography clung to his wanderer's staff. Hu-
siakov, Zamosc, Lubartow, Ritchewol, Pinsk are but a few of
villages and towns connected with his life and work. He was
expelled from Pinsk, where he was preacher and rabbi; similarly in Zelechow, where on Hoshanna Rabbah his meager
store of poverty was thrown into a small wagon, and he and
his family were sent packing.

What were their complaints against him? Levi Yitzchok be-
lieved that the idea of Hasidism could enrich and elevate the
Jewish spirit; his opponents considered Hasidism dangerous.
At that time a bitter struggle ensued between Hasidim and
Misnagdim. Reb Levi Yitzchok, it so happened, came from a
Misnagdic home. But he was attracted by the Hasidic teachings
and by the Hasidic way of life. He never met the Baal Shem
Tov, for when Israel Baal Shem Tov died Levi Yitzchok was
twenty years old. But the Baal Shem Tov always lived in his
heart and in his thoughts.

Reb Levi Yitzchok was convinced that one can reach God and
man via the path of Hasidism. His opponents never doubted
his genius in learning. The rabbi of Brisk, Abraham Katzenel-
lenbogen, was a famous Misnaged. Levi Yitzchok once had an
open debate in the Warsaw suburb of Praga with the rabbi, and
even he recognized that this representative of Hasidic thought
was a genius. And also the skeptical Misnaged who watched
Levi Yitzchok's ecstatic prayer with amusement had to admit
that something began to stir in him as Reb Levi Yitzchok wept
over the prayer "And a Redeemer shall come to Zion and to
those who shall repent of their sins." Nevertheless, some
people could not tolerate the fire which imbued Reb Levi
Yitzchok's remarks.

Levi Yitzchok, or as he was known by his family name,
Derbaremdicker, "the merciful one" (the term which he always
used in referring to God), swallowed all these insults and
disappointments with rare calm. He would pray that no harm
come to those who had ill-treated him. Once, when a woman
dumped a sackful of garbage on his head, he continued his

measured stride to the synagogue as though nothing had happened. He raised his eyes heavenward and asked God not to punish the woman. "What do you have against her?" he asked. "She was only fulfilling the command of her husband."

Historians of Hasidism who display minimal understanding of this movement and its meaning in Jewish history treat the personality of Reb Levi Yitzchok of Berditchev with astonishing sympathy. In the chapter devoted to Reb Levi Yitzchok in his *History of Hasidism,* Simon Dubnow seemingly abandons his cool scholarly detachment. He too considered Reb Levi Yitzchok of Berditchev "different."

The fact is that nothing could extinguish Reb Levi Yitzchok's ardent love for his fellow Jew. He felt he had to assume partial if not total responsibility for the fate of the individual and the community. The biblical Noah did not impress him as a representative righteous man. He cannot even serve as an example for an ordinary Jew. Noah was not sufficiently concerned about his fellow human beings. He was too much preoccupied with himself. Abraham was the first to compassionately embrace world and man. And Abraham did not express his restlessness by building an ark for himself and several other intimates; Abraham built ideas that would prompt a revolution in men's minds. He demanded justice even for the wicked men of Sodom.

Kind and mild with others, Reb Levi Yitzchok was severe and stringent with himself. Of himself he demanded more humanity, more decency, more Jewishness. He said that the Torah begins with the second letter, *beis* ("Bereishis"), and a Talmud tractate begins with page two—to show us that no matter how much we study and speculate and purify ourselves, we still have not come up to the first letter, the *aleph,* and we are always still at pre-beginning.

During his lifetime Jews considered him the devoted defender of the Jews. And that is how we regard him constantly. In our millennia-long history there is hardly another person who so continually and enthusiastically defended and justified the Jews. There was never even an interruption in his unend-

ing praise of the Jews. With boundless energy Reb Levi Yitzchok sought to persuade all of us that the speck of shadow in
the Jewish conscience was due to persecutions and loneliness,
exile and edicts. But in the depths of his soul the Jew was good.

Once, on the eve of Yom Kippur, while the congregation had
already gathered in the synagogue for *Kol Nidrei*, Reb Levi
Yitzchok, holding a candle, looked for something under a
bench.

"Who are you looking for, Rebbe?" he was asked.

He replied: "I'm looking for a drunken Jew, and I simply
cannot find one." And at once he began a conversation with
God. "Look, God, and see what a precious folk your Jews are.
You commanded them to eat and drink on the eve of Yom
Kippur. You even promised them that whoever eats and drinks
on the eve of Yom Kippur is like one who has fasted on Yom
Kippur. If other nations of the world had such a day, how
many would now be sprawling in the mud, how many now
would be wounded and killed?

"But look at Your Jews. During the day they obeyed your
commandment and prepared holiday feasts. Now, as the sun is
setting, all of them are here in the *beis medresh*. No one is
drunk. Everyone is standing on his feet, clean and holy, ready
to do repentance with his entire heart. For this alone don't they
deserve that You should grant them a good year?"

Another time, on the morning of the eve of Passover, after
the *chometz* had been burned, Reb Levi Yitzchok of Berditchev
went out to the marketplace. Meeting a gentile who made his
livelihood smuggling merchandise over the border, Reb Levi
Yitzchok asked him:

"Do you have any imported silks?"

"Yes, I do," the smuggler replied.

"How much do you have?" Reb Levi Yitzchok of Berditchev
asked.

"I can get you as much as you want," the gentile replied.

Reb Levi Yitzchok departed from him and met a Jew, whom
he asked:

"Do you have any *chometz*?"

"*Chometz?*" the Jew trembled. "God forbid, Rebbe! I've burnt everything!"

Whereupon Reb Levi Yitzchok of Berditchev addressed God: "Oh, what a good and wonderful people You have. The Russian Czar is a mighty king who has mighty armies, weapons, and prisons. He has prohibited the importation of merchandise from other countries. He has placed guards on the border who keep watch day and night. But, nevertheless, all kinds of merchandise is brought in, which is being sold frank and free. And You, dear God, You've written in Your holy Torah one verse, 'No leaven shall be seen,' and there is not one crumb of *chometz* to be found in any Jewish house!"

Even incidents that could have prompted gloom and rage did not cause Reb Levi Yitzchok from Berditchev to stray from his path. Once he saw a wagoner greasing the wheels of his wagon while praying with tallis and tefillin. The fact that the man was praying even while greasing his wheels elicited Reb Levi Yitzchok's admiration and amazement. The maskil, the enlightened Jew, who smoked his pipe on the Sabbath and admitted to Reb Levi Yitzchok that he smoked even though he knew that it was the Sabbath, caused the rebbe to address God and express his delight because the maskil would not tell a lie under any circumstances.

One time Reb Levi Yitzchok needed a shofar blower for Rosh Hashanah. Among the candidates were Hasidim and learned Jews who were well versed in the laws and purposes of shofar blowing. But Reb Levi Yitzchok chose a simple Jew who admitted to him that while blowing shofar he prayed to God to send him a proper match for his four daughters for whom he had no dowry.

"That's the sort of shofar blower I'm looking for!" Reb Levi Yitzchok cried out. "This man's motives are proper and true."

In a generation which had already become somewhat distanced from the original path of the Baal Shem Tov's Hasidism, the personality and conduct of Reb Levi Yitzchok brought back experiences of olden times. An incident that took place in Reb Levi Yitzchok's synagogue on Rosh Hashanah is reminiscent of

the story of the shepherd lad with a whistle in which the Baal
Shem Tov heard the most profound prayers.

Once, during the Rosh Hashanah *Musaf* service; Reb Levi
Yitzchok suddenly stopped and waited. He had broken off
prayers, he later explained to the congregation, because by the
door in the outer hallway sat a man who had always lived in
the village among gentiles and did not know how to pray. He
barely remembered snatches of the alphabet. The man began to
cry and plead with the Master of the Universe to help him
create the prayers out of the letters of the alphabet. That is why
they had to wait.

Just like the Baal Shem Tov, Reb Levi Yitzchok of Berditchev
also surrounded himself with the poor and with the common
folk. When he went from bakery to bakery on Passover in-
specting the *kashrut* of the matzas, he was sincerely concerned
lest the baker overtax the women and children who had been
hired to work. "Naturally, it's an outrageous lie, concocted by
our enemies, that we Jews bake matzas with gentile blood. But
baking matzas with Jewish blood, with the blood of the poor
little Jewish children, is also strictly forbidden."

Reb Levi Yitzchok empathized with the sufferings and joys of
the Jew, and sought to ease his lot while simultaneously lifting
his spirit. The zaddik of Kozhenitz was amazed at Reb Levi
Yitzchok's ability to weave holiness into weekday matters. And
Abraham Ber Gottlober, a Hebrew writer of the Haskalah
period, notes in his memoirs how ecstatic Reb Levi Yitzchok
became when he succeeded in bringing a bit of joy into a
beclouded Jewish spirit.

Solicitude for the daily needs of the Jew and the heartfelt
belief that he was capable of climbing higher in humanness and
Jewishness are the themes of Reb Levi Yitzchok's book, *The
Sanctity of Levi*. Despite the fact that it was first published in
1798 in Slavude, Reb Levi Yitzchok's book is not outdated.

The Sanctity of Levi is a collection of sermons on the weekly
portions of the Torah; I consider them more timely than many
of our contemporary collections of sermons. Reb Levi Yitzchok's sermons actually breathe with contemporaneous Jewish

problems. The Jew and the world, Jewish anguish, the "why" of our existence. Brutal question marks are put forth. And in the attempt to provide answers, Reb Levi Yitzchok combines intelligence and feeling.

The God of Israel comes down to Gimpl and to Berel; he needs them. God needs man. He is King when you and I crown him King. He incorporates our will, just as we must incorporate His will into ourselves. The chapter from *Ethics of our Fathers* that Jews recite during summer Sabbaths has to be interpreted correctly and precisely. "Know what is above you" means that man should be aware that what is done in heaven above is done by you, through you, and only for you.

Not only can we not survive without God's love and warmth, but without us God Himself would remain lonely and forlorn. Yet in his book of sermons the mystical interpretation of God and Jew does not become a supernal melody in the hands of Reb Levi Yitzchok. It is applied in a practical direction: if Jews are indeed such a strong foundation of divinity, one is forbidden to speak ill of them.

"No man is permitted to speak evil about any Jew." This is not only a law, but a part of the cosmic order of creation. Though conditions and circumstances may disturb and distort the life of the Jews, they can by no means eradicate the sense and substance of the age-old Jewish way of life.

The man of Berditchev, Reb Levi Yitzchok, the son of Sarah-Sosye, guaranteed the Creator that if He would be "kindly and beneficent" and help His people in a time of need and pain, then the dust that had gathered in the hullabaloo of daily existence would vanish. Occasionally, an awful question surfaces in his book which perhaps other teachers of Judaism had avoided, but which Reb Levi Yitzchok of Berditchev posed with the utmost boldness: "Why is this beloved people of Israel drowning in blood and tears?"

This Job-question did not drive him to bitterness. Unlike Job, Reb Levi Yitzchok did not sit down on the ground and fall into deep silence or incurable pessimism. Nothing could rob him of his confidence and joy. When the scribe wrote the engagement contract for his son, and entered the traditional formula that the wedding would take place, God willing, on such and such day in Berditchev, Reb Levi Yitzchok tore up the contract.

"Why Berditchev?" he called. "One should write that the wedding will take place, God willing, in Jerusalem, unless of course the Redemption will not have taken place, then the wedding will be celebrated in Berditchev."

And he stood and argued with God.

III

It is true that the first Jew in history had already instituted an audacious tone in his conversations with God. Open up the Pentateuch and you will still marvel at Abraham's great courage in discussing the imminent upheaval of Sodom with God. In the thousands of years that separate us from that scene (which is actually a continuing dialogue between Jew and God), such conversations between heaven and earth frequently took on quite a stormy character.

No one, however, posed such open and bold complaints as did Reb Levi Yitzchok of Berditchev. In his demands he threatened. When the secular ideas of the Enlightenment started to spread in the Jewish community, he had an announcement proclaimed in the shuls of Lukov, Kotzk, Radzimin, and Zelekov, that he, Levi Yitzchok, wanted it to be known that there was a God in this world.

But he also stood up to God. Once, when the shofar was being blown and the sounds did not come out well, he did not even want to ponder the reason for this heavenly accusation. "Then it means, Master of the Universe, that You don't want to accept my shofar sounds," he called. "Well, in that case, let Ivan blow the shofar!"

At another time, when the *Nesane Tokef* prayer was being recited on Rosh Hashanah, he demanded of God reciprocity. "If you want to be the King of Kings," he addressed God, "and sit in truth upon Your throne of glory, then You must also be good to us. For if You don't conduct Yourself the way You should, then we will give You no peace. We won't leave You alone, and Your heavenly throne will cease to be tangible and true."

There was no choice but to have God summoned to a *din Torah*, or rabbinic judgment, with the Jews. And Levi Yitzchok was confident that he would win. God had exiled His people even before their measure of sins was full. The prayer, "And for our sins we were exiled from our land," can be interpreted as *"before* our sins had reached full measure were we driven from our land." According to the law, then, we have earned the right to be redeemed prior to the set date.

In another *din Torah*, Berel the tailor from Berditchev had a complaint against God. Reb Levi Yitzchok, who understood Berel very well, felt that Berel was right. What had the tailor done? He had stopped praying; he had stopped fulfilling the mitzvot. He said he wanted to have nothing more to do with Judaism because he felt that a horrible injustice had been done to him. He was a pauper. He and his family suffered from want. Moreover, he had to bear the insults and humiliations of the gentile landowner. Was he overplaying his act of accusation against God?

"I, Levi Yitzchok," the rebbe of Berditchev told the tailor, "render my judgment that *you* are in the right and not the Master of the Universe."

On Yom Kippur, Levi Yitzchok announced from the pulpit, "Today Your Jews want to go with You to judgment, dear God. We have a great and legitimate complaint against You. All our troubles and sufferings stem from the fact that we serve You as Jews. Were we not Jews we would not have to suffer so many torments. And if we suffer on account of You, it is Your duty to help us. And if that is the case, why are You silent?"

Reb Levi Yitzchok reproached God by saying that He did not obey the laws that He Himself had drafted. "Woe, woe," Reb Levi Yitzchok sighed, "if a simple, average Jew drops his tefillin, he quickly bends down and kisses them. He is terribly distressed and fasts. And You, Master of the Universe, for eighteen hundred years Your own tefillin, wherein it is written that You love Your people Israel, have been lying around in the dirtiest mud, shamed and mocked. How can You do this?"

Reb Levi Yitzchok put fire and ecstasy into his *din Torah* with God, as he did in all his other activities. According to him, the most important factor in every mitzvah is the ardor with which it is done. That is how we interpret the talmudic phrase "the essence of the mitzvah is the kindling," which pertains to the Hanukah lights. The flame with which one approaches God and man is crucial.

As though he himself were kindled, Reb Levi Yitzchok cried out on Rosh Hashanah: "Today is the Day of Judgment. Today You judge us. But I, Reb Levi Yitzchok, say that today You, God, will be judged. We, Your children, who march to our martyrdom with Your Name on our lips, today we are bringing You to judgment."

Once, on Yom Kippur, during the closing *Neilah* service, his face radiated joy. When the fast-day was over he told the congregation why he had been so pleased.

"During Yom Kippur there was a virulent accusation against the Jews in heaven. But towards evening, during *Neilah*, two Jewish women were talking in the women's gallery. One said that she was confident that their prayers for a good year would be answered. 'Why are you so sure?' asked the other woman. To which the first responded, 'How could it be otherwise? The way we wept and pleaded today, even if we had been standing before a robber in the woods, he would have had compassion on us.' These remarks of the Jewish woman," Reb Levi Yitzchok of Berditchev added, "made a very great impression up in heaven and silenced the accusers."

Even in the word *kippurim* Reb Levi Yitzchok found an explicit hint about the *din Torah* to which he had the right to summon God. "*Kippurim* is the word used in the Torah for the holy day," he said. "*Yom Kippurim* is in the plural because *both* have to beg for forgiveness. We the Jews from God. But God too has to beg forgiveness from us."

It was Reb Levi Yitzchok of Berditchev who sang the famous

song "Dudele" to God. "Wherever I go, You; wherever I stay, You. East, You; West, You; South, You; North, You; again You, always You." For the past two hundred years his folksy *Kaddish* has stirred Jewish fantasy with its originality and sweet melody. But even in this *Kaddish,* Reb Levi Yitzchok spoke sharply and severely with God.

Jewish chosenness obligates not only the Jew but primarily God. After all, it was He who had chosen His people. "To whom do You speak?" he sang in the prelude to the *Kaddish.* "To the children of Israel. To whom do You talk? To the children of Israel. . . . And that is why I ask You: What have You got against Your people Israel? Why do You constantly afflict only Your people Israel?"

Despite this remarkably daring petition, no one saw blasphemy in these reproaches and awesome complaints against God. Reb Levi Yitzchok was considered holy by the people even during his lifetime, and in the course of time the aura of legend began to wrap itself around him. Among all the teachers of Hasidism only he achieved the Baal Shem Tov's popularity. East European Jewry felt that Reb Levi Yitzchok was one of those rare people in our history who delved deep into the depths of Jewish being and gave dramatic expression to the Jewish pain of generations. His metaphysical world outlook never ceased to be accessible to the ordinary Jew. The magic of his word made complicated questions of destiny transparently simple. Ephemeral daily mundaneness breathed with eternality because of him, and mysticism became a component of our daily hustle and bustle.

In Reb Levi Yitzchok there was a fusion of gargantuan challenge against heaven with ardent, heart-stirring faith. Reb Nachman of Bratzlav, who analyzed his contemporaries with his keen critical sensibility, was certain that Reb Levi Yitzchok had surpassed them all. The rebbe of Liady, Reb Shneur Zalman, stated that God was the Righteous One in heaven but Levi Yitzchok is the righteous on earth. Rabbi Mendele of Kotzk observed that Levi Yitzchok of Berditchev caused the heavenly gates to open with love; these gates, however, were shut when he departed from this world. And perhaps the most profound estimation of Reb Levi Yitzchok was that of Rabbi Baruch of Mezhibuzh, who said, "According to Reb Levi Yitzchok, God did not completely fulfill His obligation to any Jew."

IV

In our generation, which experienced the horror of Auschwitz, the personality of Reb Levi Yitzchok emerges forcefully before us. And his teaching, laden with warm love and fervid sorrow and wrath, becomes remarkably significant at the present time.

During the four decades that separate us from the Nazi nightmare, various attempts have been made to interpret the "why" of the annihilation and to explain the Holocaust. Many of these interpretations unexpectedly shifted gears and centered the blame on the destroyed Jewish communities. Raul Hilberg, Hannah Arendt, and Bruno Bettleheim are perhaps the better known among the Jewish scholars, sociologists, and psychologists who have dealt with this issue. They came to the conclusion that the murdered Jewry of Eastern Europe, despite all its creativity and periods of luster, did not pass the test of character and did not excel in greatness of heart—neither on the eve of the Holocaust nor during its darkest hour.

The theories and speculation of an entire group of Jewish thinkers and theologists are not any more encouraging. Immediately after the horrible tragedy of Treblinka and Maidanek was exposed to the world, Martin Buber developed his approach to the appalling mystery of the destruction in several talks. The absurdity of the gas chambers was supposedly given a philosophical and theological interpretation. That which was incomprehensible and traumatic was supposedly explained rationally. And Buber's attempt continually gains adherents in our day among those who consider Judaism a theological system and do not comprehend that the Jewish struggle throughout the generations cannot be boxed into the frame of a theology out of harmony with Judaism.

Naturally, the language is different in the religious publications that deal with the terror of Auschwitz. These articles also contain selected biblical verses and quotations from the Talmud and from religious texts. But their contents and conclusions are essentially the same: a justification of the decree. God is right, and His judgment is right. All the gnawing, haunting questions are rejected as heretical. Those for whom superficial faith does not suffice, those who dare to ask and demand, are labeled as blasphemers. The sinners are we and our parents.

Forty years after Auschwitz Reb Levi Yitzchok of Berditchev deserves to be placed in the center of our thoughts and feelings. He can provide direction and orientation when values have become lost. Here he is, the ardent defender who even in the darkness saw the light in the Jewish soul; and here he is, the fearless accuser who put forth his disquieting demands against the heavenly Judge. Reb Levi Yitzchok of Berditchev's *din Torah* with God has its terrifying continuation in our generation which experienced Auschwitz.

5

The Difficult Mountain Ascent of Reb Bunim of Pshishkhe

I

RABBI BUNIM OF PSHISHKHE'S path was actually in conformity with the historic path of Polish Jewry. Rarely were Jews in Poland pleased with the status quo. With all their significant achievements, Polish Jews did not stop searching nor did they cease delving into the depths and ascending to the heights. And when Hasidism grew in scope and popularity, the Baal Shem Tov's disciples, who spread his teachings over central Poland's towns and villages, were not satisfied either. Driven by a vibrant and creative restlessness, they demanded greater profundity of Hasidism. They declared that although battling the opponents of Hasidism was no longer necessary, continuing the struggle with one's own self and with one's own conscience was still important.

Pshishkhe, a small town in Congress Poland—as the provinces of the dismantled Polish kingdom surrounding Lublin and Warsaw were called during that time of crisis—became transformed into a great center of Jewish thought. Hasidism developed in a mountainous region, and mountains and hills were characteristic of the landscape even in the flat part of Poland. The way of life and the ideas forged there were no doubt influenced by this landscape.

The mountains of the ancient Jewish biblical past were linked

with the mountains familiar to the Jew in Poland; they helped
the Jew to construct a world view permeated with mountain
elements. If according to the well-known remark of Reb Abraham of Sokhotchov, the trees of Poland wanted to say *Kedusha*,
the prayer of sanctification, then surely those mountains could
have asked the fervent question accented in Psalm 24, "Who
shall ascend to the mountain of the Lord?"

"The mountain of the Lord?" could have been various places
and possessed various meanings. It could have been Mount
Moriah, on which Abraham, the father of Jewish history,
showed future generations, with stirring pain and granite
strength, that the Jewish path to eternity leads through the
Akedah, the Binding.

It could have been Mount Sinai, engraved upon the Jewish
historical memory as the mountain of revelation that stood in
flaming fire as God's word to man hovered over it.

It could have been Mount Carmel, where the barbed Jewish
argument with the world exploded, and where the awesome
loneliness of the Jew in the world was revealed in its absolute
starkness.

It could have been the Mount of Olives, where the luminous
words of redemption will emanate in the future; and where,
according to the prophets, from the thickest darkness a bright
dawn will shine forth.

But it could also have been Mount Nebo, where Moses, the
father of prophets, had seen the Promised Land from afar.
Here he could have come to the conclusion that visions,
although spread in anguish and yearning, do not cease to fill
the life of man with sense and substance just because they are
not fulfilled.

The truth is that other Hasidic schools of thought besides
Pshishkhe attempted to link Jews and Judaism with one of
these mountains. For Reb Levi Yitzchok of Berditchev the
Akedah motif was the most moving and crucial for the Jewish
people, past and present. For Reb Shneur Zalman of Liady,
Mount Sinai was the locus of the mighty drama of the past and
future of the people of Israel. Reb Jacob Joseph of Polonoi felt

that the dispute on Mount Carmel had never ended and that it echoes continuously in the Jewish consciousness.

For Reb Jacob Isaac, the Seer of Lublin, the messianic pronouncement from the Mount of Olives was real and strikingly relevant. And the stories of Reb Nachman of Bratzlav seem to have been inspired by the deeply human drama on Mount Nebo; his tales showed that the tremulous dream, the magic of hope, and the pain of disappointment interweave in the fabric of life, which may be passing cobwebs or everlasting monument.

But in Pshishkhe they clearly did not want to help the Jew make sense of the whirlwind of the mountain. "Go look for yourself!" they said. "Go scramble up. Go climb from mountain to mountain and discover for yourself which are the eternal mountains!"

Fifty years earlier, in the Carpathian Mountains of the Ukraine, the Baal Shem Tov had taken the Jew by the hand and supported him in his ascent up the mountains. But in Pshishkhe they felt that each Jew must develop his own creative potential and by his own efforts gather strength to ascend on high.

"According to Reb Meir of Apt," Reb Bunim said, "the rebbe's broad shoulders were created to support the Jews. But I don't have faith in these broad shoulders of the rebbe. Every Jew must open his heart and his own sources of strength by himself."

Polish Jews have always chosen the difficult path. That is why Pshishkhe is so characteristic of Hasidism in Poland. Pshishkhe made demands, Pshishkhe cut into one's conscience, Pshishkhe set conditions. Pshishkhe gave the Polish-Jewish center, which found itself in a state of political and economic decline, the feeling of self-confidence and belief in its own potential.

Naturally, in Pshishkhe they did not utilize the concept of "dignity." But the Hasidism that developed there is doubtless one of the most dignified movements in the history of the Jewish spirit. The national and social movements that developed among Polish Jewry in the nineteenth century, and whose features were clearly delineated in the period before the Nazi German Holocaust, bore within themselves the distinct signs of Pshishkhe. Pshishkhe Hasidism successfully introduced Polish Jewry to the remarkable strength of challenge and decision.

II

During the last few generations, many of the important thoughts formulated in Pshishkhe have been ascribed to Kotzk—that is, to the Hasidic path characteristic of Reb Menachem Mendel of Kotzk. However, in all fairness, it should be stressed that Reb Mendele of Kotzk drew his inspiration from Pshishkhe. It was *there* that he learned to delve deep and search constantly for truth. It was *there* that he learned not to fear Koheleth's warning that the more one knows and understands the more it hurts. "He that increaseth knowledge increases pain" (Ecclesiastes 1:18). Reb Mendele's daring remark: "So what! Let it hurt! One should also know!" Stems straight from the spiritual method of Pshishkhe.

But demanding of oneself and haunting dissatisfaction proved to be too bold and too conceited for several teachers of Hasidism. It was a time of fear and terrible insecurity for Polish Jewry. Poland had undergone a crisis that virtually destroyed its foundations. Poland went from one breaking point to another and, at the beginning of the nineteenth century, from one power to another. Still, it clung to a shadow of independence in its Warsaw dukedom—and then lost its independence altogether.

The provinces of Congress Poland were constantly in a state of political, social, and economic chaos. At first, they were controlled by Prussia, then by the Russian Czar, and after that by Napoleon. And so the marching boots of the French armies resounded on Polish highways.

In chaotic times Jews could hardly expect an improvement in their desperate situation. There was no justice and there was no judge. Anarchy was a normal condition. The Jewish populace turned out to be a burden and a problem for any new occupying power. The Jews could be blamed for every failure; and from them all kinds of exorbitant taxes could be extorted, even one for wanting to marry, for lighting Sabbath candles, and for breathing air.

No wonder, then, that the Jewish masses embraced the encouraging message of Hasidism with deep enthusiasm. In Congress Poland, Hasidism did not have to wage too bitter a battle against its opponents. In the sea of troubles in which Jews were drowning, Hasidism taught solace and hope. Hasidism shouted into one's ear: "Jews, do not despair!"

Despite all the subtle differences and the characteristic nuances that Hasidism in Congress Poland brought into the original Hasidic teaching during the generations prior to Pshishkhe, the movement was still seen as a faithful continuation of the Mezhibuzh word and song.

The semidistinct, semisecretive pronouncements and visions which Reb Jacob Isaac, the Seer of Lublin, had outlined for the public were full of encouragement. Indeed, that is why he was called the Seer. In Lublin, a bridge was constructed, a bridge of vision over the abyss of persecution and anguish. It was simultaneously dream and reality. And via this bridge one could span bitter reality and stride confidently to the bright era of Redemption.

The Seer showed the way. After him came many thousands with faith and ecstasy who desperately needed the sparks of hope which had been kindled. The Seer's disciple, the first to settle in Pshishkhe, not only bore the name of his rebbe—Jacob Isaac—but also spread the same teaching of promise and consolation. At a time of suffering and darkness, he taught, the task must be to enhearten the anguished Jewish soul.

Reb Jacob Isaac, the disciple of the Seer, made himself part and parcel of the masses of Jews who came to him from near and far to be warmed by his personality and teaching. He shared their grief and taught them to become exalted in the song of faith. That was why he was called "The Jew." The Jew of Pshishkhe, the one who behaved not like a rabbi or a rebbe but merely like a plain Jew—one of the downtrodden, persecuted, believing, Messiah-longing Jews. "In any case," he said, "when the Messiah comes he won't embrace the rebbe first, but the plain, ordinary Jews."

Reb Simcha Bunim entered the Hasidic world during this period of chaos and crisis, and in the town where Jacob Isaac, "The Jew," developed his clear system regarding the present and future of Jewry and Jewishness. Reb Simcha Bunim apparently brought with him all the traits with which Hasidism had enriched Jewish life. He seemingly came with the same spiritual baggage that the teachers of Hasidism had carried in the Ukraine and in Poland. It seems that he appeared with Hasidism's traditional vigorous yes to the world and life, with its waves of sparkling joy, and with its conviction that the way to God was accessible also to the average man.

Yet there was a new tone in Reb Simcha Bunim and in his message. He stressed that climbing up to the mountain of the Lord is not so simple, and that this ascent needs constant effort. He demanded much from man and Jew: a high degree of humanity and profound Jewishness. He was not pleased when the regime, thanks to strenuous Jewish intervention, canceled its earlier prohibition forbidding Hasidim to travel to their rebbe.

"Perhaps it would have been better," he said, "had the government put a wall around every rebbe's court, guarded by a band of strong Cossacks, and not let Jews cross the threshold of their zaddik. That way they would have learned to live 'by their own bread and water' and their own strength."

While everyone was certain that Hasidism's purpose was to declare that it was easy to be a Jew and easy to be a Hasid, Reb Bunim asserted that this was entirely baseless.

"This is utter nonsense. It is hard to be a Jew, and very hard to be a Hasid. The Jew must always feel that he is born anew, and he must always feel that each breath he takes is new. Even the very first verse of the Torah, 'In the beginning God created,' teaches us that world and man are still in the process of creation. World and man are still not completed. And if one

wants to be a Hasid, one must listen seriously to the call for a
new creation, a new self-creation."

At first glance it seemed that the bold, new concept of Reb
Simcha Bunim—or as he was called, Reb Bunim—would distance him from the masses. And indeed there were those who
were frightened off by him and by his new interpretation.
Despite the cloud of fog which mists the great Hasidic wedding
that took place in Ostilye in Volhyn, where leading zaddikim
and Hasidim had gathered, the fact remains that they planned
to proclaim a ban against Reb Bunim and his Pshishkhe Hasidism. The argument went thus: Was this the proper time to
make great demands of the Jew? Wouldn't it be preferable in
this troublesome time to maintain our age-old faith and not
speculate in matters too deep and too complex?

But Reb Bumin prevailed in his path. The Jewish masses in
Poland began streaming toward Pshishkhe. Chroniclers attest
that young people clung to him. His method was a continuation of the spiritual culture of Polish Jewry, which had always
rejected compromise and was built upon stringent demands.

This system of Hasidism was essentially Polish Jewry's revolt
against the tendency to lead a life that required and demanded
little. Moreover, when one stands at the abyss of trouble and
suffering, superficial optimism does not suffice. Even in tragedy a gigantic challenge is mandatory.

"The sufferings of Egypt" is a phrase from Exodus that
depicts the Jews' tribulations under the yoke of Pharaoh. Reb
Bunim interpreted it as "the patience, the indifference, the run-
of-the-mill tolerance with which Jews endured the tragedy."
(The Hebrew root *sevel* means both "suffering" and "patience.") Excessive patience is harmful. Shallow mediocrity is a
sin. Never mind, he said, "one can also learn conduct from a
thief. Consider how a thief handles himself. He's not lazy. He
goes out to steal in the dark of the night. And even when he
finds the door locked, he forces it open."

Reb Nachman of Bratzlav introduced fire and escstasy into
Hasidism. Reb Shneur Zalman of Liady showed that the gate of
Hasidism is open too for those who wear the crown of learn-

ing. Reb Bunim of Pshishkhe raised Hasidism up to the peak of the mountain. But he also said that the mountain of the Lord is in essence the mountain of man, and that the mountain of man is the mountain of the Lord.

III

The very appearance of Reb Bunim in the Hasidic community prompted amazement. Before becoming leaders, other Hasidic zaddikim had all been rabbis, teachers, itinerant preachers. Reb Israel Baal Shem Tov was a teacher; Reb Jacob Joseph of Polonoi, a rabbi; Reb Dov Ber of Mezeritch, an itinerant preacher; Reb Jacob Isaac, "The Jew" of Pshishkhe, a teacher. Levi Yitzchok of Berditchev was a rabbi. Reb Bunim's father was also a wandering preacher from Voidislav.

But, surprisingly, Reb Bunim was a businessman. He was employed in the forest enterprises of the Bergsons of Warsaw, a family of merchants. Reb Bunim, a bookkeeper and merchant, would often travel to Leipzig and Danzig, where he associated with "progressive" people. He spoke Polish, German, Latin. Even Hasidic folklore does not hide the fact that he wore western dress and attended the theater.

Indeed, in Danzig he obtained the books for his study of pharmacology. Examined by the governmental commission, Reb Bunim was one of the first Jews in Poland to win the right to enter an academic profession. When he settled in Pshishkhe and opened a pharmacy, he became a follower of "The Jew," the rebbe of Pshishkhe. But the town intellectuals—those who pored over talmudic tractates and those who immersed themselves in philosophical texts—gathered around the pharmacist. They argued over Maimonides' views and sought an approach to Judah Halevi's philosophy and to the Maharal of Prague's mysticism.

Reb Bunim's attention was divided between the pharmacy and philosophy. And in this remarkable circle, people were certain that the pharmacist preferred philosophic speculation over his drugstore. It was said that after Reb Bunim had passed the pharmacist's examination and received a sum of money from the governmental commission to purchase necessary professional handbooks, he went out and bought the *Zohar* and immersed himself in the Kabbalah.

Naturally, there was also grumbling. There were Jews in Pshishkhe who thought the most important thing for a Jew was observance of Judaism. And they looked with distrust at the ones who assembled and constantly asked questions. Most of the people, however, realized that the pharmacist was capable of opening a new chapter in Hasidism. And so "Bunim the pharmacist" became the rebbe. First he hesitated and declined to be considered for the post. Much time passed before he finally accepted the call.

Once, when his wife was sitting by the window, she said: "Bunim, a wagonload of Hasidim is coming to see you!"

"Eh, what are you talking about!" he replied. "You know that that's not my business!"

But during his philosophic research he began to realize that only a pharmacist has the capacity of pointing out that in life one must perpetually weigh and measure. The scale and the yardstick must constantly be applied to one's own deeds and to one's own behavior. Hasidism must have someone who is involved with the world, who knows the sciences of the world, and who has seen the sinful cities.

"I've been in Danzig," he remarked, "I've seen where moral improvement is needed."

He had his own interpretation for the Hebrew word *adam*, which means "man." The root, he said, stems from *damah*, "to imagine." Man must have the power of imagination. Only when one is in the city, in the very midst of the tumult of life, and knows not only the light but also the shadow, can one know how to wage the battle with oneself and "straighten the young trees that have become crooked."

With the passing of years, this new system grew sharper and more incisive. "Intent" (*kavanah*) became a concept with multi-faceted interpretations. Intent not only in fulfilling the mitzvot of Judaism; intent not only in praying, but also in immersing oneself in thought. Hasidism is not only feeling but also thinking. Hasidism is not only heart but also mind. Hasidism did not come to eradicate the contradictions and conflicts that burden man. Just the opposite. Hasidism means living with these contradictions. One has to serve God with both thought and feelings. One must be innocent and clever, holy and mundane, simple and complex. One must hover in the heavens and be bound to earth. One must become involved with the community at large—and still remain alone. "If one is only a wise man, one becomes a heretic," Reb Bunim said. "If one is just a Hasid, one can become a thief. And if one is merely good-hearted, one can become a libertine."

The attribute of modesty so idealized by Hasidism's first teachers was also seen in a completely different light. The tiny letter *yud* in the Hebrew alphabet shows that one must not become too proud and haughty. On the contrary. Try to adorn that little *yud* and you will soon realize that it ceases to be a *yud*. The same is true for a Jew. When he is adorned by pride, he ceases to be a Jew.

"The numerical value of the letters in *ram*, the Hebrew word for 'high,' equals that of Amalek, the eternal enemy of the people of Israel," Reb Bunim said. "But this doesn't mean that a Jew should be lower than the grass. Every Jew must consider himself an only child of God and believe that the Creator has no one else in the world but him. One should also have the feeling of pride. Along with the conviction expressed in the words, 'And I am but dust and ashes'—in other words, I am zero—one should also be absolutely confident that 'for me the world was created'—that the entire world was made only for me."

Is it difficult to resolve these two mutually contradictory concepts? Of course. "But that is why," Reb Bunim added, "our jackets have two pockets. In one we hold pride, and in the other, modesty. And we make use of each trait according to circumstances and need."

Of himself Reb Bunim would say with self-irony: "What a generation and what a leader! In today's impoverished and empty generation, even Bunim can be a leader." But yet he also said that he would not change places with Abraham. "What would God gain if Abraham were just like Bunim, and Bunim just like Abraham! It would be much better if Bunim would ascend and exalt himself—and indeed Bunim is capable of this."

One might have thought that Reb Bunim had intentions of toppling the entire structure upon which Hasidism was based. For faith in the rebbe and in his power to work wonders was considered an important principle by Reb Dov Ber of Mezeritch and Reb Elimelech of Lizensk.

"If he achieves a certain level," Reb Bunim argued, "*every* Jew can work wonders. And it is not necessary to first go to the rebbe and behold his miracles and wonders. It is much more important for the rebbe to be one of the congregation, to mingle with them, and to take part in the political and social life of the Jewish community."

Reb Bunim was a member of the governmental commission for Jewish affairs. Thus, with his own activity he showed that the *beis medresh,* or House of Study, was not the only place for the rebbe. It is possible for conversations to be transformed into prayers and for prayers to be transformed into conversations. The secret is not concealed in the world of secrets. The secret inheres in man himself.

"It's a wonder," he would say, "that during the Korah affair Moses demanded that the rebellious Dothan and Abiram be brought before him. He should have gone to *them,* gone down to the people with the intent of raising them up. The sinful man of flesh and blood is not at all as weak and helpless as others tell him he is. Every Jew is a hero. Even after Adam was driven from the Garden of Eden, the Torah still says, 'He expelled Adam,' which means that even after he was expelled he still remained—Adam."

Pshishkhe Hasidism placed honesty to oneself at the very center of the system. Even the worst of sinners are capable of finding their way back to God and to themselves. Lost are only those who deceive themselves.

"I could bring all the Jews back to the good and proper

path," Reb Bunim once said, "if they would only apply to themselves the measure of truth. And there is absolutely no excuse for claiming that it is difficult to delve deep into one's own conscience at a time of want and loneliness. 'Thou shalt not steal' always meant that you should not steal from yourself, just as you must not steal from anyone else. Naturally, he who works hard at it can achieve this kind of honesty. But the proviso is utmost earnestness."

When Reb Bunim's shofar blower made long pauses between the shofar blasts on Rosh Hashanah to enhance his devotion and piety, Rabbi Bunim told him: "Fool, blow the shofar." For exaggerated humility becomes nauseating at the moment when one is demanding justice in heaven and on earth. At a time of destiny, courage, boldness, resolution are demanded. In Pshishkhe it was called "holy impertinence"! The call that went out from Pshishkhe was: "Don't stop in the middle of your uphill climb." According to Reb Bunim narrow concepts and a narrow mind are the worst of curses. "There is an essential difference," he said, "between the fool and the wise man. The fool says what he knows, and the smart man knows what he says."

Pshishkhe held that man and Jew's chief task was to be a lifelong student, to constantly feel the thirst for knowledge, the hunger to know, and the desire to grow. In explaining the Hebrew term for "scholar," *talmid-chacham*, Reb Bunim said that a *chacham*, "a wise man," is the one who always remains a *talmid*, "a student." The rebbe fulfils his obligation to his Hasidim when he remains a student all his life.

Reb Bunim sat and studied not only with the Jews who craved to hear his word; he studied by himself too. He pondered how to remain a pharmacist and a rebbe, a scholar and a Hasid. He studied and taught himself not only how to solve and discover conflicts and contradictions, but also how to comprehend these contradictions and upon them build a life both meaningful and valuable.

Like many of his contemporaries, the Galician maskil Isaac Miezes wrote about the rabbi of Pshishkhe with utter amazement. "How strange it is!" he remarked, "A Hasidic rebbe who is immersed in speculation just like a philosopher."

When Reb Bunim became blind in his old age, he did not feel at all depressed. "All my life," he said, "I've been teaching myself how to see in the dark. On the contrary, only now, when I am blind, do I have the great opportunity of seeing people and things with an inner light for the first time. No, I have no need for eyes."

Before his death, he told his wife, who sat at his bedside: "Do not cry. All my life I've been teaching myself how to die."

In the precise analysis which has yet to be made of the character traits of the Jew in Poland, the contributions of Pshishkhe to the formation of the Polish Jew will have to be properly considered. The Jew who with his dreaminess was bold and militant. The Jew in whom there thrived a rare admixture of zestful idealism and a sense of raw reality. The Jew who was all poetry and yet soberly estimated the prose of every situation. The Jew who, regardless of which party he belonged to, or in which movement he sought expression of his ideas and aspirations—whether in Agudas Israel, Zionism, or the Bund—challenged himself to do the daring and unusual.

In Pshishkhe he was taught to challenge reality. In Pshishkhe he was shown how his own conscience matures in storm. In the flames that rose in the Warsaw Ghetto uprising, hovered letters of the parchment written one hundred and fifty years earlier in Pshishkhe.

IV

Perhaps this is why Reb Bunim loved the parable so much. It is true that every parable has a moral, but it does not necessarily have to have one moral. A parable flashes with all kinds of symbols. It shimmers with all sorts of colors. All kinds of intentions can be ascribed to it. A parable incites one's thought to sharpness of mind. It forces one to pose questions. For the question is crucial. The dialogue between God and man began with a question. And there is good reason why the Midrash holds that Abraham achieved truth through questions.

The following parable is one Reb Bunim would tell young people when they visited him the first time. It concerns Reb Isaac ben Reb Yekl from Cracow. Reb Isaac had no end of troubles: want, poverty, anguish. Naturally, despite all this, he did not lose his faith. Once he was told in a dream to set out for Prague. There, beneath a bridge near the royal palace, he would find a great treasure. When the dream was repeated a second and a third time, Reb Isaac set out on the difficult journey.

Arriving in Prague, he went to the bridge and saw a large contingent of soldiers guarding it day and night. Naturally, he could not start digging then and there for the treasure he had seen in his dream. Morning after morning he would come to the bridge and as if in a delirium would march back and forth until the onset of night.

Finally, the head guard asked him, "Who are you looking for?"

In all innocence Reb Isaac told him what he had seen in his dream and the reason for his coming to Prague.

The soldier laughed and told him: "In other words, on account of a dream you've dragged yourself this far? That's what you get for believing in dreams. If I believed in dreams I too would have to travel far, because I was told in a dream to go to Cracow, enter the house of a Jew named Isaac the son of Reb Yekl, and look for a treasure hidden behind his stove."

Reb Isaac listened to the soldier, returned to Cracow, and indeed dug up the treasure behind the stove in his own house. Later he built a synagogue in his name: Isaac ben Reb Yekl's Synagogue.

"That is the parable—and what is the moral? One thing is clear. The treasure cannot be found elsewhere. Not under the bridge and not by the rebbe. The treasure will be found at your own place. Each and every one of you." With these words Reb Bunim would end his parable. Then he would turn to the young people who came to him and say: "Children, go back home. Go and seek!"

And here is another parable, this one about a priest. A rich

landowner once set out on a journey and noticed a drunkard
sprawled in the mud. He ordered his servants to lift the
drunkard from the ground, lead him to the palace, and wash
and dress him in priestly vestments. The servants were also
ordered to treat him and speak to him as though he were
actually one of the priests.

When the drunkard became sober, he couldn't understand
what was happening to him. He wondered what he was doing
in the palace and how he had gotten these priestly vestments.
It hardly seemed possible that he, the drunkard, was indeed a
priest. But on the other hand, he thought, if he were not a
priest he wouldn't be treated as such.

Then he decided to look into the priestly books to see if he
could read what was written there. The king's servants
brought him the books he requested. Although he couldn't
read a word, he still wasn't fazed. He thought: "I am surely a
priest, but then why can't I read the priestly books? Actually,
it's no problem. Obviously, all the priests are just like me. And
none of them can read these books either."

This parable can be interpreted in different ways. If you
wish, you can see that life abounds with elements of games
and theatricality. If you wish, the parable teaches that those
who don't attempt to make sense out of the confusion of events
are ludicrous. Perhaps, too, the parable exposes how popular
is the inclination to make complex problems simplistic, and
how wrong is the notion that we have to make no effort at all to
learn and to know.

On Rosh Hashanah Reb Bunim also chose the form of a
parable. "Once upon a time," he declared, "there was a prince
who sinned against his father. The king became angry and
drove the prince away from home. Years passed and the king
began to long for his son. He ordered the most important of his
dukes to look for the prince all over the land. After much effort,
the duke finally met the prince, barefoot and in tattered
clothes, at an inn.

The duke bowed and said, "Your Majesty! Your father, the
king, would like to make amends. He has empowered me to
ask what you want of him."

The prince burst into tears and replied, "If my father wishes to bestow his favor upon me once more, I ask that he give me a pair of shiny new boots."

In this incisive parable one can note a hint to the Jew not to squander his precious days and exchange them for small, worthless things and for pitifully miserable requests that lack zest and will. One can also infer not only that small-minded concepts lower man and expose him in his utter ludicrousness, but that if man forgets to demand, then the entire creation loses its breadth of greatness.

In one sharp aphorism Reb Bunim expressed the essential element of the path he introduced in Pshishkhe. He said that he aspired to write a book entitled *Adam*. It would treat the history, the life, the suffering, and the hope of man. Reb Bunim never wrote this book. In fact, he wrote no books whatsoever. His thoughts, interpretations, and parables were written down by his pupils. Nevertheless, with his life and deeds in Pshishkhe Reb Bunim wrote one of the most profound interpretations of the problems and struggles of man.

V

In Polish Hasidism they continued with the Pshishkhe system even after this little town had ceased to be a Hasidic center. Paraphrasing Reb Bunim's remark, one might note that Pshishkhe learned to live even after it had vanished. The energy of Pshishkhe pushed and pursued Reb Mendel of Kotzk to stringently demand that Jews constantly relive the Sinai experience in the depths of their consciousness; that they ceaselessly make demands upon themselves and shout "not yet" to themselves ("We have not yet studied, we have not yet prayed, we have not yet fulfilled, not yet, not yet," in the words of the famous song of Kotzk); and that there is nothing more whole than a broken Jewish heart.

Reb Mendel of Kotzk derived his passionate and obstinate impulse toward truth, his heroic and tragic struggle against judgment and fate, and his deeply human challenge not only "to shake the foundations of the earth" but even to lift up heaven itself, from Pshishkhe. Reb Mendel of Kotzk declared

that until the advent of Pshishkhe, Hasidism was an interpretation of the Baal Shem Tov. But after Reb Bunim of Pshishkhe
opened up the wellsprings of his teachings and wisdom,
Hasidism became an interpretation of Pshishkhe.

The distinct echo of Pshishkhe is heard in Reb Isaac Vurker's
remark that the Jew must develop a strong will and the
strength to be capable of doing the following three things: yell
without voice, dance without movement, bow down with an
uplifted head.

In the style of Pshishkhe, Reb Itche Meir of Ger declared that
the Jew who relies only upon faith is lazy. Indeed, this is how
he phrased it with Pshishkhe acumen: "He is lazy, that's why
he relies on faith." If the condition of Jews and Jewishness is at
stake, Reb Itche Meir accented (he is known in Hasidic literature by the name of his book, *Hidushey ha-Rim*), we must even
bang our head against the wall and do the impossible. He did
not withdraw his remarks or change his tone even later when it
was shown to him that one cannot bang one's head against the
wall. Reb Itche Meir of Ger held steadfastly to his position:
even though one cannot, one *must* do it!

The precipitous breadth of Pshishkhe emanates from Reb
Hanoch Henech of Alexander's profound interpretation of the
verse, "And the mountain burned with fire up to the heart of
the heaven."

"This is not flowery exaggeration," he explained. "The heart
can become heaven. If the Jewish heart blazes with fire, then
indeed it becomes heaven."

As has been stated, however, Pshishkhe is not just Hasidism. It penetrated into the blood and the entire fabric of Polish
Jewry. Even the most beautiful chapters of modern Hebrew
and Yiddish literature are saturated with the spirit of
Pshishkhe. One cannot understand I. L. Peretz, Nachum Sokolow, Hirsch David Nomberg, or Aharon Zeitlin without the
influence of Pshishkhe. One cannot explain the specific character that Zionism, religious orthodoxy, or Jewish socialism assumed in Poland if one does not immerse oneself in the
teachings of Reb Bunim.

And unless one digs down into the roots of Pshishkhe, one cannot capture the spirit of Polish Jewry during the last generations; one cannot comprehend the Polish-Jewish community's bold and notable struggle for its right to live as Jews; one cannot imagine the unstilled creative fervor it possessed in periods of pessimism and despair; in short, without Pshishkhe one cannot understand the drama of the community's craving for the impossible, a drama that Polish Jewry wrote even in the hour of its decline when—despite reality—they told themselves that this was by no means "the end of the road."

In Pshishkhe, "the mountain of the Lord" took on the primordial meaning of volcano on which even the fiery, flowing lava cannot remove man's resolve to ascend to the heights.

6

Kotzk, the Hasidism of Polish Jewry

I

WHAT WAS SO UNUSUAL about the Hasidism of Kotzk? Why is Kotzk intriguing not only to followers of Hasidism but also to those far from the Hasidic tradition and way of life? Why is Kotzk constantly cited as a system that introduced storm and creative restlessness into Jewish life? What did the Kotzk rebbe and the Kotzk teaching have which imbued their brand of Hasidism with a remarkable tension, a Hasidism that did not lose its value and relevancy for the Jew despite the destruction of Polish Jewry and changed circumstances in Jewish life?

Judging by the stature of Kotzk Hasidim, one might assume that Kotzk was a metropolis or a large, densely populated Jewish center. On the contrary, Kotzk was actually a small town in Poland, near Lublin. When Kotzk ascended in Jewish history, no more than two hundred Jewish families lived there. The phenomenon of Kotzk becomes even more interesting when one recalls that its founder, Reb Menachem Mendel Morgenstern, was very different from the other Hasidic teachers to whom Jews flocked during his or earlier generations.

Unlike the Baal Shem Tov, Reb Mendele, as he was called, did not stroke and soothe the anguished Jewish spirit. Unlike Reb Nachman of Bratzlav, he did not get carried away by the fantasy of his poetic word. Unlike Reb Levi Yitzchok of Berditchev, he did not impress himself upon people's hearts with his ardent defense of Jews. Unlike Reb Shneur Zalman of Liady,

Reb Mendele did not wrap his Torah in a deep mysticism that could inspire trembling and awe. Unlike Reb Bunim of Pshishkhe, he did not even tell wonder stories whose plots would captivate his listeners or enchant them with hidden meanings. During the years that Reb Mendele of Kotzk associated with his followers, his attitude and manner of speech were severe. Despite all the light that sparkled in them his remarks and aphorisms were frequently tense and nebulous.

But even this period of severe and strained contact with people lasted only twelve years. Then began his period of seclusion, when Reb Mendele locked himself into his room and was not always accessible to those who yearned to hear his message. The life and activity of the Kotzk rebbe ended with this twenty-year period of withdrawal.

This period is clouded with the mist of various theories, but no matter where the key to his withdrawal is found, one thing is certain: in the years that Reb Mendele was sequestered within himself, he was sparing of words. Only the glow of his personality radiated to the astonished world outside.

When, then, was it in Kotzk that left such a lasting stamp upon Jewish history? And why doesn't the dust of time settle over the teachings of Kotzk Hasidism, especially since Jewish Kotzk is in ruins and so many nineteenth century Jewish movements seem to be faded and timeworn today?

II

Penetrating Kotzk means weaving oneself into a fabric where the border between the usual and the unusual is obliterated. At first glance everything appears to be simple; indeed, simplicity itself. We encounter the same phenomena that are characteristic of the Hasidic movement during the first half of the nineteenth century. But yet we face a dense secret, hardly explicable and comphrehensible via scholarly analysis.

Like many other Hasidic teachers, Reb Mendele too came from a Misnagdic home. His father, a glazier, wandered from village to village in quest of livelihood, and his sensitive son strove to get out of the straits in which he grew up.

In later years he would say that of all he had learned, what impressed him most were the verses depicting the thunder and lightning heard and seen at the Divine Revelation at Sinai. It seemed to Reb Mendele that he himself stood at the foot of the mountain awaiting a new revelation. In Pshishkhe he sought a solution to questions that haunted him. Those who were drawn to Hasidism were nourished by the sources of Torah and wisdom that Reb Bunim of Pshishkhe had opened. Not because they expected miracles from the rebbe, but because they felt that the essence of Hasidism was to awaken the hidden strengths in the Jew. Hasidism showed that the Jew can lift himself, the Jewish people, and Jewishness only when he makes an effort of will and spirit. In Pshishkhe they followed the views and conclusions that the Maharal of Prague had arrived at generations earlier. They fused heart and mind, Talmud and philosophic speculation, mysticism and literal interpretation of the Bible.

Once again, in those pre-genesis years of Kotzk, towns and villages of the vanished Jewish geography of Eastern Europe pass before us: Goray, the birthplace of Reb Mendele; Zemosc and Lemberg, where he studied; Tomashov, where he married. Indeed it was in Tomashov that something crucial occurred. Reb Bunim departed from this world, and restlessness and expectation became noticeable in those orphaned communities because of the now-empty chair.

At that time, one of Reb Bunim's most important pupils—Reb Itche Meir, who later founded Ger Hasidism—remarked openly that only Reb Menachem Mendel was worthy of continuing the chain of Pshishkhe. Hasidic sources state that Reb Itche Meir and Reb Mendele strolled and talked for hours at night in the woods. The night was full of secrets, and secretive was their conversation. When the morning star appeared, Reb Itche Meir, one of the sharpest minds in the history of Polish Jewry, poured water on the hands of Reb Mendele—a sign that he recognized his authority—and said: "Reb Mendele is the true Jew."

When Reb Mendele began in his unique fashion to make his

way in the Hasidic movement, and Tomashov was developing as the new center in Hasidism, Reb Itche Meir asserted: "Just as there once were thunders and lightnings when we received the Torah at Sinai, we now receive Torah with thunder and lightning here in Tomashov." These words were apparently inspired by the Revelation at Sinai, which for the new Hasidic leader was not just a vision from the past but a present-day drama.

We say "drama" because what began in Tomashov went beyond the bounds of the commonplace; it was not simply another rebbe and another Hasidic court. A new intellectual system and a new social movement were formed. In Tomashov, the Hasidim ceased having normal family lives. They left their families for many months to live by themselves and penetrate their own inner world. The days were spent in physical labor, with earnings contributed to a common fund. At night they studied the Talmud, burrowed into philosophic texts, and argued about God, man, and Jew. They held that it was important to remain true to one's inner calling. No one should imitate anyone else, or do something because others were doing it.

They wanted their sacred intentions and fiery enthusiasm to be felt not only in prayer but in everything that encompasses one's life. They would often rebel against values which at an earlier time had appeared to be a component of Hasidism. They wanted to improve the state of Jewishness and the human condition. Merely raising the terrestrial did not satisfy them; they explicitly wanted (as was articulated by the teacher of these daring ideas) to lift up the heavens.

Reb Mendele concluded that the path he had outlined was a difficult one, and only special individuals would be capable of following it. Attracting large masses of followers did not interest him.

"I don't want more than two or three hundred Hasidim," he said. "But I crave that the Baal Shem Tov's soul flutter in them. Instead of skullcaps, I want them to wear leaves of trees and belts of green boughs. I want them to be amazed and overwhelmed by the secrets of heaven and earth, and to cry out with the ecstasy of the psalmist who sang (chapter 24): 'The earth is the Lord's, and the fullness thereof.' "

Naturally, all this also prompted opposition. Critical voices were raised. The Hasidim in Tomashov were accused of being overly immersed in philosophy and too little in Jewishness as it should be expressed in daily life; they were accused of being overly preoccupied with offering new interpretations of things which needed no explanation at all.

The rabbi of Warsaw, Rabbi Jacob Gezuntheit, was severely critical of the group. Along with the enthusiasm which this new Hasidism inspired among the young and the astute, a protest movement also developed within the Hasidic camp. But Reb Mendele did not change his ways because of this. The locale, however, was changed: from Tomashov, where the disputes became increasingly strained, Reb Mendele moved to nearby Kotzk. And herewith begins the remarkable chapter of Kotzk in Jewish history.

III

Much has been written about Kotzk Hasidism. Even in our generation scholarly appraisals are constantly being published. But it is characteristic that the rebbe of Kotzk wrote no book at all. When asked why he did not write one, he replied after a long deep silence:

"Let's assume that I've written and published a book. Who would look into it? Torah scholars know more than I do. What could they learn from me? This leaves us with our people, none of whom have any time to look into a book. All week long they are harried with concerns about livelihood; the only day they have left is the Sabbath. But on Sabbath one must also learn and pray and eat the Sabbath meal. So the only spare time is after lunch. He lies down to rest, takes the book in hand, and opens it. Since he is already satiated with the just-completed meal, a sleepy feeling comes over him, the book slips out of his hand and falls to the floor. So, I ask you, why should I write a book?"

Reb Mendele believed that teaching orally would enable him to have greater and more apparent influence on his pupils. Words articulated with frank and sincere conviction can penetrate more deeply into the heart. The Bible that he always had with him, and in which (as he told his congregation) one could find instruction and direction, taught him that more important than writing words upon paper was to "write them on the table of your heart" (Proverbs 3:3).

The truth is that his teachings and remarks were remarkably terse. They were actually comments, aphorisms, fragments of thoughts. Frequently needle-sharp, they pricked the conscience. In this respect Reb Mendel of Kotzk remained faithful to his own personality and to the creative expression and style of Polish Jewry.

Polish Jewry had not constructed superbly organized systems either in the field of Halakhah or in the field of thought. The great contribution of one of the first geniuses of Polish Jewry, Rabbi Moses Isserles, consists of his halakhic annotations and succinct glosses. Rabbi Solomon Luria's illuminating interpretations of talumdic literature are short, brilliant comments. Rabbi Samuel Eidels's astounding erudition and psychological intuition were set into short lines—annotations which helped unlock the secretive world concealed in talmudic legends.

Hasidism too remained part of this age-old tradition. How was the Baal Shem Tov's teaching revealed? Via story, word, and gesture. How did Reb Bunim of Pshishkhe find his way to man's heart? With a parable, an allusion, a spark of thought. And those who introduced new values and modern forms to Polish-Jewish creativity in the crisis of the twentieth century also utilized this style, which reflected the spiritual personality of the Jewish community in Poland. I. L. Peretz, David Frischman, and Hirsch David Nomberg did not write lengthy works. Thought fragments were characteristic of their writings. Even Nachum Sokolow's occasional verbosity was actually just a loose bundle of fragments of broken, severed thoughts.

The rebbe of Kotzk's words and teachings were not written

by him but by his students. The only surviving autograph document is a letter—the only known letter extant. Dated Tomashov, on a wintery Friday in 5588 according to the Jewish calendar ("Eve of the holy Sabbath, the Jethro portion"), 1828, it was addressed to his beloved friend, as he is called in the letter, Reb Itche Meir of Warsaw.

Despite the rabbinic Hebrew fashionable at the time, the short letter breathes with a stirring simplicity. Each line glows with deeply human warmth. Reb Mendele expresses his anxiety at not having heard from his friend.

"I can't restrain myself and remain silent. My heart trembles because I haven't had a letter from you in three months." Continuing, he says that he suffers because not everybody understands him. Still he feels encouraged by the closeness of the young people, for "they seek light for their thoughts." In a stirring line, Reb Mendel reveals his family's state of indigence. He admits that he would write more often but has no money for stamps.

"I will tell you the truth, and I am not ashamed to admit it, but there are times when we don't have enough money to pay the postage costs. That is why I could not send you any message about myself."

Other sources also provide us with details that substantiate this bitter fact. From afar the rebbe of Kotzk was recognizable by his terribly shabby clothes. He frequently rejected proferred assistance. "What, you want to give me money?" he once angrily told a Hasid who attempted to give him a coin, and spat out in disgust.

His pupil, Reb Yechiel Meir (who later became the rebbe of Gostinin), was also poverty-stricken. Once, when he happily informed Reb Mendele that he had won a great sum in the lottery, Reb Mendele seized his collar and looked at him reproachfully.

Reb Yechiel Meir began to stammer and justify himself. "But it's not my fault that I won."

Reb Mendele kept staring at him relentlessly. Only when his pupil had distributed his entire winnings among his needy friends did the rebbe of Kotzk calm down. Reb Mendele's conduct here was consistent with his outlook: material presents burn and hurt those that take them. He would say that in a gift given by a man of flesh and blood there is flesh and also blood.

Such terrible poverty and want might have depressed the spirit and brought on an atmosphere of passive dejection; yet from here came thought fragments whose spiritual dynamism transformed Kotzk to a place to which people made pilgrimages. Disregarding Reb Mendele's explicit request not to have a crowd around him, people went to Kotzk from near and far— the average man in the street, as well as scholars and the scions of fine families. Opponents could not weaken the pulling power that this little Polish town possessed.

The Yiddish folksong stated: "To Kotzk one does not travel, to Kotzk one takes a pilgrimage." The people too, in their characteristic fashion, persuaded themselves that they could store up experience after a visit to the Kotzk rebbe. They felt that the discomfort of the weeks-long journey was worthwhile. When read today, nearly one hundred and fifty years later, memoirs of that period convince us that even in the rich thousand-year history of Polish Jewry, Kotzk was a one-time phenomenon. Reb Henech from Alexander felt that Kotzk was a commentary to Pshishkhe—but what a magnificent commentary it was!

IV

The Kotzk teaching that stresses the importance of dissatisfaction fascinates us. Since the dawn of its history Judaism has been vehemently opposed to imitation or superficiality. Abraham, the first Jew, made his mark in history by vigorously smashing accepted gods and idols. The most disquieting character portrayal of a dissatisfied man is Moses—dissatisfied with himself, dissatisfied with his fate, dissatisfied with his people, dissatisfied with the world, dissatisfied with the shocking contradiction between vision and reality.

Each and every one of the prophets was a dissatisfied man—

dissatisfied with himself, with the reigning system, with society. Jonah is the tragic example of a prophet who is cast from port to port, from country to country, from land and from water in his raging against the people's satiated self-satisfaction.

But all of them who brought God's word to man were like this. Driven by perpetual restlessness, they provoked storm and protest in their desire to build new worlds. Amos, the shepherd who became a prophet, felt that a famine must come to the land. But he added that "it will not be a hunger for bread or a thirst for water" (Amos, 8:11), but a dissatisfaction of a completely different kind. When Jeremiah lashed out with his bitter rebukes, he did not even spare his own parents (Jeremiah 20: 14-18).

Repentance, a motif which our thinkers constantly reiterated, actually means being dissatisfied with what one has achieved and keeping one's conscience in a state of permanent exertion. When the Jews lived in their own land, and later when they were exiled to foreign shores, they responded to the calls of "tearing one's heart" and "building a new heart and a new spirit." One encounters such calls in the world of symbols of the prophet Joel and in the exalted visions of Ezekiel.

With the passing of the centuries—and as a way of being able to bear the burden of existence—the phrase "content with his lot" was developed. The Jew who is satisfied with himself and with his lot was supposed to serve as a prototype. But in fact this phrase referred only to material possessions; it was supposed to shout into the Jew's ear: Don't break your neck amassing wealth!

The concept "content with his lot" was never meant to apply to the realm of the spirit. No one ever placed a limit on spiritual ascent. Even Simon ben Zoma, who made this phrase popular (*Ethics of the Fathers* 4:1), was far from being a self-satisfied person. Indeed, he was one of the most restless men of the spirit among the builders of the Talmud.

Simon ben Zoma was untiring in his desire to get to the bottom, to the root of things. He held that Adam seethed with the need to ask and look and strive, even though it would bring on countless torments. Consider, ben Zoma said, how big and strong were the efforts and torments of the first man (*Berakhot* 58). The Talmud tells that ben Zoma belonged to a small but bold circle of thinkers and seekers whose striving to penetrate the secrets of creation thrust them into the most dangerous paths and byways of human thought (*Haggigah* 14).

In Kotzk they believed that even in times of hardship and darkness one must not feed on illusory and meretricious tranquilizers. They opposed those who thought that a superficial satisfied smile on a Jew's face would uplift him and the people. Jewishness is insurgency, and Hasidism must be storm. Hasidism dare not remain satisfied with what is happening around us and within us. In Kotzk they concluded that Jews who study Judaism without concomitant effort, or pray today because they prayed yesterday, or even assume that Hasidism means simplifying the task of being a Jew—such people cripple and distort the substance and character of Jewishness.

Reb Mendele's incisive remarks, spraying sparks and fire, were cast in seemingly offhand fashion, but they were stirringly consistent. First of all, how does one develop in one's own conscience the feeling of responsibility for the community? The High Priest of ancient times can serve as an example. The laws that regulate his life can serve as a guidepost for those who gather in Kotzk. Like the High Priest, man must lift himself higher than his limited family circle; he must be removed from his family and not feel closer to relatives or intimates than to any other Jew.

What is the source of the folk expression, "a zaddik in fur," Reb Mendele asked. And he responded: "There are two ways of getting warm when it is cold. Either heat up the oven or wear thick, warm clothing. In the former, you bring benefit to others as well as to yourself. Everyone in the house then feels warm. But in the latter, only one person feels warm. There are zaddikim (Hasidic leaders) whose principal concern is to warm themselves—ever mindful of arming themselves with more and more mitzvot. The focus of their concern is themselves.

The welfare of the community at large does not interest them. And that is what is meant by the ironical gibe, 'a zaddik in fur'!"

In the view of the Kotzk rebbe, persuading oneself that one has already achieved something was considered a defect, a sin. The person who assures others that he can answer all the questions shows that he has grasped nothing, that he is far-removed from knowledge. This too is the import of Ecclesiastes (7:23), where human thought is expressed in all its complexity. To the claim of the first chapter in Ecclesiastes that the more one knows the more torments one suffers, the rebbe of Kotzk added in Pshishkhe fashion:

"So what! Let it hurt, but increase knowledge!" The rebbe held that one should not fear criticism. When he was faulted for having Hasidim who did not walk in the traditional, paved path like other Jews, he replied, "Horses go in the middle of the paved road. People go on sidewalks."

For Reb Menachem Mendel of Kotzk, seeking, asking, and demanding seemed to be the *alephbet* of Judaism. "I would never want to serve a God," he would say, "whose ways can be understood by every foolish nobody." For spiritual ascent—or, as he would call it, "holy service"—one must toil hard. It can not simply be pulled out of one's sleeve.

"If someone says, 'I didn't labor, but I have found'—don't believe it! Don't believe that one can ascend higher without irksome strain. If someone goes around with the proud self-delusion that he is already finished, then he's really cooked!" That's the way the rebbe of Kotzk would express himself in his juicy, folksy Yiddish.

A Hasid once asked him to pray for him. To this Reb Mendele rsponded, "And you? Why don't you pray for yourself?" "I don't know how," the Hasid replied.

The rabbi pierced him with his melancholy gaze and told him categorically: "Then go learn!"

Like many other early Hasidic teachers, Reb Mendele stressed the significance of humility. But it had to be a Kotzk kind of humility. Which meant: not disparaging oneself, not eradicating one's own personality, not diminishing the value of one's behavior.

"Take Mount Sinai," he said, returning to the motif that accompanied him all his life. "Sinai was chosen from among all the mountains because it was the lowest of the mountains. Nevertheless, Divine Revelation did not take place in the valley. Even if one considers oneself low, it must be a mountain lowness and not one of valley level. One cannot be on the mountain and in the valley at the same time. One has to remain on the mountain and strive constantly for the heights."

Reb Mendele had his own interpretation of the impulse to seek godliness. Moses summoned the people to this quest with the words: "You will find Him, if only you seek Him" (Deuteronomy 4:29). "Seeking," the rebbe of Kotzk stressed, "is in itself an achievement. And, furthermore, when you think you have found God, only then will you first begin to seek and search."

When a Jew once complained to Reb Mendele that his mind was constantly plagued by problems that give him no peace, the following dialogue ensued between the rebbe and the Hasid.

"What things do you think about?"

"I think about whether there is a heavenly judge and if there is justice," the Hasid said.

"What do you care if there is a heavenly judge?" the rebbe asked.

"What do you mean? If, God forbid, there is no judge and no justice, what purpose then is there to all of creation?"

"Why should this matter concern you?" the rebbe asked.

"What do you mean? In that case, what's the sense of the Torah we've been given?" the Hasid said.

"Nu, what do you care if there is sense to the Torah?" the rebbe asked.

"What are you talking about, Rebbe? What then *should* concern me?"

"If it concerns you so much," the rebbe concluded, "then you're a good Jew. And a good Jew may ask questions."

"Not yet, not yet, we're still at the foot of the godly mountain. We haven't arrived, not yet, not yet . . ." is the folk ditty
that caught on and spread in the little Polish town that developed into a great center of the Jewish spirit.

One day, gnawing dissatisfaction drove the rebbe of Kotzk to
shut himself off from the world and seclude himself in the
loneliness of his room. At times he wanted to see no one. But
on the days he saw his callers, he once again reminded them of
how important it was to lift oneself up, how important it was to
lift up the earth, and how important it was to "lift up the
heavens." He did not retreat from his stringent demands even
when one associate or another abandoned him. The meaning
of Kotzk was: reawakening the gnawing question with which
the dialogue between heaven and earth was begun in Genesis:
"Man, where are you?"

V

Kotzk also taught that the talmudic statement "truth is the
stamp of God" (*Sabbath* 55) does not suffice—truth must also be
the stamp of man. Truth without premises, without half-
measures. Reb Mendele asserted that everything in the world
can be imitated except truth, for truth imitated is no longer
truth. One must bend down to lift truth up. There is a midrashic saying that "truth was cast down to the ground." In
Kotzk they explained its meaning: in order to demonstrate that
one cannot achieve truth with an uplifted head but must bend
down to it.

In Kotzk they did not close their eyes to material conditions
and to their influence in forming man's character. The expression "we have come down here [to buy bread]" (Genesis
43:20)—referring to the ordeals man experiences for a bit of
bread—demonstrates that we always know how costly it is to
sustain our families. Unfortunately, it is a comedown. We
humiliate ourselves for bitter livelihood. So in our difficult
struggle for bread we have to redouble our efforts to remain
true to ourselves and to truth even while standing on the
threshold of dejection.

Hasidic Kotzk, in contrast to other movements in Hasidism, did not take seriously the belief in the rebbe and in his wonders. When faith is whole it needs no external proofs. Reb Mendele stressed that in ancient Egypt it took hundreds of years for true faith to penetrate the consciousness of our ancestors, a faith that needed no demonstration of signs and miracles.

Faith means loyalty, Reb Mendele said. If we use artificial means in concepts of faith, we falsify its substance and its truth. Faith can do without eyes, for with believing one can see more than with eyes. Showing one's piety is another form of serving falsehood. The biblical verse concerning the Revelation at Sinai, "the people saw and trembled and stood at a distance" (Exodus 20:18), was boldly interpreted in Kotzk: One can see, one can even tremble, and still remain at a distance.

Reb Mendele stated that there is an essential difference between standing in awe of the Creator and trembling before the *Shulchan Aruch*. From the verse in Psalms 81:10, "There shall be no strange gods among you," the rebbe deduced that avoiding idolatry was not enough. The import of the remark was that God should not be strange to us.

One's conviction of the greatness of being a Jew must be complete and whole. Nothing can weaken or diminish the mighty experience of Jewishness. For example, the Kotzke rebbe said, the Jew who sits in the *sukkah* and feels the rain is not worthy of being in the *sukkah*. (He is supposed to be oblivious to it.) Jewishness demands faith, loyalty. Jewishness is an experience which must overwhelm heart and soul, even when the enemy's whip is slashing one's head.

Kotzk taught that truth means: don't be so deeply engrossed in yourself. Serving oneself is also idolatry. Man does not realize that if he serves his own "self," the "self" creates a nest within him so that he is no longer whole. The "self" stands there like a wall between God and man. That is how the Kotzk rebbe understood the biblical verse: "I stand between God and you" (Deuteronomy 5:5).

In his efforts to penetrate the complicated nooks of man's

nature, Reb Mendele observed that one can immediately sense whether a person is authentic, just as one can tell the character and contents of a book by its introduction. The rebbe even looked suspiciously at the man who fled honor. One should not feel that honor is something from which one must flee. One simply should not become unduly impressed by it.

He warned too that in addition to not stealing, one must also not be a thief. And the fact that the Torah added "Ye shall not steal" (Leviticus 19:31), in the plural, to the Ten Commandments' prohibition, "Thou shall not steal," shows the Torah's explicit stress in this matter. The plural, "Ye shall not steal," means *you*—you, Reb nice Jew; you, Reb scholar; you too must not be a thief!

An old, well-to-do man once came to Reb Mendele and told him that he was preparing to go to Eretz Yisrael because he wanted his body to find eternal rest in the Holy Land.

"Woe, woe," the Kotzk rebbe shouted. "Woe, woe, how a man is so in love with his own wormy body! He's worrying about it even after his death."

The concept of truth in Kotzk encompassed everything and everyone. It was taught in Kotzk that without the yardstick of truth, there is no love for one's fellow man. It just remains a licorice-sweet outpouring of words without substance and stronghold. Loyalty can maintain itself and endure through truth.

The rebbe of Gostinin, Reb Yechiel Meir, acknowledged that he learned the trait of loving his fellow Jew from observing Reb Mendele when he was angry at his Hasidim. "The truth," Reb Menachem Mendel of Kotzk remarked, "demands something more: Not just holding on to the good and comfortable aspects of Jewishness for yourself—and the difficult ones, the strict interpretations, for others."

Also, if one constantly cries, "It's for the sake of heaven," he should be sure it indeed is "for the sake of heaven," the Kotzk rebbe said. There are people who strongly uphold the concept of truth for others. They want to favor the entire world with truth—except themselves. Solomon, the wisest of kings, advised these people that it would be preferable to acquire truth for their own use and not hold it for sale to the next person ("Acquire truth, sell it not," Proverbs 22:23).

In the thousand-year history of Jewish spirituality, new movements have often called upon the Jew to return to his roots and demanded that he remain genuine and honest in thought and deed. Kotzk was exciting because it formulated no principle out of principles. Everything had to flow from the essential fact that one is a Jew. Concepts such as dissatisfaction, faith, truth, and communal responsibility had to be as absolutely natural as the air one breathes. In Kotzk they did not speak of tormenting one's body or prescribing fasts. They made no attempt to become a Musarnik movement.

In Kotzk they aspired to remain true to the pristine sources of Judaism. For a Jew it is clear what a Jew must be. No matter how stringent the demands of Kotzk, people did not feel they were impossible. The warning "You shall be holy people unto me" (Exodus 22:30) was interpreted in Kotzk as meaning: "You shall be *humanly* holy."

To the question, "Where does God dwell?" they responded, "Wherever He is admitted." The verse "You shall live by them" (Leviticus 18:5), which prompted so many interpretations in Halakhah, was seen in Kotzk as a call for us to be Jews with a spirit of life. A living Jewishness must throb in our weekdays and in our holidays. Jews must always have ecstatic vitality, even in difficult times.

We must remember that Kotzk came to the fore during a period of dense concentration of Jews in East European towns and villages. Poland was occupied by the Czars, and pogroms and persecutions filled the life of the Jew with constantly increasing anguish and horror. Indeed, in the first half of the nineteenth century, the Jews were appalled by the Russian Cantonist law subjecting eight-year-old boys to a twenty-five-year period of military service.

Little Jewish lads were forcibly torn from their mother's arms in Russia and handed over to peasants for the express purpose of training them for conversion. No ears heard the Jewish cries of pain. Constant bans and restrictions prompted a sense of tragic helplessness and threatened to cast the entire Jewish community into a mood of inferiority and despair.

Here and there views were articulated for Jews to dilute somewhat or perhaps even abandon much of their Jewishness, to tone down their age-old lifestyle, to moderate the historic Jewish ideals and hope. During those decades Hasidism had already ceased to be the great creative power that it had been one hundred years earlier. Kotzk's exalted quality was that they diminished nothing and abandoned nothing. They believed that the persecuted and tormented Jew was capable of feeling the encouraging breath of Jewish history and of transforming the painful period of no alternatives into a drama of ascent. Great demands would create great Jews.

"In the end you will eventually hear the voices that awaken and demand," the rebbe of Kotzk said. "Thunder and lightning have often put the individual Jew and the community to the test of character and courage."

Once, on a Friday night (this took place during his period of seclusion), the rebbe opened the door to his room, where he had locked himself in. He went to the Bes Medresh, where a few Hasidim were sitting, and shouted:

"What Torah portion are we reading this week?"

"This week is *Kedoshim* ["Holy"]."

"Really? *Kedoshim?*" the rebbe repeated. "Do you know that the end of the Torah and the beginning are closely bound up? The same holds true for the entire Torah and for every weekly portion. Today's weekly portion begins with 'Ye shall be holy' and ends with 'their blood shall be upon them.' What does this mean? It means that it should cost blood. Let blood flow—but be holy Jews!"

More than any other Hasidic system Kotzk held that man stands with one foot in the nethermost pit and with the other in the seventh heaven. But at a time when doubts and despair began to gnaw at the Jewish consciousness, Kotzk also possessed an obstinate belief in the inexhaustible powers of our people to stride over abysses and with untiring challenge to lift themselves up to the seventh heaven.

VI

The chapter concerning the Kotzk rebbe's self-imposed seclusion during the last twenty years of his life must be written anew. True, during most of this period he was in his room, removed and estranged from everyone. But reading the Hasidic sources forces one to conclude that there are gross exaggerations. In those years, Reb Mendele did not cut himself off completely from contact with the world. In keeping with his never-ending perspicacity, he would say that washing one's hands of the world does not mean not being involved with it.

The remarks that he made in that time of profound concentration are pearls of thought and feeling. "It's not important that I've been accused of becoming silent," he said. "Silence can be the loudest scream in the world. It's not important that I appear to be disheveled and broken. There is nothing more whole than a broken Jewish heart."

In his period of seclusion he also remained a consistent teacher who demanded that Jews attain the fine point of truth and bring the world to that point. He asked: "Why does this rebbe or that one constantly cry to God to send down the Messiah? They ought, rather, to direct their cries for help to the Jews, because it is to *them* that the Messiah has to come."

When crowds assembled in his house awaiting his word, he stood at the threshold of his room and called: "Liars, fakers! What do you want of me? Do you think I'm going to cleanse you of your falsehoods? Why are you gaping at me like that? Do you think I'm a chimney sweep?"

At another time he complained, "I haven't the faintest idea what people want of me. All week long they do what their hearts desire, yet when Sabbath comes they put on their black kaftans, gird themselves with a black belt, put the black fur hat on their heads—and that's it, they think they're finished. How can I make them understand that I haven't come into this world to fill their stomachs and let them sleep with ease?"

Once, hearing an argument about which man was greater and how one man can surpass another, the rebbe of Kotzk declared: "If I am I because I am I, and you are you, because you are you—then I am I, and you are you. But if I am I because you are you, and you are you because I am I, then I am not I, and you are not you."

The rebbe wasn't fazed when asked how he could give advice to Hasidim with problems when he himself was so far removed from the world and its activities. He responded: "Is there a better place from which one can assess things the way they are?" And to Reb Yechiel Meir of Gostinin he confided: "We've said nothing new here in Kotzk. We just make great efforts to bring out what is buried deep within everyone."

Of Reb Jacob of Radzimin he asked this question: "Tell me, why was man created?"

"Man was created so that he can improve his soul," the rebbe of Radzimin replied.

But this answer did not satisfy Reb Mendele. "Reb Bunim of Pshishkhe gave another interpretation, which seems correct. Man was created in order to lift up the heavens."

A Hasid once asked the rebbe, "When should the door be opened up for the prophet Elijah at the Seder?"

"Elijah does not come in through the door but through the heart," the rebbe of Kotzk replied.

When he saw Hasidim dancing with the Torahs on Simchas Torah, he turned to them and said, "You're happy, it seems to me, because you've promised yourselves to really and truly study Torah from now on. Your joys can't possibly stem from the fact that you assume you have *already* learned. For who can say that about himself?"

We are more persuaded by a letter that Reb Itche Meir sent from Warsaw to the rabbi of Pultusk than by the bizarre and groundless theories that have gathered surrounding Reb Mendel's period of seclusion. In his letter Reb Itche Meir writes:

"I was in Kotzk last Sabbath. . . Reb Mendele spent three Sabbaths with his Hasidim. The rumors being spread are surely created by malevolent people for whom Kotzk is a thorn in their eyes."

A book about Reb Mendele by Pinchas Zelig Glicksman, published in Poland before World War II, cites letters written by other visitors to Kotzk who agree with Reb Itche Meir. Rabbi

Aaron Walden, author of *Shem ha-Gedolim he-Chadash,* relates that even after Reb Mendele had secluded himself from visitors he still was the leader of his congregation of Jews and "admitted those who knocked on his door."

Reb Isaac of Vurke constantly inquired of the rebbe about various matters and problems and sought advice and direction from him. The same was done by great masses of Jews in Poland and Lithuania who streamed to Kotzk. Reb Mendele took a stand on difficult and complicated decisions that Jews had to make at a fateful hour.

Contrary to the belief spread in various Jewish circles that doing military service would help the Jews of Czarist Russia in their struggle for equality, the rebbe of Kotzk considered military service a burdensome edict.

"We will in any case be considered strangers," he said. "Nothing will help." As was his wont, he supported his stance with a biblical verse, explaining that "For your offspring will be a stranger in a land that does not belong to them" (Genesis 15:13) means: "In a land that does not belong to Jews, they will constantly be considered as strangers no matter what they do."

On the other hand, he disagreed with those who protested the Czarist decree that Jews must dress exactly like all other residents of the land. He felt that it was not worth wasting time and energy on this issue. Jews should devote their zeal to essential matters and not to external garb. During the years of the Crimean War in which Russia was ensnared in the middle of the nineteenth century, Reb Mendele opposed Russia with all his heart and prayers, for could Jews feel any differently about an evil regime?

If before the Holocaust the uniqueness of Kotzk in Hasidism and in the historic path of East European Jewry was apparent, then Kotzk achieves an even greater prominence at the present writing, forty years after the axe of destruction fell upon East European Jewry. Kotzk emerges as a symbol of the spiritual struggles of the centers that embodied the Jewish creative impulse during the last two hundred years and felt that they were responsible for their people's destiny.

Reb Mendele's period of seclusion also manifests itself in the perspective of time, especially in view of the ashes of Treblinka and Auschwitz, within the framework of symbol.

Indeed, that is how Polish Jewry was: like Reb Mendele of Kotzk, estranged from surroundings and yet fused with them. Staring out at the past, and yet engrossed in the future. Disheveled, and yet wonderfully systematic. Scattered into splinters, and yet possessing a dream of wholeness. Raging and rebelling, and yet anchored in tradition. Seething in tumultuous bustle, and yet focusing upon their own spiritual experience.

A distorted light has recently been cast upon the shtetl (I refer to the Polish-Jewish shtetl), which is a component of East European Jewish history. The shtetl is represented as a miniature world that existed cut off from the outside world; as a medieval institution that survived to modern times but was superannuated and moldy despite all the old-fashioned charm it was proclaimed to have. But this is far from the truth. The Jewish shtetl underwent crucial changes and transformations, and in the nineteenth century (and certainly in the twentieth) it was indeed locked into general life and breathed with the outside world.

Jewish civilization dominated, but there was no wall between the shtetl and the outside world. Movements from near and far unmistakably penetrated the shtetl. I'm not referring to those people who were drawn to the Haskalah, and certainly not to those who were caught by assimilation. Reb Mendele of Kotzk supported the Polish uprising against the Czarist regime in 1831. He considered it a justifiable act of protest against an oppressive system and felt that Jews must join the struggle.

That Jews obeyed and entered this freedom movement can be seen from pictures and drawings of that period, and also from the proclamations wherein rebel leaders dwell upon Jewish participation. Because of his illegal activities, Reb Mendele had to flee and hide in Austria. The same thing happened to his friend and pupil, Reb Itche Meir, founder of Ger Hasidism. Both remained briefly in Lemberg until they could return to Congress Poland. Thirty years later, the rabbi of Warsaw, Reb Berish Meiseles, enthusiastically joined the preparations for the Polish rebellion of 1863. Despite current attempts to depict him in that fashion, the pious shtetl Jew did not live in a ghetto. He was a member of the city council; he was even in Parliament.

I have spent the last few years in Latin America. It is true that in Latin America there is no shtetl, and assimilation tears chunks of living flesh out of the Jewish population. Nevertheless, it seems to me that the Jews here feel less a part of their environment and of local problems then did the Jews of the shtetl. My impression is that the Latin American Jews know less about the world than the Jews who read Alexander Zederboim's articles in *Hamelitz*, or Nachum Sokolow's articles in *Hatsefirah*, or the "Political Letters" of Itchele in the newspaper *Haynt*.

The Jews in the shtetl felt that they stood in the very midst of the political and social struggles in which the general population was involved. Everything mattered to them. During the Napoleonic Wars Hasidic leaders were even divided in their support. Some felt that Jews should help the French armies, while others asserted that in order to uphold the traditional Jewish way of life a Russian victory was preferable. But they took sides; they were far removed from neutrality. The role of uninvolved ghetto onlooker did not suffice for them.

Jewish nationalism too was not an ideology that was introduced into the shtetl from the outside. The rebbe of Kotzk criticized the help of Moses Montefiore, the Jewish philanthropist from England, who in the nineteenth century was interested in the condition of the persecuted Jews in Eastern Europe. Reb Mendele felt that this assistance was too cold and too rigid. Another time Reb Mendele said, "Unfortunately, it is much easier to take Jews out of Exile than to take the Exile out of the Jews."

As stated, in the fourth decade after the Nazi German Holocaust the rebbe of Kotzk's period of seclusion also takes on an overwhelming symbolic significance. With the storm of thought and feeling that emanated from his teachings, and the remarkable creative restlessness that characterizes his life and work, so his years of loneliness too are engraved into the history of Polish Jewry, as is the enormous, tragic experience of the entire community of millions of Jews.

Basically, Reb Mendele was not secluded from the world, nor was Polish Jewry estranged from the world. Both sought out the world and wanted to provide solutions; passionately, they sought to bring to it sense and substance.

Shortly before Reb Mendele's death, his faithful disciple, Reb Itche Meir, said: "Years ago I spotted a bit of true fire, and all my life I have placed myself under this fire."

It seems to me that these few words contain the essence of Kotzk's contribution to Jewish spirituality. When I try to speculate about which book the rebbe of Kotzk perused during his period of deep introspection, I imagine it might have been chapter 20 of Jeremiah, where the prophet states that the word of God rages in the bones like a fire.

I remember that when World War II had just ended, we marched into the Bergen-Belsen concentration camp in Germany with the Allied Army and met Jews who had been saved from the gas chambers. There, upon the ruins, the teachings of Kotzk ascended in a remarkable fashion.

In the camp barracks, we celebrated the first Sabbath after the liberation. The signs of the recent terror were still on the death-white faces of the emaciated men and women. Even postliberation Bergen-Belsen was still a gaping, unsatiated grave for countless victims of the raging typhus epidemic and for those who could not withstand the emotion of liberation and suffered nervous breakdowns.

But in everything we said and discussed that Sabbath, we constantly returned to the thoughts and words attributed to Reb Mendele of Kotzk—his remarks about Jewish existence and the Jewish path over mountain and valley ever since the Revelation at Sinai. Judah Leib Gerst, a religious writer of prewar Poland, was among the liberated. Despite the horror of his experiences in the camps, he preserved in his memory most of the Kotzk teachings, and saw the heroic character of Jewish history from the perspective of Kotzk thought fragments. And then we broke into the melody of Kotzk: "Not yet, not yet. . . . We are still far from the beginning, but surely we haven't yet reached the end."

After the painful destruction of earthly Kotzk, Bergen-Belsen—of all places—was the site of the ringing confidence that Kotzk remains an eternal component of the Jewish path through the ages.

7

Four Significant Years in the Spiritual History of Polish Jewry

IN THE HISTORICAL texts of Polish Jewry, very little space is devoted to the four years, 1866–1870, that are the subject of our essay. Some mention them in passing, others omit them altogether with indifference. But the spiritual processes of Polish Jewry during the last few generations should be closely examined. After a penetrating analysis of the traits essential for this Jewish community in the last decades of the nineteenth century—and the decades of the present century so laden with stormy events, whose wonderful efflorescence and creativity, painful twilight, and awful destruction passed so quickly—these four years surface as an unusual slice of time, orchestrally resonant with the main motifs that accompanied Polish Jewry on the last leg of its millennium-long journey.

Even in books focusing upon the history of Hasidism, Reb Hanoch Henech—whose last four years we will treat here—does not occupy center stage. Of him the following is related: he was the son of the rabbi of Lutomirsk. He himself served as rabbi in Novidvor, in Prashnitz, and in Alexander, which is near Lodz. His chief trait was expressed in the fact that he wanted to be a lifelong student. He maintained that even though man must devote himself to the entire Torah and to all the commandments, he must nevertheless single out *one* mitz-

112

vah for particular attention. Hanoch Henech himself selected the trait of a scholar's humility. One should also remember that then—in the first half of the nineteenth century—there were indeed noted teachers whom a pupil could learn from and emulate.

This was the period when the personality of Reb Bunim of Pshishkhe made its mark. The teaching of wisdom and acuity which developed in Pshishkhe spread over the cities and towns of central Poland along with the wagonloads full of Hasidim who stretched over the highways. This took place after Pshishkhe had ceased being the leading center of Hasidism, and thousands stood at the gates of Kotzk to warm themselves in Reb Mendele's glowing fire. When the day came and the great importuner of Kotzk took his dense secret to eternity, the orphaned feeling soon passed. For Reb Itche Meir of Ger soon blazed his way into the drama of Polish Jewry. And Reb Hanoch Henech was a student of Pshishkhe, Kotzk, and Ger.

The fact cannot be denied that in moments of tension and expectation, when Jews stood at the parting of the ways, they frequently turned to Reb Hanoch Henech. They argued with him, saying that one should not constantly be content with the modest role of a student. There comes a time when one must take the community by the hand and lead them—they must be shown the way.

Nevertheless, Reb Hanoch Henech always wanted to pay deference to the great leaders and sages. He had his own interpretation of the ancient tradition of giving half a shekel for the Holy Temple. The half-shekel hints at a man's soul, only one half of which should be considered a heavenly gift. With the other half one must work and toil. The soul cannot simply be given away before it becomes ripe. With this sharp/tender witticism, which remained characteristic of him, Reb Hanoch Henech confided that this had happened to him: the more time he spent with a teacher and the more familiar he became with him, the more his importance diminished. So, then, one must constantly learn and improve one's moral state.

But in 1866, when Reb Hanoch Henech was already an old man (to be exact, he was then sixty-eight), it was impossible for him to keep averring that he still wanted to remain a pupil. This occurred after the death of Reb Itche Meir of Ger. By then, none of Reb Itche Meir's thirteen sons was alive; and his grandson, Reb Aryeh Leib (who was later know by the name of his book, *Sefas Emes*, "Language of Truth"), was still very young. So the Hasidim urged Reb Hanoch Henech to become the leader of the community. He was faced with an accomplished fact.

From near and far, people began coming to him in Alexander. The little town near Lodz was the place where the spiritual heritage of the Hasidism of Pshishkhe, Kotzk, and Ger thrived. For four years Reb Hanoch Henech was the central figure in the Hasidic movement in Congress Poland, despite the fact that during this period, too, he deeply longed for those blessed and happy years when he had been permitted to study at the feet of others. And he frequently articulated this feeling. He was neither worthy, he said, nor did he want to occupy the chair which had become empty. The money brought to him as an offering he would distribute as charity to the poor. And this is the way he continued to act until he departed from the world in 1870.

The preceding is more or less what is told about Reb Hanoch Henech of Alexander in histories and Hasidic books. But, as stated, indeed the years 1866–1870 brought significant values into the psyche of Polish Jewry during a decisive phase of its existence, and set a deep stamp on the ways and byways of its spiritual restlessness.

II

Actually, this problem was not new in Jewish thought. An infinite number of hypotheses and proofs could be gathered in order to support one proposition: at the same time one could amass many opinions and arguments in order to assert the very opposite. Would the great and bold exultations of man's spirit take place in the distant future—or were the people of long ago gifted with the power and talent to ascend on high and draw upon the ever-fresh sources of their own nature? Is the task of the generations expressed in an endless striving to introduce new ideas into the weekday and holiday world, or is the pursuit of new achievements and the climbing to new heights just an illusion, since everything has happened anyway in the foggy past and everything has already taken place in ancient times?

On the one hand, we spun ideals and hopes which were related to the distant future, to the end of days. It was felt that only in the end of days would man be capable of becoming perfect. But, on the other hand, it was said that if the people of long ago could have compared themselves to angels, then we, in later generations, can consider ourselves plain people. But since the earlier group comprised plain folk, then we in later generations have not even reached the level of simple human beings.

Even in the philosophy concealed in biblical language and in its grammar, this struggle of methods found expression. In biblical language, past, present, and future have fuzzy borders. The very same word can be used to express past and future, and even the term which marks man's progress (the root *k-d-m*) can be read as relating to a distant past. This means that even the philological elements can inspire reflection. "Go out and learn." Consider! The past, no matter how attenuated it appears to us, can be magnificent progress; and that which we label as progress can actually be a backward path.

During the four years of Reb Hanoch Henech's leadership, concepts which seemed to belong to the distant past were restored with youthful vigor. Even the concept of antiquity once again took on the meaning it had had in ancient Jewish tradition. Who said that one must be old at seventy? When Moses stood before Pharaoh with his great demands, for which so much strength and vision were needed, he was eighty years old; and his brother Aaron, who was first preparing himself for his historic task, was eighty-three (Exodus 20:17)

During the decisive months when the people's destiny hung

in the balance, it was indeed the venerable elders who acted with youthful courage. The Pentateuch does not omit the important role they played in the various acts of the struggle which had to be waged against the Egyptian powers, in the desert wanderings, and in the Revelation at Sinai. This did not change later, during the period of the Judges and Kings. The Book of Joshua tells that when freedom was being shaped and the land was being prepared for the people, the eighty-five-year-old Caleb ben Jephunneh, a leading personality of that era, declared that he did not feel the burden of his years and that he was still overflowing with faith and iron will (Joshua 14:7–12 .

During the period of his glory, Solomon, the wisest of men, believed that it was important to surround himself with elders (I Kings 8:5). And in the Book of Proverbs, where Solomon's experiential wisdom is concentrated, he comes to the conclusion that old age is a crown and beauty (Proverbs 16:31). Even Job, who was consumed by gnawing doubts, did not, despite his gloomy circumstances, totally lose his confidence in wisdom acquired through the years. Job said there was something in these graybeards which is deserving of admiration. "Wisdom is with the old, and understanding in length of days" (Job 12:12).

In the vision of the prophet Joel, the elders participate in the decisive councils of the people, and they are among those upon whom the Divine Spirit hovers: "Your old men shall dream dreams" (Joel 3:1; also see Joel 1:14 and 2:16).

Indeed, according to the view handed down from antiquity, it was the old who passed the tradition on from generation to generation (*Ethics of the Fathers* 1:1). A warning was even deemed necessary not to be misled by conflicting opinions. The Talmud states that if the young tell you to build, and the elders advise to destroy, rather obey the elders and not take the advice of the young seriously, for the latter's thoughts are in chaos, and they do not clearly know the significance of building and of destruction (*Nedarim* 40).

Judaism was also at odds with Hellenistic philosophy in its

attitude to youth and old age. In Hellenism, old age was rarely appreciated. Perhaps only in Plato can one read that the experience gained with years should prompt the young to regard the older generation with respect.

In the second half of the nineteenth century, the interpretation given the biblical verse stating that "Abraham was old, advanced in years" (Genesis 24:1) was vibrantly relevant in Alexander. Every one of Abraham's days was valuable for him; no day had gone to waste. The fact that Reb Hanoch Henech was approaching seventy was accepted as a portent that he would confidently lead his people during the insecure times impending for Polish Jews. This pertained not only to the legal status of the Jewish masses but also to the spiritual dangers lurking from the improperly understood "Enlightenment" and from the trend to assimilation which had arrogantly invaded the Jewish community. With the power of the regime and the dissidents, assimilation attempted to tear Jews away from their own lifestyle and demonstrate how important it was—even if only outwardly—to adapt oneself to the surrounding world. The first step to the outside world inexorably had to lead to paths from which there was no return.

With renewed energy Alexander revivified approaches which even in the Hasidic world were considered old-fashioned. Once again the stress was placed upon "internal worship," just as at the dawn of the Hasidic movement, when the Baal Shem Tov came down from the Carpathian Mountains bearing his pure message. The stress was also laid upon "purifying oneself inwardly"; upon the strength which is decisive in the path of man and Jew—the inner strength; and upon the point which must smolder deep in one's heart—the "spark of Jewishness." Actually, Reb Hanoch Henech repeated thoughts which were ancient in the teachings of Hasidism; thoughts which even in the inner circle were considered outmoded. Everything had to be done with inner intent.

Judaism demanded the entire person, the whole "I." To be a Jew in one's heart "internally" was paramount. When a Jew once told Reb Hanoch Henech that he was an expert on

Bachya's *Duties of the Heart*, he repulsed him by saying that one must bear within oneself the duties of the heart: to feel the duty or obligation for Judaism which one carries within oneself. We all carry obligations, debts which we owe and have not paid. The person who considers himself an absolute saint and is impressed with his own great saintliness is indeed absolutely finished—and, moreover, he is no saint at all.

Reb Hanoch Henech would sigh deeply when he recited "Cast us not into old age" during the Days of Awe. But he gave that prayer a new and extraordinary interpretation: "Help us, God, not to cast away our time into old age. May we not squander our years, and may we not constantly use the excuse that we will improve our deeds when we grow older."

When a Hasid once came to him bewailing his hardships, Reb Hanoch Henech told him: "This is not the correct way. When I was a young student there was a boy who began to cry every time the teacher asked him a question. So the teacher would say to him: 'My child, when one looks "inwardly" one doesn't cry.' " Reb Hanoch Henech concluded: "If one is a Jew inwardly, one does not cry."

In the teaching developed by this septuagenarian, joy flowed with youthful enthusiasm as Hasidim took up the challenge to once more hearten the Jewish spirit. It is true that in Hasidism's teachings the sources of Joy have never dried up. But it cannot be denied that occasionally its pristine and natural strength was diminished. There were times in Pshishkhe when sober wisdom and sharp aphorism did not permit full, unsophisticated joy to embrace the Jewish spirit. This was even more noticeable in Kotzk, where tearing pieces out of one's own conscience at times smothered the outbreaks of inner joy.

With its dynamic activity, characteristic of Reb Itche Meir of Ger, all too frequently there remained no place for the exultation that spurts out of joyful ecstasy. In Alexander, thought and deed had to lead to the feeling that the Jew, linked with the entire congregation, senses in all his limbs the joy of being a Jew.

Reb Hanoch Henech used to say that the "I" permits itself to be addressed only in connection with God. In the Jew there must not be any place for the proud and puffed up "I." The accent is on "we." We people, we Jews, are happy and satisfied that we are the children of God, and that we understand and feel that we must join and enter the community at large.

In his own language and in his characteristic fashion, at a time of loss and of the burgeoning of sharply individualistic and egoistic tendencies even in the Jewish community, the rebbe of Alexander helped to preserve the social consciousness of the Jew. Although it is true that since the Council of the Four Lands Polish Jewry had developed quite a strong and alert sense of community cooperation and common destiny; nevertheless, as a result of the extreme economic and social differences—which were all the more obvious in Jewish society— this period showed that the threads which had held the Jewish community of Poland together for centuries could be torn asunder.

Reb Hanoch Henech did not quarrel with God as Reb Levi Yitzchok of Berditchev had done. Neither did he quarrel with the Jew, as was the way of Reb Mendele of Kotzk. He did not even stress that all Jews should be scholars, as Reb Itche Meir of Ger had demanded. Reb Hanoch Henech wanted Jews to be happy and satisfied with simply being Jews and belonging to the Jewish community. "Learn to do well" (Isaiah 1:17), Reb Hanoch Henech remarked, does not mean learn well or be a good scholar. It means learn to be good Jews and learn to do what is good.

Even if sadness is not an explicit sin, he stated, it leads to sin. it blocks up the heart. It covers the light. Not every Jew is capable of rising to the level of joy of a mitzvah, but every Jew can be joyful. The Jew who is unhappy at belonging to the Jewish people evidently does not feel grateful for the wonderful gift presented to him. Sadness is a deep abyss. The Jew becomes sad when he persuades himself that he deserves everything in the world. But the truth is that indeed he *does* possess everything: he is a Jew.

At that time new notions were spreading in the towns and

villages. Ater the abortive Polish revolt of 1863, when hopes of independence were dashed, the ideology called positivism—well known in Polish circles—penetrated into the Jewish community. It maintained that the dreams and ideals which had nurtured previous generations were now empty and old-fashioned and romantic—and therefore to be extirpated. Also, many Jews began to believe that one could not constantly continue a way of life that was old; one must look for a practical purpose. One must shake off the heritage of yesterday and the dreams of tomorrow. The Jewish situation would improve only when Jews became more "realistic" and took a "sober" view of the problems of the world, the people, and belief.

But in Alexander Reb Hanoch Henech made fun of these new theories with a gentle humor that perhaps comes with years but which lost nothing of its resolute expression. Nonsense, he said, absolute nonsense. In life one cannot survive without bitterness. The promises to make Jewish life sweet are but hollow dreams. In his thinking Reb Hanoch Henech found support in the ancient books. The olive oil used in the Holy Temple is drawn from a liquid which, as is well known, was bitter. Light, then, comes from bitterness. It is true that not every bitterness is light. But light is bitterness. Understanding, too, is bitterness. The Torah tells us that when Jews wanted to drink water in the desert, the water was bitter. Moses then threw wood into the water, and the bitterness was made sweet (Exodus 15:23–26).

But the wood was bitter too. This means, then, that bitterness can be sweet. Who says, who dares to say, that it is bitter to be a Jew? It is sweet, sweet as honey to be a Jew—this is what the rebbe of Alexander taught. (Sections of his teachings have been preserved and have come down to us in his charming, rich, and poetic Yiddish.) "Just remember," he once called out, "remember who your parents were and from whom you stem. It suffices to say to Jews, in the words of the Torah, 'These are the heads of their fathers' houses' (Exodus 6:14), and to reveal the fine familial lineage from whence they stemmed. And then there would no longer be any room for sadness and bitterness in the Jewish soul."

The boldness of Reb Hanoch Henech also expressed itself in those years when the modern "realistic" and "sober" tendencies began to ensnare the Jew and threatened to topple the structure of generations. He revivified the old teaching of the Kabbalah concerning the cosmos and the Jew. He made the dense language of the kabbalists more accessible, but in its revivified form the old idea still retained all its entire depth and colorful richness: the partnership of God and Jew does not work only in the Jewish congregation. It spreads itself over the entire universe. It influences the cosmos. The behavior and the inner intent of the Jew are decisive in the order of the world. They are a component of the universe. The Revelation at Sinai was a cosmic event, and no matter how lowly and dark Jewish life seems to be from our point of view, our Jewish existence is filled with cosmic elements.

Jewish existence is supernatural, as are the sun, the moon, and the stars. In a society that strove to be practical and to establish firm links with material concepts, the rebbe of Alexander introduced metaphysical notions that could be popular for the average man.

Exile too, he said, must be understood from this point of view. When we know that the supernatural is operative in our path through history, even the Exile begins to look differently. The period of exile in Egypt, he remarked, was so difficult because there our concepts remained in exile and did not rise to the heights. "The Egyptians were marching after them" (Exodus 14:10) can refer to the baseness of Egypt coming after the Jews. This baseness accompanied the Jews. It went with them in their mind and in their feeling.

In the old-new teaching developed in Alexander there was a spiritual restlessness which Reb Hanoch Henech brought from Kotzk. In his remarks one felt the breath of Pshishkhe, where the concept of dignity was placed on the very first page of the book of man. In Alexander one could also feel, although not to such an obvious degree, something of the strong-mindedness that emanated from everything which Reb Itche Meir said and did. But Reb Hanoch Henech thought it extremely crucial that every Jew should know and appreciate the importance of being a Jew, the importance of belonging to a people who influence the order of the world. One of his most profound statements was: "If the world is in a state of chaos, it is only because it has not yet opened the Book of Genesis." Only the ideas of Genesis can bring about an end to the awful chaos into which the world and man have strayed.

We say: "importance." In later generations, during the period between the two world wars, and in the tragic years of the Nazi German Holocaust, more modern terms were used. During that time of fear, the Jewish community also considered its fate against the background of the universe, the world, and man. The call which the Warsaw Ghetto sent out on the eve of its last uprising does not omit—even on the brink of the awesome tragedy—mentioning the important and decisive place which Jews assume in man's movement to a more humane world.

Neither the yellow patch nor the gas chambers were able to rob those who perished in the German vise of the feeling of national pride. They could not take from them the consciousness that along with its moving tragedy Jewish chosenness also possesses great historic fervor. But it must be underscored that this unshakable, ironclad conviction of the importance of being a Jew became most exalted during a fateful period of spiritual crisis and was revivified with youthful vigor in the teachings of Reb Hanoch Henech of Alexander.

In Jewish pain and sighs, he stated, one often notes the feeling of happiness which flows out of the Jewish soul. Reb Hanoch Henech confided that he often heard this sighful joy, occasionally from a poor worker who rushed quickly into shul on the eve of the Sabbath, and at times from a butcher who quickly closed his shop, cast off his butcher's apron and garb, and spiritually renewed, prepared himself to greet the Sabbath.

III

Along with the resolve to bring the Jew ideas and concepts from long ago, Reb Hanoch Henech also sought to introduce new values into Jewish life. He criticized things which he thought worthy of criticism. As strange as it may seem, there was hardly anyone in the Hasidic world who poked fun and joked so much about events which he deemed worthy of eliminating from Hasidism and Jewish life. If it may be said that the Polish-Jewish community excelled in its tendency toward criticism and self-criticism—and Polish Jewry did not cease prodding its own conscience even at the gates of Auschwitz—it should be shown that in the second half of the nineteenth century this trait bore the special stamp of the rebbe of Alexander. The fact that his criticism was not leveled with anger, and did not emanate from a man who stood outside, left a lasting impression. Even in his jokes and mockery he remained "internal"—gazing and looking from within. Even his call to demolish had the confidence of building.

"I've never seen a pseudo-rebbe," he would say. "What do I mean by a pseudo-rebbe? A man who grows long side-curls, puts on a silk caftan, white socks, and so forth. And if someone dons this garb, why by so doing he has already become a rebbe! For nowadays this is what the rebbehood consists of!"

As if this acerbic remark were not enough, Reb Hanoch Henech offered his own interpretation to the word *chatzerot*, which is mentioned in the very first verse of Deuteronomy. It is the name of a place which probably had some connection to the Korah controversy during the desert wanderings of the Jews. The rebbe stressed that this word should be interpreted literally. *Chatzerot* comes from the word *chatzer*, which means a "court." Korah and his followers wanted to establish a separate rebbe's court. The verse in Lamentations, "Let us lift up our heart with our hands unto God in the heavens" (3:41), means that it is not enough to lift our hands and clap them during prayers. Along with one's hands, the heart too must be lifted up. And it is possible to do this and achieve this. The rebbe also said that we ought not to repeat old melodies just because Hasidim sang them a long time ago. Many of the old songs have lost their essence and have become vitiated. It is high time to create a new melody.

This is just some of the sharp criticism that came out of
Alexander. But it aroused and inspired faith. It is never too
late. There is always time for improvement. We still find
ourselves in the "today," in the wonderful Jewish present.
Naturally, there are two "todays"—a today of blessing and a
today of curse (Deuteronomy 11:26). There is a today of eating
and drinking, for the decline is imminent; a today of despair
("eat and drink, for tomorrow we shall die"). But there is also a
today of life and hope—the today expressed in Hillel's dictum
in the *Ethics of the Fathers:* "If not today, then when?"

When people in the Jewish community began to doubt the
possibility of opposing the approaching crisis of values, Reb
Hanoch Henech found an encouraging hint in the Torah verse:
"The mountain was ablaze with fire up to the heart of the
heaven" (Deuteronomy 4:11). When the Jewish heart becomes
ablaze with fire, he said, it becomes heaven. The earth can be
lifted up to heaven. This is the meaning of the verse in the
Psalms: "The earth is given to man" (115:16). The earth was
given to men so that they could make heaven of it.

The nations of the world, he added, assume that heaven *and*
earth exist; that there are two worlds. We Jews believe that
heaven and earth are one, and that the two worlds are one and
indeed must remain one. Believing that there is a God in
heaven is not sufficient. One must believe that God is also on
earth. The foundation of our faith is "One"—it is never too late
to lift the earth and earthly elements up to heaven. Reb
Hanoch Henech did not want people to depend on him for this
task. Every one must make the effort for himself.

His artistic nature and his inclination to reflection found
expression in the profound parables that he occasionally deliv-
ered. When he came to the saying in the *Ethics of the Fathers,*
"This world may be compared to a corridor" (4:21), his fantasy
was triggered. He told the story of a villager who once came to
a great metropolis. As he passed a house full of lights and
merrymakers singing, playing and dancing, it dawned on him
that the owner was probably celebrating a wedding. The next
day he passed the same house and once more saw people

celebrating, playing, and dancing. The villager wondered whether the man was having another wedding. Two nights in a row? One day later the very same thing occurred. People were once again singing, playing, and dancing in that house. By now the villager could not understand this. Is it possible for one man to make so many weddings night after night? So he posed this difficult question to passersby. They burst into laughter and explained: "My dear man, this is a wedding hall which is rented to a different celebrant each night. Last night there was one group of guests, and today another group is dancing there. The party dancing today won't dance there tomorrow."

Reb Hanoch Henech agreed with those who interpreted the talmudic passage as meaning that the world may be compared to a wedding hall (and not, as some read it, to a wedding) where the dancing guests constantly change. One group of guests danced last night; still others are dancing there today. And those who dance today will not dance tomorrow.

But in the continuing change, the only constant is movement. The cosmos belongs to this ceaseless, unending movement. And Jews and Judaism are part and parcel of the cosmos. While in the surrounding environment concepts were confused and the need to introduce changes into Jewish life was generalized in a superficial manner, the old man of Alexander introduced clarity of thought and pointed the way for the Polish-Jewish community in the last decades of its existence. Thinker and poet, the Alexander rebbe made the mystical verses of *Anim Zemiros*, written by the thirteenth-century kabbalist Rabbi Judah of Regensburg, comprehensible for the Polish Jew. The concepts of old age and youth, of twilight and dawn, strode forth out of mysticism in Alexander and fused in the heart and spirit of Polish Jewry at a time of breakup and storm.

IV

For four years, 1866–1870, Reb Hanoch Henech was the central figure of Hasidism in Congress Poland. But during those four

years bricks were laid for the spiritual structure of the Polish-
Jewish community. It was apparently the rebbe of Alexander
who said that the difference between the Vilna Gaon and the
Baal Shem Tov is that the former left books and the latter left
people. And Reb Hanoch Henech also helped to mold the
personality and character of Polish Jewry in the last great hours
of its history.

In the special knack that the Polish-Jewish community had
for weaving elements of antiquity into the rhythm of modern
life, in the talent it had for singing new songs with old
melodies, and in its resolute decision to spin the dreams of old
in the raw and hard prose of changed circumstances, one saw
the mighty influence of that septuagenarian who was undoubtedly one of the youngest people in the history of Hasidism,
and perhaps the youngest in all the spiritual and social movements in our rich, millennia-long history.

One of the great mystics of modern times, Rabbi Abraham
Isaac Kook, Chief Rabbi of the Land of Israel, said that the
Jewish task had always been and would always be to renew the
old and sanctify the new. This rare ability contains many of the
secrets of our existence.

In the Hasidism of Alexander, during the short four-year
period of Reb Hanoch Henech's leadership, Polish-Jewish spirituality came closest to the synthesis which Polish Jewry had so
passionately sought. There it was shown that heaven and earth
can become one; that worlds which were split can fuse and
become one again. There it seemed that even the conflict
between materialism and the spirit can end; that the border
between old age and youth can be eradicated; and that old and
new can lose their polarity.

The concluding words of the biblical verse "Moses spoke to
the entire congregation of Israel the words of this song *until
they ended*" (Deuteronomy 31:30) were interpreted in Alexander
as follows: "until the Jews became whole." (The Hebrew reads
ad tumam; the word *tum* can be interpreted as "ending" and
also as "perfection.") Men must be taught and taught until

even generations split in their attitude and personality can become whole.

It is true that Polish Jewry never achieved that longed-for synthesis. Its creative restlessness pulsated until its final era, and even in its last path. But indeed that creativeness makes the Hasidism of Reb Hanoch Henech of Alexander one of the most significant and remarkable chapters in the history of Polish Jewry.

8

Ger, the Last Great Chapter of Polish Hasidism

I

DURING THE TWILIGHT of Polish Jewry, Ger Hasidism was not alone in the Hasidic world. Rich and colorful pages were also written during that period by the Hasidim of Alexander and Kozhenitz, Pabyianitz and Modzhitz, Radzimin and Radzin, Sokolov and Ostrovtze, Skernievitz and Grodzhisk, Belz and Bobov. Many other trends in Hasidism also developed their spiritual treasures in that creative period which was also an anguished time of imminent Holocaust.

Ger, however, was the Hasidic movement in the heart of Poland—the region known as Congress Poland—around which the great masses of religious Jewry gathered. Even if some people held that Hasidism's former vigor had waned, Ger Hasidism still maintained its pristine momentum.

The Ger *shtieblekh* ("little prayer–rooms"), as Ger quorums were called in that world that is no more, were an important part of the spiritual panorama of Polish Jewry. Messages by the Ger rebbe written in his scholarly hand, in a learned Hebrew replete with modern terminology, were sent to all points of Ger's geography. His letters were devotedly read to the Hasidim on Sabbaths and holidays, and meticulously interpreted across the length and breadth of Poland.

All the trends active in the Orthodox strata of Polish Jewry found expression in the religious Yiddish daily, *Dos Yiddishe Togblat*, published in Warsaw until the outbreak of World War II. Nevertheless, the newspaper was dominated by Ger thinking and temperament, and it reflected the Ger position on contemporary issues.

When the Ger rebbe left for periodic visits abroad, and especially when the last rebbe of Ger, Reb Abraham Mordecai, went to Eretz Yisrael in the thirties, tens of thousands of Hasidim came to see him off at the Warsaw railway terminal. Even government circles realized that Ger was a strong and meaningful movement among Polish Jews. Polish writers and intellectuals were attracted more to Ger than to all other Hasidic sects. Ironic and mocking comments existed; nevertheless, Ger compelled one to ponder the remarkable influence which its spirituality cast upon the weekday world.

Jacob Schatzky's *A History of Jews In Warsaw* depicts the Polish writer Sawicki's meeting with Reb Itche Meir Alter, the founder of Ger Hasidism, in the latter half of the nineteenth century. Schatzky tells how impressed Sawicki was with Reb Itche Meir after discussing Jewishness and Hasidism with him. Indeed, until the Holocaust the Ger "court" was subjected to portrayals and analyses by Ger Hasidim as well as by outsiders. Even when criticism was leveled, it could not be denied that past and present met in Ger Hasidism and that down-to-earth matters were exalted with the Talmud and the *Zohar*'s philosophy and faith.

Considering Ger Hasidism some forty years after the destruction of Polish Jewry, one concludes that there was good reason for the rise of Ger Hasidism in those towns and villages which, in the storm of historical circumstances, forged their own path to God, man, and Jew.

Even if we agree that there is some exaggeration in every psychological analysis of the various Jewish centers, we must admit that in the whirl of political, social, and economic conditions, the Jewish dispersion—despite all the threads which bound up the widely scattered communities—took on specific and singular traits wherever it went.

During the course of centuries Polish Jewry assumed attributes that set its own specific stamp upon this community. The type known as the *batlan*—the idler or unworldly man—so familiar to us from depictions in Yiddish literature or folklore, was actually a rare phenomenon among Polish Jewry. In the Polish-Jewish community the *batlan,* if indeed we wish to term him thus, had a sober outlook upon the world and life, while the impassive, expedient man was frequently capable of becoming lost in dreams.

In the history of Spanish Jewry, the acute, philosophic mind of Maimonides was intolerant of poetry; and the lyrical, poetic nature of Judah Halevi categorically rejected the cleverly fashioned rationalistic ideas. Following the historical path of Polish Jewry, the "iron mind" of Rabbi Moses Isserles enjoyed flights on the wings of fantasy. His poem in honor of Shevuos—a kind of wedding contract between God and the people of Israel—can serve as a document of the innocent, folksy creativity of the sixteenth century. Rabbi Samuel Eidels, whose every line testifies that he lived in an aura of legend and in the enchanted world of poetry, made great efforts to fit the fantasy of legend into the frame of Halakhah, a tendency which frequently transforms his explanations of the aggadas scattered in the Talmud into a tender, lyric commentary on sharp and difficult laws.

These traits, which for hundred of years were forming the psyche of Polish Jewry, received their clear and visible expression in Ger Hasidism as they perhaps never had in any other spiritual movement that matured on Polish-Jewish soil. In Ger they were simultaneously practical and dreamy. They made sober calculations and spun winged fantasies. Undeniably rooted in the reality of daily life, they demonstrated the correctness of the Maharal of Prague's statement that Jews have their roots in heaven.

Ger was a little town. In Polish it was called Gora Kalwaria. To get there from Warsaw, one boarded the narrow-gauge railway which in Polish Yiddish was nicknamed the *koleike.* But in that small town and on that miniature railway, the last great chapter of Polish-Jewish Hasidism was developed. By looking at Ger, one sees Polish Jewry in the hour of its twilight with greater clarity.

This Hasidism was nurtured on the Baal Shem Tov's teachings of feeling, but it also contained Reb Bunim of Pshishkhe's sparks of sophisticated thought. This Hasidism brought consolation and encouragement to the lonely Jew, but it also impelled him to study and immerse himself in the hidden and revealed aspects of Torah learning. It was said that Ger is and must be a continuation of Kotzk—the anguish of Kotzk had gone over to Ger.

Ger Hasidism did not create a synthesis of contrasts, it stubbornly attempted to link them. Like the Hasidim of Pshishkhe, in Ger they climbed the mountaintops. And like Reb Mendel of Kotzk, they also descended into the abyss of searching and asking. It was constantly stressed that Ger was a continuation of Pshishkhe and Kotzk. But in Ger they said a resounding, energetic, and aggressive yes to man and life. The height of the mountains and the depths of the abyss could not and were not supposed to diminish the importance of the earth. Despite its flatness, the daily struggle for existence takes place on earth; and it is here, after all, that the greatness of God reveals itself to man.

Ger Hasidism excelled in its activity. Ger Hasidim were mobile and dynamic. Bold, profound thought was not supposed to trigger doubts, hesitations, or a spirit of passivity. It dared not take away from the Jew his natural, creative, and boundless optimism. On the contrary, it was supposed to awaken and stimulate, prod and inspire. Ger was the Hasidism of the initiative of the Six Days of Creation. The Sabbath-day rest gets its holy reflection, it was said in Ger, when one feels in it the vigorous breath of the weekday that precedes and follows it.

Although he himself was a faithful disciple of Reb Mendele of Kotzk, Reb Itche Meir, the founder of Ger Hasidism, did not explicitly follow the path of his great teacher. He did not lock himself into seclusion, nor did he ask this of others. He taught his adherents that the foundation of the Jewish people was the community at large. And the individual Jew is obligated to link his deeds with the community—for only when the individual is bound up with the community is there sense and meaning in the individual's life.

During the thousand-year history of Polish Jewry the problem of the individual and society was always central. This is apparent in the notes and emendations that Rabbi Moses Isserles brought into religious law. Over a period of centuries, the Council of the Four Lands, a uniquely Polish-Jewish institution—the like of which was not to be found anywhere else in Jewry—took the Jewish individual by the hand and showed him how to follow the path of the general community. Hasidism too, with its concern for the individual, taught the Jew that when he becomes part of the entire group he will cease being lonely and forlorn. It seems that the societal motif with which the Hasidic movement was born strove to achieve its perfect expression in Ger.

Moreover, while everything was tottering in Polish-Jewish society, in Ger they marched determinedly toward the individual and the community. Ger Hasidism developed during a stormy time in Poland and in the Polish-Jewish community. The drama of the Polish struggle for independence in the nineteenth century and indeed Poland's period of independence are linked with Ger Hasidism. The last heroic page in the history of Polish Jewry is virtually incorporated into the last great chapter of Polish Hasidism.

II

Reb Itche Meir Alter set the stamp of his strong personality upon Ger Hasidism; because of him it spread in Ger. Although many other founders of movements within Hasidism were active in various undertakings (Reb Bunim of Pshishkhe was a pharmacist), Reb Itche Meir was different. He was a merchant, and he continued his business enterprise even after he became the rebbe.

With his father-in-law, Moses Chalfan-Lifschitz, Reb Itche

Meir ran a tallis (prayer-shawl) factory in Neistodt near Raveh. When the factory was liquidated after his father-in-law's death, he became a book dealer in Warsaw. For a while he was a partner in a Jewish printing establishment, and then the manager of an apartment house. Later, he opened a vinegar factory. After Reb Mendele of Kotzk departed from the world and the Hasidim demanded that Reb Itche Meir lead the community—a demand which he had so often rejected—he could no longer refuse and finally agreed to settle in Ger and receive those who thirsted for his words. But even then he did not interrupt his business affairs. He purposely wanted to support himself and his family with the work of his own hands.

Reb Itche Meir disdained both the traditional payments given to Hasidic rebbes and the salary paid to rabbinic judges in Warsaw. Why? One answer may be his wish to be faithful to the principle of the sages of the Talmud, who preferred to be shoemakers or blacksmiths rather than use the Torah as a means of livelihood. But surely this was not the only reason for Reb Itche Meir's remaining a merchant even after he became the rebbe.

This was not only a personal decision. Actually, he wanted to set an example and teach the people that one must be involved and live with the community, that one must trade and pursue one's livelihood like all other Jews.

Once, during Passover, he told his Hasidim in Ger: "I want you to know that I don't want any money from you. Also, I'm not looking for honor. My sole desire is that I bend your hearts to heaven during the few years that I remain here. If there is anyone here who disagrees, I'll ask him not to come to me anymore. And those who come to ask me to pray for livelihood or to have children, they'd be better off going to other Hasidic rebbes. Ger is not the right place for them."

The example that Reb Itche Meir set was well understood by his contemporaries. Not only Hasidim realized why the rebbe of Ger wanted to have the same occupation during the week as his Hasidim. The Ger rebbe's decision to support himself by his own labors was widely commented upon by the enlightened and by maskilim. Samuel Zevi Peltin, the editor of the Polish-Jewish journal *Israelita*, an organ for assimilated Jews, published an enthusiastic article citing the merchant-rabbi as an example for our "Hasidic brethren."

Even if it is incorrect to contend that Reb Itche Meir was the first Hasidic leader to do communal work—actually Reb Bunim of Pshishkhe and Reb Mendele of Kotzk, as well as others in earlier generations, had participated in communal affairs—it is still a fact that Reb Itche Meir was totally immersed in community activities. Actually, he was supposed to live in Ger, but he spent more time in Warsaw, where work for the public good literally swallowed him.

The rebbe of Ger felt responsible for everything that happened and might happen in Poland in general and to Jews in particular. Because of his involvement in political activities he even had to change his family name from Rottenberg. When the Czarist regime, which regarded any political activity in occupied Poland with suspicion, declared Reb Itche Meir's multifarious communal work illegal, he changed his name to Alter. He was forced to leave Poland for a certain period and hide in Austria.

But nothing could weaken his resolve to work for the public welfare. He was a member of various state commissions, where fateful questions concerning Polish Jewry were considered. Along with edicts that threatened to cut off Jewish livelihood, they also dealt with projects that were supposed to open the doors of education and "civilization" to Jews.

The regime wanted to compel Jewish children to attend secular Polish schools. They forcibly attempted to make the Jews adopt the Western mode of dress. Using various pretexts, they sought to obligate Jews to serve in the army. And among the Jews were those who enthusiastically welcomed the official attempts to introduce these new "modern" lifeways to the Jewish masses.

These were tumultuous years for Polish Jewry. Jewish society found itself between the vise of Czarist might and the fires of the patriotic uprising of 1863, when the Polish people raised the flag of freedom and political independence. And it seemed strange to outsiders and insiders alike that the rebbe of the Ger Hasidim took an active part in these stormy conferences.

That the voice of Rabbi Jastrow was heard during the deliberations was accepted as self-evident. People also were accustomed to meeting the rabbi of Warsaw, Rabbi Berish Meiseles, at these state commissions. But the Ger rebbe's participation was not seen at once as an expression of the Hasidic Jew's right to be represented where his fate was discussed—especially when the rebbe dared to articulate an opinion that conflicted with that of the representatives of the enlightened and the assimilated. Reb Itche Meir was even arrested once because of his courageous remarks. He was released only after thousands of Hasidim gathered by the walls of the prison and demanded that the Ger rebbe's right to speak on behalf of his followers be recognized.

But Ger Hasidism represented a new direction and a new system in Hasidism not only because of its ramified communal activity. The sword and the book, which according to an old midrashic saying descended together to the earth, also descended in tandem in Ger. The book, however, was not thrust aside because of communal activities. In Ger the Hasidim studied. In Ger one immersed oneself in Talmud and commentaries. In Ger they strove to make a scholar of the Jewish merchant and artisan, or at least to inculcate in him the will to learn and become more learned.

Reb Itche Meir devoted himself to writing Torah commentaries and editing responsa on halakhic problems—new interpretations entirely in the Ger spirit. He is known in the Hasidic world by the name of his profound books, *Hidushey ha-Rim* (an acronym for Rabbi Itche Meir), which brilliantly treat a series of talmudic tractates.

If some people resented Hasidism as the nest of the naive, common, and ignorant elements of the population, Ger demonstrated that Hasidism is also capable of sparkling with true intelligence and with stunning learning prowess. Even opponents had to admit that when it came to genius, perhaps no one in Polish Jewry was comparable to the Ger rebbe.

This unusual combination of practical business sense, de-

voted communal activity, and astute learning brought a trait
into Ger Hasidism that defies description. It may be termed
insolence. It may be called strength of character. It may be
labeled tenacity of principle. If one wishes, it may even be
called *chutzpah*, "nerve."

Ger Hasidism possessed an insolence and chutzpah not
apparent in other Hasidic movements. But what remained
characteristic of Ger was the kind of insolence and nerve that
did not contradict the elements of modesty and humility basic
to the Hasidic teachings. At the funeral of his mother, Reb Itche
Meir, broken with grief, declared with utter frankness:

"I beg you to forgive me when you learn in the true world
that your son was not worthy of being a rebbe. I too feel that
I'm not worthy of it. I too feel that the people are fooling
themselves and making a terrible mistake."

The insolence and nerve that attained their most moving
expression were exemplified by a passing remark of Reb Itche
Meir's. It deserves to be set on the title page of every discussion
of the remarkable Ger Hasidism. Once, at a communal confer-
ence, an edict against Jews was being discussed. The participants felt that since all doors for intervention had been closed,
revocation of the edict was no longer possible. But the Ger
rebbe obstinately stuck to his position. And when others told
him that one can't knock one's head against the wall, he
countered: "Even if we can't knock our heads against the wall,
when it pertains to Jews and Jewishness we *must* knock our
heads against the wall."

As stated, *Hidushey ha-Rim*'s contribution to our religious
literature is evident principally in the field of learning and
pilpul. But Hasidic thought too was enriched by the treasures
of Reb Itche Meir's spirit. His Torah remarks constantly reiterated the community motif. Concerning the Exodus passage on
the plague of darkness, "No one saw his brother, and no one
got up from under him," the rebbe stressed that if one does not
notice his own brother, one cannot stand, one cannot rise, and
one cannot ascend to the heights.

The rebbe explained the verse from the Song of Songs, "I
sleep but my heart is awake," by saying that even when Jews

want to sleep, their hearts must remain awake. Regarding Hillel's aphorism in the *Ethics of the Fathers,* "If I am not for myself who will be, but if I am only for myself, what am I?" the rebbe of Ger regarded the second statement as fundamental. If I do not consider myself as part of the general community, then what am I?

Reb Itche Meir once said that he who constantly feels real danger is no longer frightened by the danger of the moment. The verse in the Psalms, "Leave off evil and do good," bids us not only to retreat from evil but not even to probe the nature of evil. It is better to do good.

The commandment is do! Life cannot be utilized for philosophic speculation that leads to nothing. Once, on Rosh Hashanah, the Ger rebbe explained why we must cry when we come to the line, "Man is created from dust and his end is dust." If one has not lifted oneself up with devoted deeds for the community, and has only lived for oneself alone, then the dust remains till the end of one's life. And that is a cause for weeping.

Ger Hasidism matured in this fashion amid Polish Jewry in the latter half of the nineteenth century. And now, as I search for a phrase that would perfectly reflect Ger's inner spirit, I recall the talmudic remark ascribed to Samuel of Babylonia: "The trails and footpaths of heaven are as clear and familiar to me as the trails and footpaths of my hometown, Nahardea." But there is one difference: Ger wanted the Jew's trails and footpaths in various lands and towns to have the clarity and transparency of heaven.

According to the founder of Ger Hasidism, the High Holidays prayer, "He who reveals the depths in judgment," means that in law there is depth, in law there is mercy, in daily conduct there is exaltation. The community and the individual become exalted through practical, concrete deeds.

III

The chapter of Ger Hasidism opened with Reb Itche Meir Alter. The golden chain of Torah and thought, of word and deed, was extended by his grandson Reb Judah Arieh Leib, who is also known by the name of his book *Sefas Emes* ("Language of Truth"). Educated by his grandfather, he carried within him Reb Itche Meir's spiritual heritage and his outlook on the world and life, on man and Jews.

The thoughts expressed in *Sefas Emes* help us understand Ger Hasidism during the years of its growth. According to Reb Judah Arieh Leib, Korah's great sin was that by rebelling against Moses, he set himself apart from the community. When Abraham argues with God about the destruction of Sodom, he asks, "What if there are fifty righteous men within the city?" By the phrase "within the city," the Torah means that if one is indeed righteous, one must move "within the city" and be involved with the community, feel its pain, be immersed in its problems.

How did prophecy arise among the Jewish people? We find the answer in Deuteronomy: "A prophet in your midst from among your brethren"—because of brotherly contact with the rest of Israel. The prophet was a teacher and brother. And Mordecai of the Book of Esther is worthy of special attention in all Jewish generations. Mordecai bowed down to no one. He courageously came out in defense of his people. In every generation there are and there must be Mordecais who bend a knee to no one.

In Reb Judah Arieh Leib's book, the concept of the "inner point" has a profound meaning. The "inner point" is what connects the individual Jew with the soul of the community, its experiences, its beliefs and hopes. The "inner point" is the source of faith and also the source of action. The Land of Israel, its holiness and its redemption, is also in the category of deed and activity. Through great deeds of selfless devotion Jews can be brought out of Exile and the Exile can be taken out of the Jews, even though the latter is much more difficult to accomplish.

Ger Hasidism in Poland comes to a close with Reb Abraham Mordecai, the son of Reb Judah Arieh Leib. During the pre-Holocaust years, Reb Abraham Mordecai Alter continued the Ger tradition with the unflagging energy of Hasidism's beginnings. Its activities spread to all realms and corners of Jewish life. Ger established yeshivas; Ger raised scholars. But from Ger also emerged men of deeds, people who moved in the daily tumult of business and labor.

Ger Hasidism was active in politics, in social undertakings, in the building of Eretz Yisrael. In the world of Hasidism, Ger was among the first where love for the Land of Israel expressed itself not only in devoted prayer and in mystical fervor, but also in concrete practical achievements.

The rebbe and his Hasidim went up to the Land of Israel. They bought land, they established settlements, they built houses, they constructed factories. Reb Abraham Mordecai Alter said, "In a designated time and at a designated place there are deeds that surpass even studying Torah."

I knew Ger Hasidim. Until the outbreak of the Second World War, I worshiped in a Ger shtiebel in Warsaw. Ger's style and temperament were ever fresh in the hearts of those who came in contact with it. Today too Ger is dynamic and flourishing in Israel, where it vigorously and stubbornly cares for its continuity.

Writing about Ger forty years after the destruction of Polish Jewry means seeing the inner spirit of the Polish community in the last hundred years of its history. It means seeing the remarkable fusion of humility and insolence which took on such distinct forms during an extraordinary time of storm and twilight. It means accompanying the Polish-Jewish community in its struggles and heroic efforts. It also means listening to its moving dialogue with God and man.

9

The Contribution of Spanish and Polish Jewry to Jewish Culture

I

THE COMPARISONS SEEMINGLY surface on their own: both the Spanish and Polish Jewish communities, which once flourished and now are gone, made extraordinarily significant contributions to Jewish culture. Both left their marks because of their dynamic vitality and the bold challenge and profound thought which matured in their respective centers. Both perked up the Jewish spirit during several centuries of cultural activity. Both at times shocked and at times dealt kindly with Jewish sensibility; and both breathed a fresh and energetic spirit into Jewish life.

Both the Spanish and Polish Jewish communities compassionately sought a solution to the problems which since ancient times had distressed man and Jew. Both brought forth the awesome "why" in the hour of tragedy, and both stubbornly rejected the possibility that senselessness and chaos predominate in the process of history. Both too, in periods of fervent belief, carried on a gigantic struggle with God, fate, and conscience; and both were supremely confident that they had been assigned the responsibility of guarding the lost and wandering souls, and of orienting and pointing out paths and alternatives for all the people in the Diaspora.

Spanish Jewry focused on a verse in the only remaining

chapter of the prophet Obadiah, where the land "Sefarad" (Spain) is mentioned. Although we are not certain that *Sefarad* referred to Spain, the use of the term in the Bible was supposed to testify to the ancient lineage of the Spanish Jewish-community and to the cloak of dignity and responsibility it bore ("The dispersion of Jerusalem that is in Sefarad," Obadiah 1:20).

Polish Jewry too found an old legend that showed that heaven had decreed it to be the home and center for Jews and Jewry. A mysterious note that fell down amid the wandering refugees revealed the meaning of the word "Poland" (in Hebrew, *Polin*); the note said, *"Po lin"*—meaning: "spend here the night of your exile!"

Maimonides, the great philosopher of Cordoba, rooted himself in our spiritual culture with the *Guide to the Perplexed*. But surely he is not the only Spanish Jew who plays the role of a guide to the perplexed. Other teachers preceded and followed him; they labored in various fields of creativity to help man and Jew to find the way to God and to himself.

In this fashion, Nachman Krochmal is no exception in the history of Polish Jewry. His efforts to show direction and outlet for those who could not extricate themselves from the thick morass of questions and problems lie at the very root of Polish-Jewish society. When Krochmal presented to his students in the fields of Zhulkiev the poetic, idealistic method later detailed in his *Guide to the Perplexed of Our Times,* he remained faithful to the generations-long tradition of Polish Jewry. It was timely for those who erected the tower of Jewish law, for those who turned to the heartfelt teachings of Hasidism, as well as for those who thrust open the doors for the Haskalah, the Enlightenment.

Even during the twilight hour impending for both communities, everyone was confident that substance and stronghold sufficed to save them from the raging flames of destruction. Don Isaac Abarbanel, the last of the refugees from the Spanish Inquisition, raised the bright lantern of salvation in his *Commentary to the Bible* which he composed during those years of fear and horror. And the twentieth-century Vilna poet Hersh

Glick, while standing amidst the ruins of the Jewish people in Poland, cried with stirring confidence: "Our footfalls will thunder—we are here."

In both Spain and Poland some held that heroism was a necessary ingredient in man's life. Even more, heroism must round out the existence of the individual Jew and the community. The rabbinic deciders of law, the philosophers, and the poets of Spanish and Polish Jewry constantly return to the theme of *Kiddush Hashem* (Sanctification of God's name, or martyrdom). *Kiddush Hashem* seemed to be the beginning, the daily reality, and the exalted fervor.

For Hasdai Crescas, rabbi of Saragossa, whose son was killed in the anti-Jewish riots in Barcelona, the Binding, mentioned in Genesis at the dawn of Jewish history, showed the Jews the path they would have to tread for countless generations. According to Rabbi Menachem Zemba, the rabbi of Warsaw, whose wife and daughter perished in the gas chambers of Treblinka, *Kiddush Hashem* was forged out of the firm Jewish law. With his characteristic clarity, Maimonides defined the act of *Kiddush Hashem* in his letter of consolation to the Jews of Yemen: "If a Jew was killed just because he was a Jew, and would have remained alive had he not been a Jew, then he perished for *Kiddush Hashem*." There is no doubt that in both Spain and Poland Jews knew how to chant the melody of faith in times of loneliness and oppression, and how to transform the ashes of ruins into morale-boosting monuments of spiritual heroism.

Without these two centers of Jewry one cannot comprehend Jewish culture. If not for the bricks that the Jews of Spain and Poland set in place, it could not be what it is now. The fact that a time span separates both communities adds color and accents their intrinsic character. The last one thousand years of Jewish life are marked by the creativity of these two Jewish centers. This does not mean that we should denigrate the merits of other, larger and smaller communities for maintaining Jewish existence and enriching Jewish culture during the last thousand years. But despite the importance of various Jewish spiritual centers and settlements during the last millennium, it remains a fact that the places of honor in Jewish life and creativity were taken by Spain and Poland.

Moreover, one gets the impression that in the mystery in which Jewish history is wrapped, the hour of destiny bound these two geographically distant communities. For at the very time when Jewish life was brutally torn asunder in the Iberian Peninsula—in the first decades of the sixteenth century—Jewry in Eastern Europe began to flourish with youthful energy. Jews were said to have settled in Poland hundreds of years earlier— but as long as the spiritual center in Spain was active and vital, there was no impulse to prod Polish Jewry to burst into the Jewish world with an overwhelming vigor, a vigor which remained characteristic of Polish Jewry until the terrible days of Auschwitz and Maidanek.

Both communities, of course, were intimately bound up with the circumstances and surroundings of their time. Despite the castles they built in the air and the special skill they developed for living and breathing with only the sky above their heads, both communities were like the ladder of Jacob's dream, anchored fast on earth.

Spanish Jewry felt at one with Moslem society in those provinces within the Moslem orbit, and cooperated with Christian circles in those cities and towns under Christian hegemony. Polish Jewry was incorporated into the economic and cultural processes which the Polish people experienced, and was influenced by the political and social movements which stirred the strata of Polish society. If one is unaware of the political and cultural panorama of medieval Spain, one cannot possibly understand Samuel ha-Nagid's poetry or appreciate the literary theories of Moses ibn Ezra. Similarly, one cannot understand the contributions to Halakhah (Jewish law) of Rabbi Moses Isserles, or the flashes of Torah insight of Rabbi Bunim of Pshishkhe, or even the dramatic satire *Night at the Old Marketplace* of Isaac Leib Peretz, if they are not seen in conjunction with the various convulsions which Poland experienced.

Nevertheless, the creativity of these two communities was

thoroughly Jewish. Jewish feeling pulsated through both; both plumbed the core of Jewish thought. Rabbi Solomon Luria of Lublin studied the Talmud text as meticulously as Rabbi Solomon ben Abraham Adret of Barcelona serveral centuries earlier. Rabbi Israel Meir HaCohen of Radin, better known as the Chofetz Chaim, called upon the Jew to purify himself in the wellspring of noble Jewish virtues, just as the Sephardic Rabbi Bachya ibn Pakuda had done generations earlier in his *The Duties of the Heart*. The struggle between heaven and earth, waged with moving courage by Rabbi Mendel of Kotzk, was actually a bold challenge to transform matter into spirit and to raise man to God by force. This was also the leitmotif of the *Zohar* and the path that the Kabbalah had taken in Guadalajara with Rabbi Moses de Leon. The fantasy which took the Hebrew poet of Zgierz, Jacob Cohen, to the world of ancient Jewish kings was fashioned out of the same wings upon which Judah Halevi of Toledo soared to Jerusalem, singing longingly that his heart was in the east though he was in the west.

Jewish creativity in Spain spanned more than five centuries; likewise, for nearly five hundred years Poland was the leading center of Jewish spirituality. We now have the perspective of time to assess the contribution of the Golden Age of Spanish Jewry; but we cannot yet assess the full scope of the contribution of Polish Jewry to Jewish history and culture. However, even a perfunctory attempt to treat this theme reveals both harmonious integration as well as blunt and sharp contrasts.

II

It is an incontrovertible fact that both Spanish and Polish Jewry were seriously concerned with enriching spiritual life. The biblical verse "Man lives not by bread alone" (Deuteronomy 8:3) can serve as a fitting epigraph for the two destroyed centers. In both, Jews waged an exhausting struggle to maintain their physical and material survival.

Being a Jew in medieval Spain was by no means easy. The periods of tolerance were often swiftly and mercilessly interrupted. In the eleventh century, Samuel ha-Nagid's son Yehosef perished with most of the Jewish community in the bloody anti-Jewish riots organized by the Muslims in Granada. Almost a century later Maimonides was forced to leave Cordoba for fear of attacks by the fanatic Almohades. Many of the poems written during the very flowering of the Golden Age of Hebrew poetry in Spain sound more like dirges. The poet Solomon ibn Gabirol bemoaned the fate of his people, "Sold to strangers and whom no one wants to redeem." Judah Halevi, who, in his attempt to find refuge with Muslim and Christian rulers, always had the wanderer's staff in his hands, noted that there is little difference between the "Ishmaelities" (Muslims) and the "Edomites" (Christians) when it concerns their attitudes toward Jews. With brutal cruelty the Inquisition and then the Expulsion of 1492 closed a page of history which even earlier was replete with painful disappointments.

In Poland, the situation of the Jews was no brighter. Despite the pro-Jewish decrees of the early dukes and kings, the history of Polish Jewry throughout the centuries can be viewed as a chronicle of persecutions, pogroms, and expulsions. Even when no incitement to murder was specified by the Poles, they applauded economic boycott.

Nevertheless, throughout the entire difficult and often superhuman struggle for survival, there was no letup in either center of dynamic quests in the spiritual realm. Characteristic of both is a line of verse by Solomon ibn Gabirol: "Though my body treads on earth, my spirit soars to the clouds." The deeper one is immersed in the creativity of both communities, the more one is convinced that their chief concerns were to determine how Jews and Judaism could maintain their pristine freshness and how Jewish creativity could be eternally fruitful.

Today, scant attention is paid to the outmoded cosmologica theories of Ibn Gabirol's religious epic, *The Royal Crown (Kete: Malkhut)*, which is indeed the poet's crown in his literary heritage. One is, rather, captivated by the mighty song which soars up to the Creator. Yet when the poem was written, the scientific hypotheses recorded therein were the last word in the human intellect. From Ibn Gabirol's creations the reader wa supposed to feel that "the soul of souls, the beginning of every cipher, the foundations of every building," inheres in the Divine Revelation as interpreted in Judaism. Heinrich Heine said of Solomon ibn Gabirol that his rose was God, but the truth is that in contrast to other religious poems of medieval Europe the Divine is not abstract in Gabirol's poetry. It is bound up with the Jewish people, their beliefs and ecstasy, their hopes and dreams.

Maimonides' purpose is quite apparent in his *Guide to the Perplexed*. The great teacher of Spanish Jewry did not use flowery language and could not abide poetic forms. His diction was terse and clear. His *Guide* was written in the form of a letter sent to his pupil, Joseph ibn Aknin, and to all students and Jews who thought it worthwhile to delve into Greek philosophy, even if it conflicted with the teachings of Judaism and even if it harbored thoughts and concepts that endangered Jewish life and tradition.

The *Guide* neither attempted nor sought to dethrone Aristotle, an impossible task in an environment where man's rationality reigned supreme. But Maimonides' *Guide* does state convincingly that there is no force that can destroy the foundations of Judaism. If you wish, the philosopher said, you can see that the contrasts between Aristotle and Judaism are not so formidable. If you wish, you can stroll safely and securely with your intellect and understanding over the paths and byways of Judaism. If you wish, you can easily recognize that in Jewish teaching everything has a reason, that logic is decisive, and that the roots of philosophy, research, and scientific analysis are ensconced in the Jewish faith.

Literary critics of modern Spain are confident that Judah Halevi's *Kuzari* was the first novel written in Spain, indeed in all of Europe. In other words, the masters of world fiction owe a great debt to the Jewish thinker and poet of Toledo.

Indeed, though the *Kuzari* is based on historical facts, its theme is developed in the form of a story: The king of the Khazars—a people who lived on the shores of the Black Sea in the eighth century—decides to cease serving idolatry. An enormous thirst for God overwhelms him, and he invites representatives of various faiths to his palace to discuss questions of God, man, and the universe. The king's invitation is accepted by representatives of Christianity, Islam, and Judaism. A freethinker joins them, and a discussion commences that lasts for days and nights: it keeps the king and those who read Judah Halevi's book in suspense. Five hundred years later a German thinker, Herder, remarked that the dialogue developed in the *Kuzari* has elements of literary mastery and impressed itself upon the heart and conscience of its readers.

It is important to add that *Kuzari* is the title of the book in its Hebrew translation. Judah Halevi wrote his work in Arabic, the language accessible to intellectuals and the broad populace. In the Arabic original the title itself already spoke of "the truth of the scorned faith." The premise of the work was that Judaism can survive all trials. Even those who postulate the argument of feeling will find substance and stronghold in Judaism. In Judaism there is warmth and heart. Jews are the heart of the world.

The Spanish-Jewish center was very much concerned with the people's faith and culture; the major works created there contain the motifs which transformed that settlement into the "Crown of the Jewish Exile."

A good example would be the remarkable personality of Rabbi Moses de Leon and the kabbalists of Spanish Jewry whom we have to thank for the *Zohar* as it has been transmitted to us. In the *Zohar*, Jewry, which in Judah Halevi appears as the embodiment of feeling, and in Maimonides as an expression of understanding, becomes totally wrapped in mystery. Moreover, when trends of mysticism dominate the people—and the spiritual creativity of Spain during the era of Moses de Leon was webbed into mysticism—Jewish teaching provides direction and can lead one into the sphere of mystery.

The *Zohar* is written as if it were a commentary on the Pentateuch. Yet, with the overwhelming truth of intuition, it emphasizes that apparently simple passages in the Pentateuch should not be interpreted on a simple level. Nothing is simple.

Not the Torah, not creation, not man, and not the Jew. The secret of the Divine penetrates everything and everyone. We all move in the realm of infinity. There too hover "the Holy One, blessed be He, Torah, and Israel."

Lack of historical perspective prevents us from singling out works which should be considered the concentrated expression of Polish-Jewish culture. Still, we can readily assert that in Poland too, where attention was paid to matters of the spirit, concern for the people's destiny and culture penetrated mind and heart. Polish Jewry began to tread the paths that Spanish Jewry had previously trodden.

I know that the method of *pilpul,* or hairsplitting talmudic analysis—the mode of piling one question on another, and the purposeful entanglement in the thickets of thought—which was entrenched among Polish Jewry from the beginning of its development, cannot be compared to the clarity and precision of Maimonides' teachings. But in both the Polish and the Spanish Jewish centers human thought was elevated to a place of honor. Both have the impulse to ask questions. Neither fears the most outlandish premise. With a different system or, better yet, with no system at all, and in an entirely different language, the great Polish Talmudists and masters of Jewish law—Rabbi Moses Isserles, Rabbi Solomon Luria, and Rabbi Mordecai Jaffe, the author of *Levushim*—expressed the same profound amazement at the possibilities of the intellect with which we are endowed. Everything, they contend, can be comprehended and explained with the mind.

The tale, the genre which Judah Halevi chose to go hand in hand with poetry, was also popular with the teachers of Hasidism. In the world of Hasidism, Reb Nachman of Bratzlav, Rabbi Bunim of Pshishkhe, and others held that it is easier to open up man's fantasy and will with a story. The founder of Hasidism, Reb Israel Baal Shem Tov, traveled about in the region of Mezhibuzh and Sharograd telling stories. But here it is not only a matter of form. Like Judah Halevi, the Hasidic builders, teachers, and disciples drew from the wellsprings of feeling in Hasidism.

Open any page in Reb Levi Yitzchok of Berditchev's *The Sanctity of Levi*, or the *The Language of Truth* by Reb Judah Aryeh Leib of Ger, and you can easily see that you are plucking the same strings of tender love for the people of Israel which can be found in the *Kuzari*. And surely there is a bridge between the *Zohar* and the teachings of Hasidism. In the Carpathian Mountains, the Kabbalah became accessible to the average Jew. Complicated concepts were simplified, so that the East European Jewish spirit could be introduced to the mysticism of the sophisticated Spanish-Jewish men of spirit. But the sparks came from the *Zohar*. And the belief that one can rise up to God with heart and feeling and concomitantly come closer to man and Jew, and the conviction that mystery flutters in Jewish pain and flows in Jewish joy—all these wipe away the distances of time and place, and fuse the Hasidism of Eastern Europe with the teachings of the Kabbalah of Jewish Spain.

The analogy between Spanish and Polish Jewry impels us to examine the Haskalah movement and modern Hebrew and Yiddish literature from the same prism. Naturally, these modern movements were the products of a changed era. Ideas that found their expression in the nineteenth and twentieth centuries remove us from concepts characteristic of the medieval period. But is it really difficult to find points in common which both Jewish centers have in the modern era? Is the difference that great?

Micah Joseph Lebensohn of Vilna did not board a ship as did Judah Halevi in order to sail to the Land of Israel. But in the poem that Lebensohn dedicated to Spanish Jewry's sweet singer of Zion, we hear the pounding of the waves which brought the yearning poet to the Holy Land. Micah Joseph Lebensohn accompanies Judah Halevi on his bold journey. He shares with him the experiences which in folk legend were transformed into symbols of the heartfelt intimacy that binds the Jew to the sand and stones of the Land of Israel.

Perhaps Isaac Leib Peretz read the religious poems of Isaac ibn Ghayyat of Lucena; perhaps not. But his short story "Three Gifts" accents the motif of *Kiddush Hashem* with the same fervor which stuns us in the works of the Spanish-Jewish poet and intellectual. "Three Gifts" depicts with the same reverence the profound mystery of the Jewish soul, and casts light upon the ethereal beauty of magnificent Jewish self-sacrifice, so in contrast to the surrounding world of specter-laden shadows. Moreover, even the scholarly, Hebrew-laced Yiddish so characteristic of I. L. Peretz is quite close to the Hebrew of Isaac ibn Ghayyat.

In the twentieth century, the sharp wit of Hersh David Nomberg of Amshinov sparkled in the same fashion in Yiddish. The same ironic and bitter laughter and philosophic/ sarcastic cry of pain also rang out in the streets of Toledo, where the stunning talent of Abraham ibn Ezra shone forth. The laughter of both writers was mixed with tears; both approached past and present with a highly intellectual critique; and both wandered from land to land and town to town with understanding humor. And among all those who were part of the circle of *Zohar* mystics during the centuries which separate us from the kabbalists in Spain, surely it is Hillel Zeitlin who shows that he has stepped directly out of the spiritual climate of Guadalajara.

The kabbalist Hillel Zeitlin diligently studied the *Zohar* in Warsaw and, as he confided in his essay "Between Two Worlds," sought in Kabbalah an interpretation for his dreams. Upon Kabbalah concepts he built his view of Judaism, and he wove sayings from the *Zohar* into his newspaper articles. When he was led to Treblinka on the eve of Rosh Hashanah, he did not go alone. Reading Zeitlin's remarks that appeared in the underground Ghetto newspaper before his deportation, one gets the impression that an entire group of medieval Kabbalists marched with him on his last journey. And accompanying them on the road to Treblinka was the section of the *Zohar* that laments the Exile of God's Divine Presence.

In the attempt to compare the spiritual contributions of the two now-destroyed Jewish centers, we should note that both communities ascribed importance not only to the spiritual essence of their works but also to the language in which they expressed their thoughts and feelings. The builders of Jewish culture in Spain could very easily have devoted themselves entirely to Arabic, the language accepted in the intellectual world of their time and actually uniting continents through its extensive usage.

It is true that many significant works of the leading representatives of the Golden Age of Spanish Jewry were indeed written in Arabic. But the vast majority of these thinkers and intellectuals also wrote in Hebrew, a language that they considered precious. They did not neglect the language of the Bible and Mishnah, but treated it with tenderness. Their concern for its purity showed extraordinary devotion. Because of this love of language they even fell into fits of jealousy.

Menachem ben Saruk and Dunash ben Labrat waged a passionate debate over the rules of Hebrew grammar, a debate that generated proponents and opponents, and which even took on the character of a bitter war within the Spanish-Jewish communities. Jewish ministers of state and men of wealth were participants in this dispute.

Moreover, in an era when high state authorities suggested that Jews use Spanish, which was at that time in its developmental stage, Jewish men of spirit remained true to the historic language of their people. They did not utilize it solely for penitential prayers, religious poetry, or holy themes. They explicitly transformed it into a language for profane and secular themes. The difficulties in this field were vast. The writers had to create new terms, invent new forms, and instill a gracefulness compatible with the aesthetic demands of that era. Nevertheless, they embraced Hebrew with body and soul. "Our language is a wonderful tongue!" cried Judah al-Harizi ecstatically. Solomon ibn Gabirol implored the remnants of Jacob not to forget "the chosen language."

This was not merely the passion of a few individuals. Many significant groups in the Jewish community were drawn into the stream of love for the language of the prophets. True: they did not use Hebrew for everyday purposes. They spoke the languages of their surroundings. But their hearts were with

Hebrew. And it is to the historic credit of the Spanish-Jewish community that in the hands of its masters Hebrew was enriched in expression and form and was placed at the center of modern Jewish creativity.

In no smaller measure did the Jews of Poland express their concern over language. Perhaps at first not so much attention was devoted to grammar. In Hasidic literature, too, no great efforts were made to write grammatically. But perhaps because of that the language of the Bible was not constricted. It breathed folksiness. Therefore, in the hundreds of years of Polish-Jewish history, side by side with the spiritual wrangling one can see, as well, open conflicts regarding Hebrew usage. Should biblical diction predominate, or can the language be elastic, move freely, and mirror the speech of the masses?

There was a sharp dispute among the Misnagdic (anti-Hasidic) rabbis, Hasidic rebbes, and representatives of the Haskalah not only concerning Jewish values and problems of Jewish thought. The various philosophies and theories which aspired to gain influence in Jewish life were expressed in the linguistic form of the polemic itself. For the enlightened writers of the Haskalah, who faulted the idea and lifeways of Hasidism, the linguistic form was a component of their satire. Joseph Perl's *Revealer of Secrets* can serve as a striking example. Imitating the special Hebrew of the Hasidic rebbes was in its own right an important weapon in the conflict of ideas.

Polish-Jewish writers did not resort to a foreign language when they wanted to gain access to the broad masses who did not understand Hebrew. Yiddish was kneaded and shaped with numerous elements that came from Hebrew and was warmed by the traditions of generations. Yiddish became a part of Jewish life, Jewish personality, and Jewish culture. Even more, Yiddish itself became culture.

Despite the assimilationist tendency which captivated various groups in Jewish society, the love for Yiddish among Polish Jews is seen in the long process of linguistic development from the sixteenth-century Bible commentary, *Tsena U-R'ena*, to the sophisticated prose of Joseph Opatoshu or of I. J. Singer. This attests to the importance which was acorded to Yiddish. They knew very well, as I. L. Peretz remarked in his poem "Monish," that "my song would sound differently had I sung goyish."

They knew in Poland, just as they had known long before in Spain, that in the effort to consciously preserve Jewry and Jewishness, language is not necessarily an instrument but is indeed substance. The truth is that in Spain an attempt was also made to transform Spanish into a part of traditional Jewish culture. This was done with Ladino, which utilized Spanish vocabulary and was written in Hebrew characters. They brought grammatical rules from Hebrew into Spanish and enriched its philological treasury with expressions from the Bible and the Siddur. Even though Ladino did not experience the wonderful flowering of Yiddish, it nevertheless demonstrates that in both centers the concept of Jewish culture was much broader and deeper than it seems to be in our own day.

III

But there are differences too—and these are obvious even in a superficial consideration. In Spain, Jews paid no attention to historical research, probably because they were supremely confident that Jewish life in Spain would always continue and never become something of the past. Spanish Jews were so much enamored of the physical and spiritual climate of Andalusia, and they felt so much a part of the land and its inhabitants, that despite the too frequent outbreaks of hatred, they could not believe that Spain would ever be linked with the yesterday of Jewish wanderings.

Even when harsh reality left no more room for illusions, and the Inquisition and the Expulsion were in progress, they took with them the keys to the houses they left behind. They had hopes of an imminent return home. They evidently believed that Jewish life in Spain would never end. It was a continuous today.

But no matter what the reason, it is a fact that Jewish creativity—so fruitful on Spanish soil—was almost nonexistent in the field of historical research. Abraham ibn Daud indeed unfurled the glory of the Jewish past, when Jews lived independently in their own land. Abraham ben Solomon and Joseph ben Zaddik depicted more contemporaneous events, especially the bizarre period of the expulsions. Judah, Solomon, and Joseph ibn Verga, in their chronicle, *The Rod of Judah*, described the dreadful tragedy that befell Spanish Jewry. Along with their anguished cry of woe, they informed us not only that blood and tears flowed in Jewish martyrdom, but that from it also emanated the light of glowing human decency.

The Book of Genealogy, by the astronomer of Salamanca, Abraham Zacuto, seems to be inspired by the thought that stars shine both in heaven and in Jewish history, and Zacuto immersed himself in the roots of Jewish genealogy. But this can by no means be compared to the glorious page which the Spanish-Jewish center contributed to other aspects of our culture.

Polish Jews, however, were always interested in historical research. Already in the sixteenth century, when Jewish culture in Poland was flowering, David Gans wrote an impressive account of general and Jewish history in his book, *The Plant of David*. True, David Gans was born in Germany and wrote his chronicle in Prague. But he studied in Cracow with the great halakhist Rabbi Moses Isserles, who had a strong interest in science and history and had a great influence upon Gans; and it is surmised that Rabbi Moses Isserles urged him to dig deep into the past. "He was the teacher who educated and raised me," David Gans asserts.

The Cossack slaughter of the Jewish population in the seventeenth century has left in our historical memory fast-days, penitential prayers, and supplications. It also left a chronicle, *Deep Mire*, by Nathan Notte Hanover, which perhaps is first among all the testimonies of destruction ever written in the history of European Jewry. Surely there is good reason that this work, with its warm and heartfelt style, was translated into many languages and has not become obsolete as a historical document of the first order.

Modern times have produced new scholars who consider historical studies a supremely important part of Jewish culture. Both in ancient times and in the pre- and post- Holocaust periods, Polish Jews devotedly and diligently explored the past. Meir Balaban and Isaac Shiper are probably the best known among the Polish-Jewish historians. But the fact is that gathering material for Jewish history was a popular task in Poland. Young and old believed that it was their duty to lay bricks for the building. In the ghettos too, upon the ashes of ruins, and despite the danger of death, Jews remembered to record events. Emmanuel Ringelblum, in the Warsaw Ghetto, was the historian of a community which considered the writing of history a great and sacred mission.

When we turn to Spanish Jewry, we frequently encounter the somewhat inaccurate claim that their culture was the product of but a few individuals. The talented and seeking few would not have been able to find inspiration for their works had they not been confident that there was broad interest in their thought and that their ideas would have wide repercussions.

Indeed, Solomon ibn Gabirol complained about his loneliness in an indifferent environment, and Abraham ibn Ezra had to pound on the doors of men of wealth and beg for financial support. But they too could not deny that a certain segment of the community paid attention to matters of culture. But this does not mean that culture among Spanish Jews attracted the masses. Most did not read poetry, philosophy, or the kabbalistic writings. The wonder of Jewish culture in Spain was the achievement of an elite—and the segment of the Jewish community which felt the need to nourish themselves with these writings was an elite too.

This is not the place to analyze the reasons why Jewish culture was widespread among the masses of Polish Jews. Perhaps it was prompted by the invention of print, which caused a spiritual revolution in Europe when Spanish Jewry was already moribund. Perhaps it is the great achievement of Yiddish, which brought the treasures of culture to all levels of the folk. A modern Yiddish poet once declared in one of his poems: "I write, you write, we all write, and through writing we are raised aloft." Actually, the same thoughts were expressed by Nathan Notte Hanover during the times of Chmielnicki. In his chronicle, *Deep Mire,* he states: "There was more Torah among the Polish Jews than there was in the entire Jewish dispersion."

In Hasidic books even the convoluted Kabbalah was popularized. In Poland even the average man in the street was deeply immersed in Jewish culture. The philosophers of Jewish Spain would no doubt have been astounded at hearing simple people arguing about the principal concepts of Jewry and Jewishness, unafraid to offer opinions on topics which have been complex ever since ancient times.

In Poland there developed a dynamic and vigorous social movement which was lacking in Spain. The Council of the Four Lands was the communal organization that united Jews from all the Polish provinces under one leadership and bound them in the awareness of cooperative responsibility. This council matured them not only for political and national activity but also for cultural activity; it taught them to fulfill the tasks that pertained to matters of the spirit. The folk movements that developed among Polish Jews in the nineteenth century, and the political and social parties that were active up to the eve of the destruction, give a special character and a specific trait to the Polish-Jewish center.

The papers published not only in Warsaw but also in smaller towns, the periodicals of various organizations, the journals devoted to Talmud, Hasidism, and modern literature, attest to a culture in whose foundation and growth an entire people participated. The Friday editions of Yiddish and Hebrew newspapers, which contained information as well as important material in the realm of ideas, movingly demonstrate that Jewish culture lost none of its depth even though it was popularized. Popularity does not stand in antithesis to profound thought. The shimmering rainbow of political and social ideologies perhaps reduces the monumental architectonics of

Polish-Jewish culture. But this helped to spread culture and prompted the participation of the entire community.

This sketchy outline brings forth yet another difference in the analysis of the cultures that developed in the two centers: along with its abundant spectrum of sounds and colors, Spanish-Jewish culture possessed a harmony and order lacking in the culture of Polish Jewry. In their energy and zest, and in the haste of their initiative and excitement, those who built and developed Jewish culture in Poland were not concerned with constructing systems. The art of systemization was alien to them. Speaking of the Passover Seder, the Maharal of Prague once said that the special talent of the Jewish tradition is seen in its introduction of order (*seder*, in Hebrew) in a historical event which seemingly developed entirely without a sense of order. The Exodus from Egypt is a conglomeration of events where everything went against logic and system. Nonetheless, out of this knot of bizarre events Jews formed a Seder. The same may be said about the culture of the Jews in Poland. Without system, without order, without harmony, the cultural drama of Polish Jewry possesses the extraordinary higher order of life itself, even though life seems incredibly chaotic and terribly complicated.

Surely other differences can be noted. It is remarkable, however, that in the mystery of Jewish history both centers blend: in the act of *Kiddush Hashem* the contrasts were done away with. In its last hour the dying Jewish masses in Poland also drew courage and faith from the sources of the spirit which flourished in the Spanish-Jewish center. The *Ani Ma'amin* ("I Believe") with which Polish Jews went to the gas chambers was sung with a modern melody. But its content is sourced in concepts that stem from the teaching of Maimonides, the great teacher of Spanish Jewry.

10

An Encounter with the Golden Age of Spanish Jewry

I

MY FIRST ENCOUNTER with the Jewish creativity of medieval Spain took place decades ago. In my youth in prewar Warsaw, my father would sit and study difficult passages of Abraham ibn Ezra's illuminating biblical commentary. Although Ibn Ezra excelled in erudition and even more so in brilliant acumen, my father also admired Ibn Ezra's poetry and owned the edition prefaced and annotated by the maskil and scholar, Abraham Kahana.

Even though I did not fully understand all the religious poems in that collection, I did grasp several fragments, which elicited a smile mixed with bitter sadness. For example, the rhymed epigram where Abraham ibn Ezra complains about the hard lot of a wandering beggar. He states that when he knocks on a rich man's door in the morning, he is sent away with the excuse that the grandee has already left; and when he knocks in the evening, he is dismissed with the alibi that the rich man has already gone to sleep. Ibn Ezra concludes, how unfortunate is the poor man "who has come into this world without a lucky star." I always felt a kinship to this epigram, which reminded me of the Jewish humor of laughter through tears. That epigram also mirrored the want which beset many Yiddish and Hebrew poets of *my* circle.

158

It is superfluous to add that the chief place of honor in my father's library was reserved for the volumes of Maimonides' Code of Law (known as the *Mishneh Torah*), a monumental ingathering of Jewish Halakhah. After becoming entangled in the thickets of the Talmud, I would breathe free and easy reading this work. I thought that there was good reason for the Code of Law to be termed the "strong hand." This was not only because the Hebrew letters of "hand" (*yad*) have the numerical value of 14, after the fourteen major sections of the work, and because it deals with the fourteen basic themes in which Jewish law was systematically set by Maimonides. The best reason was that the books take the reader and guide him with a firm and sure hand through the dense and frequently unexitable forest of the age-old Halakhah.

On Saturday nights in Warsaw—evenings which now seem to be in a distant world—I used to lecture to young people thirsting for knowledge. At times I would speak about Judah Halevi, Spanish Jewry's poet of Zion. Despite its grace and charm, Judah Halevi's Hebrew was too richly ornamented for my listeners—and for myself as well. Nevertheless, Judah Halevi's sighs, his tears, his anguished outcries, were moving and frightfully familiar: "My heart is in the east, and I in the depths of the west."

Not only was his poem moving and impressive, but so was his life, in which truth was fused with legend. The final scene of his life is doubtless a mixture of truth and wonderful folk fantasy. For Judah Halevi there could be no other path to eternity. In conformity with folk intuition, death had to take him as he was kissing the stones of the Holy Land, while weeping his heart out with sadness and longing.

But I must confess that I first realized the true dimension of the masters of the Golden Age of Spanish Jewry only during the last twenty years, when—as a direct result of the wanderings which our generation of storm and haven-seeking had to undergo—I was cast upon the shores of Spanish-speaking Central America. At the University of Panama I was appointed to teach Spanish-Jewish history and Jewish contributions to

Spanish culture. Only now have I become cognizant of the
remarkable and, I might even say, bizarre aspects of the
Golden Age of Spanish Jewry.

What most intrigues a East European Jew about Spanish-
Jewish life and creativity is the ease and naturalness with
which the Jews there linked the holy and the profane, the
Sabbath and the weekday. Just as the little flames of the
dripping Havdalah candle penetrated the consciousness of the
East European Jews, so did the blessing they said at the end of
the Sabbath, "He who separates the holy and the profane."
That is, the Jew was fully conscious that a thick wall separates
the realms of the holy and the profane.

In Isaac Leib Peretz's play, *The Golden Chain*, Rabbi Solomon
wants holiness to encompass the weekday world too. With the
power of his ardent word, then, he attempts to raise his
Hasidim and, with stubborn daring, to prevent the Sabbath
from departing the Jewish homes. But in the fervor of the
rabbi's belief there lurks the fear of weekday specters which
can uproot everything linked with Sabbath and holiday, for
they can subjugate everything that is divine and holy.

The masters and teachers of Spanish Jewry, however, had no
fear of the weekday. Along with his commentary to the Talmud
and his religious poetry, Samuel ha-Nagid composed frivolous
verse. And Judah Halevi, in addition to his passionate prayers,
which to this day are recited in the Sephardic ritual on Yom
Kippur before *Neilah*, also rhapsodized about the bride who
charms everyone with her beautiful eyes. Solomon ibn Gabirol
was the author of the profoundly religious poem, *The Royal
Crown*, with which our *Kol Nidrei* prayers conclude. In it he
reverently sets the kingly crown upon the Creator of the world.
Ibn Gabirol exalted himself with philosophical thoughts formulated by Plato and succeeded so well that after several hundred
years he prompted incredulity. No one believed that the same
Solomon ibn Gabirol had gone from one extreme to the other
and was also the author of *Fons Vitae* ("Source of Life"), a
philosophic tractate in Arabic based upon a Platonic model.

Later generations viewed Maimonides as a complex man, yet

there was nothing in his thought or works which seemed complex by Maimonides' standards, or by those of most of his contemporaries. One could faithfully follow and forge Jewish law and at the same time admire Aristotle of pagan Greece as a divine philosopher and teacher. The Havdalah ceremony is an ancient one, but in the Golden Age of Spanish Jewry, they apparently stressed the theme of separation less than did later generations of East European Jews. In Spain, the sanctity of the Sabbath spread over the shadows of the week, and the distinction between the sacred and the secular was virtually unknown.

No less remarkable is the stamp which the masters of Spanish Jewry placed upon the Spanish language itself. East European Jews knew that they were virtuosos of their host nations' languages. The poet Julian Tuwim, who was born and raised in a Jewish family, was doubtless one of the greatest masters of Polish poetry. In the field of the historical essay, none can compare to the Polish prose of Shimon Ashkenazi. And Osip Mandelstam and Boris Pasternak uplifted Russian poetry during strained times for Russian literature.

What happened in Spain, however, is surprising even for the Jewish course through history, a history replete with surprises. In Spain, the Jews laid the foundation for the Spanish language. Even the term *Sefarad* (found in the prophet Obadiah, and by which Jews refer to Spain) has been incorporated into Spanish civilization since its inception.

We have now discovered that Judah Halevi was the first known poet to write poetry in Spanish. Not too long ago such a theory of literary history would have sparked a storm of protests in Spanish academic circles. At the beginning of the twentieth century, a famous Spanish literary historian, Marcellino Menéndez y Pelayo, alerted the scholarly world in Spain to his "suspicion" that Judah Halevi was the first to write poetry in Spanish. Skepticism greeted this revolutionary theory, and Menéndez himself added all kinds of qualifications to his discovery. He stressed that his supposition might be correct and carefully added, "Who would have expected this?"

In the twelfth century, when Judah Halevi lived, the Spanish language was still considered the vulgar vernacular of the common masses. No man of talent or of intellectual caliber was willing to descend from the heights and exchange Arabic or Hebrew—languages then accepted in Spain as fit instruments for the expression of feeling and thought—for a primitive and semibarbaric dialect.

Today, no one doubts any longer that Halevi, Toledo's yearning poet of Zion, truly laid the foundation of Spanish poetry. At the end of his Hebrew poems Judah Halevi would occasionally add several strongly secular verses in the Spanish vernacular. Here is one brief example:

> Vayse meu corachón de mib.
> Ya, Rab, si se me tornarád?
> Tan mal meu doler li-l-habib.
> Enfermo yed, cuándo sanaràd?

> [Seeping away from me is my heart.
> O God, won't it ever return to me?
> My longing for my friend is great.
> Is he ill, and when will he healed be?]

Most of the credit for developing the Spanish language must be given to the so-called translators' school of the twelfth century. This group, created in Toledo, was charged with rendering into Spanish the collected scientific discoveries of previous eras. Not only did this school of translators erect an impressive tower of culture in medieval Spain, but the Spanish language itself was nurtured and developed there.

The greatest Christian authorities in this field now attest that the makeup of this school of translators—which, incidentally, was an official institution given moral and financial support by the kingdom—was overwhelmingly Jewish. Jews worked there; Jews translated from Latin, Arabic, and Hebrew; Jews were the editors. And to further enhance the surprise, it should be added that these were not ordinary Jews, but rabbis, rabbinic judges, cantors, and other religious functionaries.

A rabbi was also the author of a book of moral proverbs in Spanish. *Proverbios Morales,* an important work in medieval Spanish belles-lettres, is considered a classic which thrust Spanish literature, and indeed the Spanish language itself, forward. *Moral Proverbs* was written by Rabbi Shem Tov of Carrión (in Spanish: Sem Tob de Carrión), which is in the heart of Castile.

In these poems, dedicated to Don Pedro I, the ruler of Castile, the rabbi presented the king with a clever, incisive lecture on humanity and decency in an elegant form. Rabbi Shem Tov taught Don Pedro the wisdom of life not in rabbinic fashion, but with a bold, worldly approach. He also taught the king that he, as ruler, must preserve and honor the language which the masses were using in Spain and which also deserved to be the language of kings and dukes.

The Jewish concern with the Spanish language did not cease with the Expulsion. Along with the wanderer's staff, the exiles of Spain also took along the language that their parents had cultivated and pampered. As though it were a precious treasure, the refugees preserved the language of Toledo and Barcelona in Turkey and in Greece, the lands where they found haven.

Ladino is unique in the history of the Jewish dispersion. It is an extraordinary drama of enduring love for the spiritual values of a land which many refugees themselves excommunicated—they swore and adjured their children and their children's children never to return there again. This linguistic heritage passed from generation to generation among the exiled Jews. In Ladino they sang lullabies; they prayed in it; they expressed their sufferings and hopes; they laughed and cried, they lived and died with it. In Ladino they wrote stories and commentaries to the Torah. Unto this very day books and papers are published in Ladino. Ladino newspapers can still be purchased in the kiosks of Tel Aviv. The Sephardic Jews wanted (and still want) to preserve the sound of this old language which their ancestors disseminated.

Comparing the Sephardic loyalty to Ladino with the Ashkenazic love for Yiddish is superficial and false. Those who

stubbornly clung to Ladino had no intention at all of creating
and developing a new language for Jews. Those who spoke
and wrote Ladino actually strove to carry on the tradition of
Spanish, the language developed by their ancestors in Castile
and transformed into an integral part of their weekday and
their Sabbath.

II

Many of the evaluations of Maimonides' works seems to be
quite cliché. Even Ahad Ha'am's essay, in which the philosopher of Cordoba is delineated as the prince of rationality, does
not seem to be thoroughly convincing. Similarly unconvincing
is the appraisal written by Israel Zinberg in his *History of Jewish
Literature*, where Rabbi Moses ben Maimon is represented as
the most outspoken rationalist in the history of Jewish thought.

Questions upon questions pile up. Maimonides was by no
means the first to deal with questions of faith from a rationalist
point of view. Hundreds of years earlier, Saadia Gaon of
Babylonia delved deeply and boldly into the paths and byways
of human rationality. He was not the first to bring order into
the branched-out Jewish law either. Rabbi Isaac Alfasi, too,
attempted to introduce system into the Halakhah. Even our
amazement at the grand simplicity with which Maimonides
explained complicated problems is not entirely justified. Surely
Rashi, the modest vintner of Troyes, surpassed him in the art of
interpretation and explication.

The truth is that the main problem at the center of Maimoni-
dean thought—reconciling the teachings of Judaism and the
philosophy of Greece—was treated even earlier by Abraham
ibn Daud. If we turn to Maimonides to help us find our way
out of our modern maze, as he helped those who had gone
astray in his generation, it is not because of the achievements
ascribed to him (and even those were not always accurate).
Perhaps it is the sense of wholeness we see in his works and
impact that is so crucial in Maimonides and which comes
across so forcefully and articulately to our generation, for
whom wholeness and harmony are a distant and almost unat-
tainable ideal.

Naturally, it is correct to say that in the Code of Law Maimonides is a strict respecter of law. According to him, Halakhah is the duty of the Jew and the foundation of Jewish society. In all fourteen parts of the Code, Maimonides constantly repeats that the law breathes divinity into our life; however, without law life can at times become dehumanized. The Code of Law is actually a demonstration of the authority of Jewish law, or of the abyss into which the Jew can descend when he ceases to recognize the law. The Code is in essence a mighty paean to Halakhah, a psalm to law. According to Maimonides, it is only because of law that the divine spark glows in us.

But it is no less true that in addition to this mighty reverence for law, Maimonides also possesses a stirring love for the Jews even when they do not always observe the law. While constructing this monument of Halakhah, the man who apparently was all intellect became all heart on seeing his people's suffering and pain. The man who should have been an angry accuser was also the ardent defender of his people. His "Article on *Kiddush Hashem*" is a paradigm of the tenderness with which one must view Jewish anguish and the love one needs to gather Jewish tears.

Maimonides lived at a time of trouble in Morocco. Many Jews were forced to conceal their Jewishness to save their lives. In certain circles scattered accusations were leveled against these Marranos. But it was Maimonides, the master of law, who defended them. It was he who said that no Jew should be estranged from the Jewish community if he considers himself a Jew.

His voice was raised even more forcefully in his *Epistle to Yemen,* which was sent to the Jews in distant Yemen when they suffered a deluge of persecution. This letter abounds with a faith that strengthens and elevates the broken spirit. According to this halakhist who had become a sentimental letter-writer, those who cast stones at Jews haven't the slightest concept of what Jewry is and what Jewishness demands. Even when Jews struggle for their lives and cannot fully observe the commandments, they are holy. Their pain alone breathes with endless devotion and sacrifice. And so who can, who has the right to, punish? Maimonides asserts that it is a duty to bring consolation to the suffering and with love and compassion whisper in their ears, "Jews, do not despair!" One might have expected that Maimonides' letter would also have triggered dissatisfaction and protests because he permitted conversions to Islam under duress while Jewish law forbids it. This unusual side of Maimonides was absolutely astonishing. It was too difficult to accept that the strict halakhist should fall prey to his feelings.

In several passages in his works Maimonides unexpectedly becomes a mystical poet. Maimonides had nothing to do with Kabbalah; indeed, mysticism and rationality are antithetical. Nevertheless, Maimonides spoke about messianic times like an impassioned kabbalist. He is the only one among our great deciders of law who devoted much space to the laws pertaining to the holy Temple and to sacrifices, laws which from the beginning of the Exile were removed from Jewish reality.

Neither Rabbi Isaac Alfasi, who preceded Maimonides, nor Rabbi Joseph Caro, the author of the *Shulchan Aruch*, who came after him, dealt with these laws. These two great masters of Halakhah held that a definitive Code should not present laws applicable only in ancient times, when the holy Temple stood and Jews were masters of their own land, or laws which can once more become timely only "when the time and the generation are ripe."

Only Maimonides did this. Only he devoted the last part of his Code of Law to the times of the kings and the judges who once existed and who shall come again. Maimonides felt that in the Jewish path through history the present does not exist. There is only an all-pervasive eternity. The Jewish yesterday and the Jewish tomorrow are as real as the Jewish today. Jewish expectations are a part of Halakhah. Jewish yearning is fundamental. In Jewish law redemption is essential.

In Maimonides, fantasy coexisted with mind and heart. Literally by force he conjures up a picture of the coming Jewish state and, as if it had existed in his time, handles the problems which are likely to surface. Fantasy has ceased to be merely fantasy. In his view, Messiah is no distant offshoot of the root of Jesse. The Messiah has the choice of being one of us. In fact, at this very moment he might be wandering among us and we wouldn't even know it.

In the Golden Age of Spanish Jewry the antitheses were evidently not crucial. There they apparently knew the meaning of harmony. Unlike Rabbi Solomon in I. L. Peretz's play *The Golden Chain*, in Spain they did not have to wage a desperate struggle to strike down the barrier between one attitude and another. There they wiped away the border between understanding and vision. There they were able to decide law soberly, to love with turbulent emotion, and to gaze into the distance with fiery yearning. There the masters and teachers honored the rational intellect—and believed in the resurrection of the dead. There they whispered prayers and pious supplications, while concomitantly singing profane songs about wine and love. There the priests of the holy temple of the holy tongue simultaneously built the temple of the Spanish language.

There, in Spain, unity in the human personality and in spiritual creativity were as natural as divisiveness is to us in the current twilight of the twentieth century.

And one should not wonder why those far from that singular phenomenon known as the Golden Age of Spanish Jewry regarded the astonishing harmoniousness as remarkable and even suspicious. One of the tosafists, Rabbi Moses of Coucy, appraised the works of Maimonides with the phrase, "a dream without an interpretation"—an evaluation that actually encompassed an entire era.

But indeed this transforms a timely encounter with the Golden Age of Spanish Jewry into a fascinating and enriching experience, and also into an ideal which we, in our generation, long so much to achieve.

11

The Spiritual Culture of Polish Jewry

BY CONSTANTLY USING the overly generalized concept "East European Jewry," we tend to forget that Eastern Europe encompassed several nations and various Jewish centers. This essay will deal explicitly with Polish Jewry. Admittedly, the task is not an easy one, especially since our generation still lacks the perspective to properly evaluate the legacy of the Polish-Jewish community after the destruction. Polish-Jewish culture thrived and flourished to the late 1930's. Many of us even participated actively in the fabric of its glorious past. Today Polish Jewry is in ruins. The question, then, is whether we—or our generation—are capable of an objective summary of its spiritual heritage. Nevertheless, *because* the theme is fraught with difficulty, it tempts the imagination.

There is yet another problem: the very definition of "Polish Jew." Who were the Polish Jews? It could be correctly asserted that Polish Jews are those who lived within the boundaries of Poland. But in the course of history the map of Poland underwent severe and crucial changes. The old historic Polish kingdom was united with Lithuania. Joined within its territory were Little Poland, Cracow, and Lublin; Greater Poland and Poznan; Red Russia (Ruthenia), the later Eastern Galicia with Lemberg; and ethnographic Poland, Central Poland, which was later to be called Congress Poland, and Warsaw.

But in the eighteenth century commenced the period of decline. Poland began crumbling and was divided up among its greedy neighbors. At the end of the eighteenth century it was quite off the map; only a shadow of its independence remained in a small section of central Poland. After World War I, a new, large, independent Poland rose again in 1918; and the political and spiritual unity of the great Polish-Jewish community was revived. So then, concerning which geographic, political, and cultural boundary can one speak of Polish Jewry?

The task before us is extraordinarily complex. Within the framework of my essay I will work with the following definition: Although for a certain period Polish Jews were subjects of a different power, they nevertheless maintained their unbroken historic contact with Polish Jewry and with the spirit of the Polish-Jewish cultural tradition.

I will exclude from my essay Jews who lived in regions separated from Poland who cut themselves off spiritually and culturally from the Polish-Jewish community to which they had previously belonged and proceeded to create and develop their outlook in a completely different direction.

Jewish settlement in Poland is very old. One thousand years ago, when the Polish kingdom was founded, Jews were already living on Polish soil. Coins with Hebrew letters were minted in Poland one thousand years ago. Naturally, however, many long eras had to pass before a discernible Jewish culture began to form on Polish soil. In the first several centuries of Polish-Jewish history the Jewish population grew slowly. Jewish migration into Poland was also meager; it increased greatly only in the fourteenth century. While Jews were persecuted in neighboring lands, in Poland there was a significant tolerance. Poland itself developed as a power only toward the end of the fourteenth century. Jews were an important economic factor in the rise of Polish cities and of commerce and industry.

Poland began to be a leading Jewish spiritual center. There emerged a culture with a distinct style and a unique form of expression.

Pilpul and Talmudic Culture

It should be stated at the outset: this was a religious culture. Wherever Jews lived the world over, their culture was a religious one; and the Talmud was the basis of Jewish civilization in that period. But in Poland a special method of studying the Talmud developed: the method of *pilpul*.

We are used to translating the word *pilpul* as "scholasticism," but I doubt that scholasticism truly expresses what pilpul stands for. In this method the intellect stands supreme. A goal of pilpul is to develop and sharpen the intellectual capacities of the student so that he can—independently—comprehend the proceedings and succeed in Talmud studies.

From the schoolrooms and the yeshivas the method of pilpul was transferred to all realms of spiritual life. It put its stamp on the Polish-Jewish psyche. Already at the dawn of Jewish culture in Poland the Polish Jew was the sort of person who, with his deep piety, still believed in the power of the intellect. He exercised the thinnest and finest nuances of thinking.

The first well-known talmudic genius who emerged from Polish Jewry was Rabbi Jacob Pollack, the head of the Lublin Yeshiva. He was a master of the method of Torah scholarship that, in the words of the Hebrew-Yiddish saying, "uprooted mountains." It is told of Rabbi Jacob Pollack that on one occasion his pupils tore several pages out of the Talmud folio he had been studying. However, he did not notice that they were missing. With keenness of mind he tied together subjects far removed. Rabbi Pollack wrote no books and left no new interpretations, for he feared that his pupils would lessen their efforts and become dependent upon the authority of his written remarks.

The rabbinic authorities who followed him proceeded along this same path of pilpul. I will just cite several names: Rabbi Sholom Shachne of Cracow, the master of sharp thought; Rabbi Moses Isserles, Polish Jewry's famous decider of law, who used his sharp dialectic and iron logic for his commentary to the *Shulchan Aruch*; Rabbi Solomon Luria, who was gifted with first-rate analytical powers, and paved the path for independent criticism and research of the talmudic text.

This esteem for the intellect is the reason why the builders of talmudic culture in Poland admired the great rationalist of Spanish Jewry, Maimonides. Actually, they were quite removed from Maimonides. They did not have his multifaceted philosophic preparation. But one trait united the rationalist of the no-longer-extant Spanish community and the spiritual thinkers of the newly developing Polish Jewry: respect for the human intellect.

Rabbi Moses Isserles considered Maimonides the teacher par excellence and regarded the *Guide to the Perplexed* as the profound source of philosophic knowledge. And furthermore, like Maimonides, Rabbi Moses Isserles tried to explain events in the world, in life, and in belief from a rational viewpoint. He said that man's mind may be compared to a flame which lights up the darkness; and only he who comprehends the truth lifts himself up to the highest rung.

Another talmudic genius, Rabbi Mordecai Jaffe, wrote a commentary to the *Guide to the Perplexed* and even attempted to give a rational explanation for the phenomenon of prophecy.

The Inclination to Mysticism

But this is still not a complete picture of the spiritual culture of Polish Jewry of long ago. Concomitant with the enormous reverence for the human intellect during that dawn of Polish-Jewish culture, there also developed a contrasting tendency—one toward mysticism, to the Torah of the heart. And this was an entirely new trend.

In the Jewish world of that time (and also earlier) these two trends were in bitter conflict. On the one hand, one methodology declared that we must attempt to understand all phenomena with our intellect; that we dare not permit emotional factors to play a role in our life; that the great, multihued world of man's dreams, illusions, and entanglements is merely a spider's web. Man finds uplift only by using his active intellect.

On the other hand, the second tendency found its expression in mysticism, Kabbalah, and its basic book, the *Zohar*. This methodology declared that feeling was higher than intellect; that the world of fantasy was more real than the real world; that the tremor of a yearning soul was more crucial than a thinker's cold intellect.

A virulent and dramatic debate engaged the entire Jewish world. What was Judaism? What was a Jewish world view? What is Torah? Is it a Torah of the mind or of the heart? Can everything in this world become open, clear, understandable— or must it remain befogged and sealed, an eternal secret?

In Poland these two contrasting tendencies moved in tandem. Side by side with the intellectual culture a mystical culture was developed. Side by side, hand in hand. And furthermore: in the same persons. The same sharp, sober minds could also be poetic and romantic. The iron minds were also carried away by imagination. The rationalist was a mystic; the mystic also a rationalist. The Talmud was the book of the people. But the *Zohar* too was the book of the people.

I purposely use the word "people" because one of the characteristic traits of Jewish culture in Poland is that the entire people participated in its development. Not just one stratum, and not one class—as was the case in other Jewish centers. In the Polish-Jewish community *everyone* laid the bricks for the palace of culture. Everyone studied Talmud, and everyone immersed himself in Kabbalah.

The very same Rabbi Moses Isserles who spoke about the universal meaning of an active intellect also wrote a commentary to the *Zohar*. And in the same breath he also stated that everything was concealed—that the human soul was a wonder, and the heart, a mystery.

The same Rabbi Solomon Luria, the analytic critic of the Talmud text, considered the Kabbalah the holy of holies; in an encounter with mysticism, he felt, man remains mute, without words.

Rabbi Moses Isserles and Rabbi Solomon Luria were not the only ones affected and passionately moved by the secrets of the

Kabbalah; it touched other talmudic geniuses and Polish masters of pilpul of long ago. To cite a few names: Rabbi Mordecai Jaffe, Rabbi Samuel Eidels, Rabbi Joshua Falk, Rabbi Meir of Lublin, Rabbi Joel Sirkis, the latter the author of an analytical commentary on Joseph Caro's *Shulchan Aruch*. He was even bold enough to declare that anyone who opposes the Kabbalah should be excommunicated.

True, Jews in other communities also had these two opposing tendencies within themselves; the inclination toward rationalism and toward mysticism. But in other Jewish centers this was a rare phenomenon. These people remained exceptions to the rule. In Poland, however, this contrast was the norm.

The Genius of Polish Jewry: The Contradiction

Weren't the builders of Jewish culture in Poland aware of the contradiction? Didn't they realize that an abyss separated the two world views: the teaching of the intellect and the teaching of intuition? Of course they did! They knew that both teachings were diametrically opposed and made no attempt to bridge the gap. The genius of Polish Jewry did not lie in finding an accord, in constructing a synthesis. Not then and not later. Polish Jewry was great in contradictions.

Already in the sixteenth century, at the very outset of the growth of pilpul literature, noteworthy kabbalists lived in Poland. The air was thick with pilpul and—mystery; with sobriety and—messianic dreams. A mystical literature developed which stated that man is appointed to secret tasks; that surely both the Jew and the people of Israel have a tendency toward mysticism and mysterious goals; that sparks of sanctity can spring forth from the husk of the external world, sparks of holiness and goodness.

A mystical literature developed which contained all the elements of the Kabbalah as it was developed in Guadalajara, Spain, the city of Rabbi Moses de Leon, who compiled the *Zohar,* and in Safed, the city of Rabbi Isaac Luria. The mystical spirit of the Jewish masses in Poland is reflected in the *Two*

Tablets of the Law, a book by Rabbi Isaiah Hurvitz. In this sacred book we read: "The secretiveness of the world is infinite and has no limits."

"Even if man were to live one thousand years he would not be able to penetrate the mystery. . . How awesome is man," states the writer, "how enormously secretive. He who does not see the light of mysticism sees no light at all. And he who leaves the study of Kabbalah separates himself from the spiritual essence of the world."

But more characteristic than anything else mentioned heretofore is the remarkable book wherein the boundary between the intellect and feeling is completely effaced. The title of the book is *Revealer of the Depths,* by Rabbi Nathan-Notte Shapiro. Here a dialectical mysticism emerges. A tender feeling of redemption is woven together with mathematical combinations. The teaching concerning sparks of holiness is enmeshed with rational insinuation, with dialectical calculations and hints.

The pilpul element is also woven into the ethical books that were written in Poland. Structures of dialectic rise before us along with the moral fervor that emanates from them. One can say that the Divine Presence of God manifests itself in the sermons, wrapped in mystery and engrossed in calculations.

Illogical? In Polish-Jewish culture it was logic vis-à-vis a pairing of intellect and emotion. From the hour of its dawning Polish Jewry was dominated by a profound spiritual unrest. It found no spiritual satisfaction in intellectualism. However, it didn't find a totally spiritual satisfaction in mysticism either. Polish Jewry vigorously pursued both wellsprings and drank from both of them with extraordinary thirst.

The Shabbetai Zevi Movement

To this very day we still stand amazed: how could the movement of the false messiah Shabbetai Zevi in the middle of the seventeenth century have dominated the Jewish masses of Poland in such an awesome manner? Intelligent, average Jews as well as scholarly rabbis packed all their belongings, left their homes, and with their wives and children traveled to port cities in order to wait for months and even years—waiting for what? For a cloud to carry them to the Land of Israel.

This is one of the great riddles in our history. Attempts are made to explain this mass psychosis by referring to the Polish Jews' depression after the massacres of 1648 and 1649—the slaughters committed by the Chmielnicki Cossack bands—and by referring to the rising hopes of redemption during that period of pain and suffering. The Jews had suffered in previous generations and in other lands. Hopes of redemption had previously risen in the Jewish world. Even false messiahs had appeared in earlier generations. But nowhere but in Poland was there such mass ecstasy as during the Shabbetai Zevi era.

Only within the specifically Polish-Jewish culture, which was a fusion of dialectic and innocence, of cleverness and naiveté, of pilpul and feeling, could there have developed the incomparable and incredible psychosis whose purpose was: to remove God's Divine Presence and the people of Israel from Exile.

Only by this can one explain the passionate polemic that flared up then around the great scholar Rabbi Jonathan Eibeschutz. Possessor of one of the keenest minds in the history of Jewish spirituality, he was accused and attacked for his ostensible support of the Shabbetai Zevi movement. That such a figure could have been accused in the first place of being sympathetic to the false messiah is characteristic. To this very day we are still attempting to get to the bottom of this passionate dispute.

It seems that those who were not affected by the dynamic of Polish-Jewish culture—and stood spiritually outside of its circle—were not able to comprehend the essence of its internal elements. They could not understand its deep contrasts. They were incapable of comprehending how Rabbi Jonathan Eibeschutz could have remarked, "Would that our souls could be a footstool to the kabbalists," and at the same time write admiringly about the human intellect. For those who themselves were not a part of this muddle, everything in this remarkable spiritual world had to remain hazy, incomprehensible, and in any case, suspect.

The unique Polish-Jewish culture was the product of deeply spiritual and social processes that Polish Jewry had experienced. The economic circumstances in which Polish Jewry lived undoubtedly contributed to the shaping of these processes. Polish Jewry was also affected by external influences; by contacts with Polish culture and with the historic spirit and path of Poland. Into the frame of this picture one must also insert the movement of another false messiah, the follower of Shabbetai Zevi, Jacob Frank. But the reason for this specific and singular (one might even say unique) Jewish culture is a chapter in and of itself. For the purposes of this essay, describing its essential character must suffice.

The Hasidic Movement

During the course of two hundred years Polish Jewry brought forth the teachings of Hasidism, which stirred up the entire Jewish people and has lost none of its influence even in our own generation. In essence, Hasidism is a continuation of the Kabbalah. It merely introduced greater simplicity, clarity, and flexibility into the mystical teaching. It opened up the wellsprings of feeling for the average Jew. Had Hasidism not been born among Polish Jewry, and had it not developed within the Polish-Jewish community, then perhaps it would have remained what it was at the beginning of its history: a methodology that highlights the meaning of simplicity; a teaching that accepts that the path of God leads through and from the heart—that the deepest roots of belief are not to be found in thinking but in inner religious ecstasy; a movement believing that the deepest wisdom is not to be too smart.

But Hasidism developed within Polish Jewry; and here the inevitable historic knot came into play. In a region where pilpul and Kabbalah reigned in tandem for hundreds of years, this new system had to build upon these two contradictory elements. And such Hasidism became: a blend of intellectual activity and religious ecstasy, of sharpness and fire.

In the regions that cut themselves off from the mainstream of Polish-Jewish culture, Hasidism kept its innocent simplicity for generations. But in Poland Hasidism did not rebel against intellect. On the contrary, it strived to raise the average Jew intellectually.

In Galicia, which despite its annexation by Austria in the eighteenth century still throbbed with the Polish-Jewish pulse, the rebbes' courts became significant centers of learning and talmudic pilpul. It suffices to mention Zanz Hasidism, which spread Torah learning in abundance in that region.

And in Vilna, where at the end of the eigthteenth century the influence of the joint Polish-Jewish culture was still strong, and where a separate Lithuanian-Jewish culture was in the dawn of its formation, we encounter something remarkable: the resolute anti-Hasid (or Misnaged) Rabbi Elijah of Vilna, the Vilna Gaon, immersed himself in the Kabbalah and wrote a commentary to the *Zohar*. And his opponent, the Hasidic teacher Reb Shneur Zalman of Liady, was constructing a philosophic intellectual method of Hasidism known as *Chabad,* an acronym of the Hebrew words *chochmah,* ("wisdom"), *binah* ("understanding"), and *daat* ("knowledge"). Chabad held that ecstasy alone does not lead one to God; it must be accompanied by clarity of understanding.

Characteristic of Hasidism in the very heart of Poland, the so-called Congress Poland, was the path of Reb Bunim of Pshishkhe, which was developed even further in the methodology of Reb Mendele of Kotzk. Pshishkhe and Kotzk are two small Polish towns which become important centers of the Jewish spirit.

"One does not travel to Kotzk. To Kotzk one makes a pilgrimage," was a well-known folksong. The Kotzk rebbe, Reb Mendele, is the symbol of Polish Hasidism, which struggled with itself and with the tragic contrasts in the human personality, and which sought the hidden and felt the secretive. This was the Hasidism that believed sincerely, and at the same time probed into itself with anguish—to ascend to the heights in torments.

In the beginning of the Hasidic movement the old talmudic saying "God demands the heart" was stressed. But Kotzk added that the heart alone does not suffice, because at times a horrible chaos reigns in the human heart. Can one then expect that the heart would not delude one?

Hasidism began with prayer, with voices and ecstasy. But in Kotzk they said: "If someone says, 'I toiled, I found'—believe him." One can arrive at belief through suffering and probing. Prayer must be accompanied by introspection. Kotzk is the Hasidism of tragic challenge; therefore, it is symbolic of Polish Jewry.

Hundreds of years earlier Spanish Jewry proclaimed the path of the golden mean. The middle-of-the-road way that avoids the extreme was declared to be the ideal path for man. Polish Jewry, however, vigorously cast aside the golden mean. Contrast seethed and simmered in Polish Jewry. At one and the same time, and with the same ardor, the Jewish center of Poland hurled and cast itself from one extreme to another. The following remark, made by the Kotzk rebbe, left a shattering impression not only upon Hasidic circles but also upon the length and breadth of Polish Jewry:

"Man stands with one foot in seventh heaven, and with the other in the lowest pit of hell."

And he also said: "The middle of the road is not for people. Horses, not people, go in the middle of the road."

This barb gave full expression to Polish Jewry's generations-long protest against the path of the golden mean proclaimed hundred of years earlier by Spanish Jewry. Indeed, sharp extremes are characteristic of Polish Jewry in all modes of life and creativity and in all periods. The contrasting trends etched their influence upon Polish-Jewish culture in modern times in exactly the same fashion as they placed their stamp on Polish-Jewish history at its dawning.

The Haskalah in Poland

At the threshold of the nineteenth century the Science of Judaism and Haskalah literature emerged in Poland. Scholarly books dealing with the problems of man and Jew, general and Jewish history, and philosophy were published in Hebrew, Yiddish, and Polish. But the vast majority of works written on these themes in the Polish-Jewish community are entirely different from similar books written in other lands.

The Enlightenment and its literature also took on unique forms in Poland. Here, Haskalah works did not address the tendency toward dry enlightenment so characteristic of Western European centers or even the Jewish regions of Russia. Here they did not base themselves upon one-sided rationalistic theories. In any case, the one-sided and narrowly rationalistic method was not characteristic of the Haskalah and of the Science of Judaism as they developed among Polish Jewry.

Nachman Krochmal, the representative thinker of the Galician Haskalah, floundered between the theories of speculative intellect and the gentle poetry of spirit and people that, according to his view, hovers over all periods of Jewish history. On the one hand, Nachman Krochmal taught the confused people of his generation that only through investigation can one achieve absolute truth; but, on the other hand, he let himself be lulled by the melody of the heart and was overwhelmed and immobilized beneath the wings of the Divine Presence that hovers over the Jewish path through the ages.

The enlightened maskil Jacob Samuel Bick demonstratively sold his copy of Maimonides' *Guide to the Perplexed* and was drawn, much to the astonishment of maskilic circles, to the emotion and ecstasy that streamed forth from Hasidism.

The scholar Jacob Reifman, with his total reverence for the new, enlightened winds that blew from Western Europe, was deeply immersed in the specific Polish-Jewish sphere of ideas. He did not want to nor could he separate himself from the teaching of the heart and of tradition and feeling introduced in previous eras.

The scientist and mathematician Chaim Zelig Slonimsky was accepted by all strata of Jewish readers, religious and nonobservant, because in him struggled the old and the new, the mind and the heart, and because he tied together scientific and

maskilic content with old Jewish feeling. One could not sense
the new and the strange in his writings. One might have
thought that his works were a continuation of what was
written in the holy texts. Could the same have been said about
the leading maskilim of that time in other regions?

Solomon Ettinger, the enlightened author of the play *Serkele*,
pokes fun in his fables at the backward masses who from youth
to old age run to recite the Psalms and wail at gravesites at
every opportunity. But the same Solomon Ettinger devoted his
talents to translating the very prayers he mocked into Yiddish.

Dr. Jacob Klatzkin was a Spinoza scholar. He translated
Spinoza's *Ethics* and other works by the Dutch-Jewish philosopher into Hebrew. Dr. Jacob Klatzkin was a thinker who found
himself in Spinoza's realm of ideas. But this same Klatzkin also
composed a diary wherein we read:

"Those who know me would surely not believe that I often
wrap myself in my tallis and tefillin and pray to God with holy
trembling and awesome tears just as my grandfathers and
great-grandfathers used to do. I often rise in the middle of the
night to recite the midnight service with such ecstasy and
weeping that it actually saps all my strength."

Strange and incomprehensible! A Spinoza scholar wrapped
in tallis and tefillin. A Spinoza scholar crying and wailing
during the midnight service that commemorates the Jews'
mourning and the destruction of the Temple . . .

There is no clear-cut line in the Polish-Jewish psyche.

Modern Literature

Contradictions and sharp contrasts are also apparent in the
modern Hebrew and modern Yiddish literature that developed
in Poland. Several examples should illustrate this.

Nachum Sokolow, one of the founders of modern Hebrew
literature, was doubtless influenced by the Haskalah. In everything he wrote one recognizes his desire to enlighten the
reader, to "make him conscious," as they used to say. But at the
same time and in the same breath, Sokolow was also a thor-
ough romantic. A longing trembles in his writing which is

impossible to define. A vague longing for a world which is not real. A vague striving to distances, to lofty worlds, to higher spheres. Sokolow's style along, together with its explicit Haskalah element, comprised a multicolored, ethereal mosaic.

Sokolow was accused of being unsystematic; it was said that he was too densely ramified; that he represented a mishmash of culture and ideas, of content and form. But he came out of the viscera of Polish Jewry. Generations of Jewish culture cried out of him, generations of belief and generations of doubt, generations of learning and generations of innocence, generations of calculation and generations of outpouring of soul.

The writer, poet, and literary critic David Frischman—born in the industrial province of Lodz—came into modern Hebrew literature with his vigorous and stormy essay "Chaos." In this angry and cutting critique, Frischman passionately pleaded that more elements of modern European culture and of European streams of thought enter the life and the spiritual creativity of Judaism. Indeed, it is a fact that he devoted his entire multifaceted literary talent to bringing into Hebrew the masterworks of Shakespeare and Goethe, Byron and Nietzsche, Oscar Wilde and Anatole France. But this resolute European in the Polish-Jewish panorama came into conflict with his own ideas and convictions.

Undoubtedly, his essays excel with their beautiful style, but at the same time they are examples of sharp contradiction. They contain love songs to European aesthetics but are also laments for the disappointment which European culture brings. His writings seethe with bitter satire against life in the Jewish ghetto, but a sentimental exaltation of this lifestyle also emerges from them. In "Concerning Judaism," an essay in which Frischman attempts to analyze the various concepts and methods which had developed in Judaism, he raises himself and the reader up to the extreme of mysticism. Citing Heinrich Heine, who stated that Judaism is "the civilization of the heart," Frischman accents that he believes with utmost conviction that this civilization is an eternal one. Frischman remarks: "Is it possible that I have become a mystic? If you wish it, let it be so. I know that it sounds like a paradox. But let it be, gentlemen. Paradoxes are perhaps the strongest and only truth to which I can cling."

Jacob Cohen, the famous twentieth-century Hebrew poet, was a leading figure in the secular Tarbuth educational movement. He wrote verses that were inspired by the joy of life and the spontaneous laughter of youth. But he also has poems permeated with an explicitly religious spirit. In his poems and dramas, he delves into the depths of the mystery of Jewish existence and of Jewish opposition to all attractions which come from the outside world. In fact, in some of the collections of prayers printed in our time Cohen's deeply religious poems have been included along with prayers that have become sanctified through the course of generations.

Isaac Katzenelson began his creative work in Hebrew poetry as a devotee of Hellenism, of frivolous joy. He interpreted for the Hebrew reader the concepts of Epicurus, the ancient Greek philosopher. But he underwent a moving and profound transformation. Abandoning Epicureanism, he moved closer to the Jewish view and to Jewish feeling with increasing intensity. He became the keener who bemoaned the destruction of the Jewish people in the German gas chambers. These poems of lamentation wherein Katzenelson weeps over the destruction of Polish Jewry during World War II are an expression of the enormous pain that the poet felt during this shattering Jewish tragedy. Katzenelson too shared the fate of his people. He perished in an extermination camp along with his brethren, the tormented Polish Jews.

These same sharp contradictions and cutting contrasts are apparent in no smaller measure in modern Yiddish literature. It would seem that Isaac Leib Peretz is the name that comes first to mind. Which Peretz was the real one—Peretz the intellectual, the most outstanding intellectual in modern Yiddish literature, or Peretz the ardent romantic of modern Yiddish literature? Peretz, the sophisticated poet of the drama *Night in the Old Marketplace,* or the naive singer of folksy tales? Was it the Peretz whose ear was alert to the melodies of his time, or the

Peretz who continued the old melody of the ancient past? Was it the Peretz who was drawn along with the trends of modern socialism, or the Peretz who lived in the sphere of the erstwhile kabbalists and saints? Which Peretz is the authentic one—Peretz the satirist, the mocker, or the Peretz who found no other verses to translate into Yiddish than the poem *Akdomes,* a series of mystical verses which Jews recite in the synagogue on Shavuos? Is it the Peretz who laughed at the Jewish pack of woes, or it is the one who demonstrated that in this pack of woes elements of redemptive exaltation are hidden and proclaimed the Sabbath holiness of the Jewish week?

The truth is that Peretz was a spiritual wanderer like the rest of Polish Jewry. He was drawn along in a direction, swam with it, and at the same time struggled against it. He was an artist of the mind who sought the heart; an artist of the soul who sought the intellect. Isaac Leib Peretz testified about himself: I like the thing and its opposite.

"Between Two Mountains" is the title of his famous story where a dialogue develops between the world of the intellect and the world of fantasy. In actuality, this is a conversation between Peretz and Peretz. That is the meaning of the secretive little dots which abound and multiply in his works. This is the historic dialogue of Polish Jewry.

Contradictions mark all the modern Yiddish literature that flourished in Poland in the twentieth century. It is entirely different from the Yiddish literature that developed at the same time in Russia and Lithuania. In Yiddish literature in Poland there is no wall between realism and romanticism. There is no wall between raw naturalism and dreamy poetry. The realists are romantics. The naturalists are idealists at the same time.

Fliegelman, the hero of Hirsch David Nomberg's drama, was cast between extremes. Fliegelman the intellectual expresses the seeking and the conflicts of the Jewish intellectual in Poland in the twentieth century. Fliegelman's creator, Hirsch David Nomberg, was also cast about between these awful extremes. He was at once a believer and a skeptic, a journalist and a poet, a man of sharp wit and an innocent, a rationalist and a romantic, an analytic dialectician and a dreamy yeshiva bochur.

Itche Meir Weissenberg, the father of modern naturalism in Yiddish literature, introduced into Yiddish the brutal, elemental rabble. Weissenberg portrayed the raw, workaday shtetl. He expressed the natural impulses of the Jewish masses. But the same Weissenberg also sought other and much different ways in his creativity, ways that sharply contrasted with his own naturalistic works and naturalistic world outlook. He wrote books that moved toward visionary and mystical ways, as for example his dramatic poems and his novel, *In the Deep Abyss*. Strange as it may sound, Weissenberg, the theoretician of Yiddish naturalism, also soared upon the wings of mystical fantasy and metaphysical visions. Only under the peculiar conditions of Polish-Jewish creativity could the naturalist have concomitantly been a metaphysician.

Joseph Opatoshu, whose literary career is closely bound up with the years he lived in New York, breathed the air—even in this great North American metropolis—of the distant Polish shtetl where he was born. The spiritual climate of his Yiddish short fiction is the climate of Polish Jewry. Blessed with a powerfully realistic talent, he portrays the life of Polish Jewry in the latter half of the nineteenth century. Joseph Opatoshu depicts the passions of the people who pass through his stories, their struggles, their strivings. It must be added, however, that this realism is interwoven with contradictory elements.

In his novel *In Polish Woods*, which brought him so much fame, Opatoshu brings the reader into the specific and extraordinary environment where merchants and businessmen quote passages of the *Zohar*, where sober people are preoccupied with penetrating the divine mystery and attempt to purify the sinful world of the external husks of impurity; where intelligent Jews and people who by nature have prosaic souls speak ecstatically, using the language of the Kabbalah. This realism fused with the irrational and the mystical is also characteristic of his novel *1863*, where Opatoshu describes the participation of Polish Jews in the Polish uprising against the Russians in that dramatic year.

Even to this day the name of Sholom Asch prompts discussions in the Jewish world. Asch was the subject of sharp debates during his lifetime, and the storm surrounding his personality and his work has not yet stilled decades after his death. It is a fact that Sholom Asch rebelled against the sanctified Jewish tradition and views. He brought much prejudice and false interpretation into his works, which did not express the true nature of Judaism. These prejudices against Judaism are especially depressing in the novels where Sholom Asch represented the origins of Christianity.

However, it should be stressed that another Sholom Asch exists too: the one who depicts the patriarchal and uplifted lifestyle of the Jewish shtetl in Poland with admiration and love, and portrays the gentility and lofty humanity of Hasidic rebbes with reverence. Sholom Asch wrote enthusiastically about the acts of martyrdom in Jewish history and declared that the themes of martyrdom and messianic longing spoke to him most powerfully from the age-old Jewish culture. Sholom Asch was the author of an impressive novel, *Kiddush Hashem*, which deals with the sufferings of Polish Jews during the Cossack uprising under the leadership of the brutal Chmielnicki.

Kiddush Hashem, or santification of God's Name, is also the theme of Asch's other works. Those who want to find consistency or logical thought in Sholom Asch search in vain. There is neither consistency nor logic to be found. There is seeking, there is restlessness. The author says of himself, "I inherited a restless and dreamy heart from my mother. From my father I inherited belief and faith."

Just like the hero of his trilogy, *Three Cities*, wherein he describes Jewish life in the first decades of the twentieth century, Asch constantly, untiringly searched for a path for himself. He sought an orientation in the religious and social confusion of man and Jew. Like his hero, Asch too was drawn and dragged by opposing ideologies. Asch was a writer with an idealistic world outlook, a romantic imagination, and a realistic style. He remained in conflict between the truth of beauty and the beauty of truth.

Israel Stern, master of sophisticated verse in Yiddish poetry, felt closer and more at home with the spiritual world of Hasidism than with the modern world (the period between the two world wars) in which he lived. A great expert in European culture, he was nevertheless more interested in the spiritual exaltation of Reb Nachman of Bratzlav, the eighteenth-century Hasidic zaddik. Israel Stern drew inspiration for his poetry and prose from the personality and works of Reb Nachman. The poet often visited the impoverished shtiebel of the Bratzlav Hasidim in Warsaw. There, with the Hasidim, he prayed and sang ecstatically.

One had the impression that Zusman Segalovitch, a Yiddish writer of romantic prose, worked outside of the spiritual sphere of Polish Jewry. It turned out that he was not interested in the problems of his surroundings. He lived in the world of romantic dreams. But the destruction of Polish Jewry opened up Segalovitch's closed soul. His poems published after the Holocaust are perhaps the most shattering tombstone placed upon the grave of the slaughtered Jews. The poet immerses himself in the essence and the personality of the community of which he himself was part, but where after the destruction nothing was left for the poet. "There" and "Nothing" are the names of two poems of this moving collection in which the extraordinary greatness of a world now gone rises before us.

On the eve of the Second World War Yechiel Lerer published his poem, "My Home," In this wonderful work the author succeeds in depicting the singularity of the Polish-Jewish community: the contradictions, the conflicts between old and new, as well as the entire genius of restlessness and contrast which was unique in Polish Jewry's thousand-year history.

Alter Katzizne was a poet and playwright with radical and leftist tendencies who lived in the period between the two world wars. Surprisingly, he chose the motif of *Kiddush Hashem*, Jewish martyrdom, as a theme for his drama, *The*

Duke. In the eighteenth century, the Polish duke of Vilna, Valentin Potocki, was moved by the religious and ethical fervor of Judaism and converted to the Jewish faith. His daring move triggered a storm of persecution against the duke. The Catholic Church did not forgive him for renouncing Catholicism. He was handed over to the authorities and tortured. But the tremendous torments he suffered did not weaken his resolve to remain a Jew. Duke Potocki breathed out his soul for the santification of God's Name. The martyr's faith of this exalted, righteous convert is the theme of the drama by the left-wing radical poet Alter Katzizne.

The Jewish Press

The Jewish press in Poland played a decisive role in the life and culture of Polish Jewry. It cannot be compared to any other press in the world. Not only did it inform, it led, accompanied, educated; it inspired with motherly warmth; it actively maintained the creative strength of its readers. The Jewish press in Poland was an integral part of the spiritual culture of Polish Jewry.

Daily newspapers and journals appeared in Yiddish, Hebrew, and Polish. But one must admit that fundamentally the press in Yiddish became transformed into an institution of the people. The press reflected the intellectual thirst and the emotional lyricism of Polish Jewry, its dynamism and will, its wit and irrationality. Warsaw's four leading daily newspapers were an integral part of Polish-Jewish history in the twentieth century. *Moment, Haynt, Dos Yiddishe Togblat,* and *Folkszeitung* represented various political and social movements.

Moment was independent, *Haynt* was Zionistic, *Yiddishe Togblat* was Orthodox, and *Folkszeitung* was connected with the Socialist Bund. But despite their various affiliations all were united by a deep feeling of responsibility for the destiny of the community they represented, and by a strong sense of concern for its welfare and exaltation. Their reporters were not only talented journalists but they also included intellectuals, thinkers, historians, and poets.

Several representative names should be cited:

Hillel Zeitlin, philosopher and kabbalist, author of a commentary to the *Zohar*, a man of deep moral concepts whose articles contained the breadth of four thousand years of Jewish history.

B. Yeushzon, the master of the feuilleton which expressed the conflict between understanding and intuition in which Polish-Jewish history found itself. At the same time this beloved journalist published a series entitled "From Our Ancient Treasures," commentaries and explanations of the weekly Torah portion, in which generations of wisdom and wit shimmered in a rainbow of colors.

Other journalists were Noah Prilutsky, a philologist, attorney, communal leader, and man of erudition, who reacted with characteristic style to every problem that emerged; Abraham Mordecai Rogovoy, a writer with Hasidic fervor who translated chapters of Maimonides into Yiddish; S. Y. Stupnitsky, author of a study on Spinoza, whose articles brimmed with love for Polish Jewry; Baruch Shefner, spokesman for the socialist ideology whose yeshiva education often manifested itself in his writings; Joshua Gottlieb, an essayist who knew how to weave philosophic reflections into the problems of daily tumult; Meir Balaban, the great Jewish historian, professor at the Warsaw University, who often felt the need to speak in Yiddish with his readers about historical problems and personalities; Isaac Shipper, a scholar of Polish Jewry's economic development, who was also a historian of the Yiddish theater and a writer with a poetic style.

At a crucial time, this press, which gave voice to the most diverse outlooks, also created a united front against the waves of hatred and false accusations that flourished against Polish Jewry both from governmental circles and from the anti-Semitic parties. I remember that in 1934, when Goebbels, Nazi Germany's propaganda minister, came on an official visit to Warsaw—as a guest of the Polish government—all the Yiddish newspapers ran anti-Nazi proclamations on their front pages. Thus they expressed their pain and anger at Poland's official friendship with those who incited racism. Naturally all the Yiddish papers were confiscated that day by the Polish regime. But the entire land resounded with the dignified and courageous demonstration of Polish Jewry, whose press was a fortress of culture and self-defense.

The Plastic Arts

The face and soul of Polish Jewry were powerfully portrayed in its plastic arts. Polish Jewry produced great painters whose pictures were an artistic contribution to the character and history of Jewish life in Poland. Maurycy Gottlieb, a talented painter who died in the bloom of his life at twenty-three, left an artistic heritage of extraordinary work. In his monumental picture *Jews Praying on Yom Kippur*, Gottlieb expressed the inner world that vibrated in the men and women who gathered in the synagogue on the holy day, offering their prayers to their Creator.

Henech Glitzenstein, the sculptor, painter, and etcher, expressed in a statue, *Messiah*, all the longing and hope of those Jews who went out to meet the Messiah throughout all their lives.

Arthur Szyk revealed in his paintings, miniatures, and illustrations a grandiose and dramatic history of a thousand years of Polish Jewry from the beginning of Jewish life in Poland until its tragic extermination.

Maurice Minkowski immortalized upon canvas the pain and the suffering, the torments and the disappointments, the hopes and the strivings of the Polish Jews. He painted the folk masses in their poverty and their daily toil. But with extraordinary intuition he also captured their souls, which were illuminated with high spirituality.

Samuel Hirschenberg, in his pictures, *Exile, The Eternal Jew*, and other works that made the painter famous the world over, portrayed the despair of Jewish life in Poland, which was interwoven with authentic mysterious belief. In his passionate picture, *Exile*, a mass of homeless victims of a pogrom moves in frozen silence over an endless snow-covered field. An old man moves first; following him are a crowd of women and men, young and old. Several of them are carrying children in their arms, others press the Torah scrolls to their hearts. Children and faith accompany these homeless people on their march— people who in the face of cruelty and murder have not lost their faith in God and man.

In the 1920's, Hillel Zeitlin published a Yiddish weekly entitled *Der Blitz* ("Lightning"). Every issue of this magazine was a manifestation of Polish Jewry's ideational quest. Every issue carried the cry of a mass of people; and in every issue one could feel the enormous effort, dominated by an extraordinary longing for truth, of souls who strove to deepen their intellectual qualities and to penetrate the sphere of intuition.

Der Blitz, which devoted itself entirely to seeking the divine and the human, was an articulate symbol of the spiritual culture of Polish Jewry, for which there is no equal in our history.

The Social Movement

The contrasts were also manifested in social life and in the social activities of Polish Jews. The disheveled, scattered Polish Jewry, which at first glance had so little order and system, succeeded in organizing its communities—which no other major Jewish center, past or present, succeeded in doing.

By the sixteenth century Polish Jewry had already developed an autonomy and built up its autonomous institutions. Jewish autonomy in Poland surpassed even the classic autonomy achieved by the flourishing Jewish community of ancient Babylonia. The Council of the Four Lands—the name given to the united representation of the various Jewish communities of Poland—was in that distant era already representing the Jewish population both in its internal and external forms. Nowhere else in the entire long history of Jewish dispersion did such a strongly organized community representation as the Council of the Four Lands exist.

Indeed, it is amazing. The Polish-Jewish community, which at first glance was torn, split, and searching, remarkably demonstrated its full religious and national unity during its fateful hour. So it was in old Poland, and so it was in independent Poland between the two world wars. At crucial times Polish Jewry succeeded in struggling with moving unity for its human, religious, and national rights.

Those of us who lived in Poland during the pre–World War Two years remember very well the impressive internality which shone out of the multicolored social movement in the Jewish street.

Zionism here achieved a popular character that was lacking in the vision of its creator, Dr. Theodor Herzl. The socialistic Bund was exalted with strong national fervor. And the Agudas Yisrael organization, which modeled itself after the Orthodox Jewish community of Frankfurt, had a revolutionary impulse here.

The Final Act

The extremes met and fused also in the final act of the Polish-Jewish drama. Those of us who no longer find ourselves in the midst of Polish-Jewish culture and no longer move with its dynamism cannot agree to this very day who gave the initiative for the heroic uprising of the Warsaw Ghetto.

To this day we are engrossed in the disputes and cannot decide who had the primary influence in the outbreak of the uprising: the pious Rabbi Menachem Zemba, the Zionist Mordecai Anielewicz, or the Bundist Michael Klepfisz. The truth is that all three had crucial influence.

Just as with its rise, so with its destruction, Polish Jewry remained faithful to itself and to its contradictions.

There, where intellect and mystery developed side by side, they also declined side by side. And when the axe of destruction and extermination was aimed against the deeply rooted Polish-Jewish tree, its intertwined branches remained in their generations-long fusion.

Naturally, there are other traits in Polish-Jewish culture which should be brought to the fore. But in this essay I merely wanted to indicate what strikes me as most essential in Polish-

Jewish life. Upon Polish soil no classic calm was poured out on
Jewish spiritual culture. Restlessness simmered in it—the deep
spiritual restlessness which makes history and which fertilized
Jewish life and Jewish creativity the last five hundred years.
And the effects of this restlessness still have not ceased—even
now after the tragic demise of Polish Jewry.

12

The Jewish People—What Kind of People Are We?

I

WHAT KIND OF PEOPLE are we? Moses said that we are a stubborn nation, stiff-necked and headstrong, and that we are not at all graced with understanding and perception. But the same Moses held that we are a chosen and exalted people, that we possess rare virtues, and that we are the embodiment of holiness. Explicitly: a holy nation.

In talmudic times, Jews considered themselves a very rash people. When something is asked of us, we immediately jump to carry out the request, without considering whether what we are doing is right or not—as if driven by the feverish madness of action. When we were asked to contribute for the holiness of God, we responded generously; and when we were asked to build the golden calf, we joined in the defilement with ardor and ecstasy (Babylonian Talmud, *Shekalin* II).

But one of the talmudic sages, Rabbi Simon ben Lakish, argued that there were no bad Jews at all, for even the least worthy and empty Jew is full of mitzvot and good deeds, just as the pomegranate is packed with seeds (Babylonian Talmud, *Eruvin* 19). The medieval Spanish poet and philosopher Rabbi Judah Halevi assured us in the *Kuzari* that the people of Israel are the most sensitive of all peoples. As a people we have the sensibility of the human heart. But Maimonides, who also grew up in the spiritual environment of Spanish Jewry, sought to persuade us (and himself as well) in all his works that the historic attribute of the Jewish people and of Judaism is their sharp and analytical intellect, their daring and truthseeking intellectuality.

In his interpretations of the Bible, Rashi occasionally accents that the Jews excel in the magnificent and precious trait of modesty and chastity (Commentary to Song of Songs 6:11). But for the famous kabbalist of Safed, Rabbi Isaac Luria (the Ari), crucial was the sense of memory with which the Jews are imbued and which they have to cultivate with all their might, lest it be weakened, God forbid. With this in mind, the Ari ordained that Jews should repeat every morning at least six verses from the Torah which deal with remembering: remembering events and remembering the past that must forge the future.

Samuel David Luzzatto, the profoundly original nineteenth-century philosopher, concluded that the term "merciful sons of merciful fathers" ascribed to the Jews is a faithful mirroring of the Jew: we are thoroughly compassionate. We were a merciful people during biblical times, when our farmer ancestors, after the harvest, left bundles of wheat in the fields for the poor, the widows, and the orphans; and when at sunset they would return the pledged blanket to the needy man so that he could cover himself during the cold night. We were full of compassion in all the lands of our dispersion. We built social institutions under the aegis of the community, the charity, free loans, old-age homes, and aid to the poor were principal concepts and components of Jewish life. Unto this day we are the most compassionate people in the world. We continually address our prayers to the merciful Father in heaven; we stress that in our tradition God is the all-merciful, full of grace and goodness.

However, Saul Israel Horowitz, the Hebrew essayist and journalist, who gave a shattering account of his conscience at the start of the twentieth century, rebutted all this. As a people we are by no means that interested in being compassionate. We were not merciful at the dawn of our history, when we waged wars with dozens of peoples and with ourselves, when tribe was pitted against tribe. The Jews did not show any compassion and mercy to strangers and to kin in later eras; and in the modern period compassion is certainly not a Jewish trait. Horowitz maintained that the idea that Jews are compassionate was an empty illusion created over thousands of years, a claim refuted by the hard, raw facts of history and life.

I must say that this theme, which attempts to offer a solution to the essential character traits of the Jews and of the Jewish people has always intrigued me. It awakened my interest, I remember, as far back as the years prior to World War II, when I lived and was active in the deeply rooted, ramified, and amazingly colorful Jewish community of Poland.

What kind of people are we? During the *Shalosh Seudas,* the Third Sabbath Meal between the *Mincha* and *Maariv* prayers, which we would have in the apartment of Hillel Zeitlin, in Warsaw, our topic of discussion would be the Jewish soul.

Hillel Zeitlin, kabbalist and interpreter of the *Zohar,* was supremely confident that the sparks of holiness always glow in the Jew. At times they blaze up in a divine flame; at times they reveal themselves more subtly—but like the eternal light in the synagogue the spark of holiness burns in the Jewish soul and in the Jewish character.

Nevertheless, those of us who listened with awe to our teacher and master dared to argue with him. In that period of storm and stress in our thinking, we were not thoroughly convinced of the correctness of his argument. We responded: Doesn't Maimonides teach us that though every Jew is capable of reaching the level of Moses, he can also descend to the level of Jeroboam, that traitor and man of intrigues who after King Solomon's death broke the unity of the Jewish nation and led the ten tribes to idolatry? In general, can it be established that in all periods in history the sparks of holiness warmed the Jew? Weren't there also long periods of decline in our march through history, when the Jew as individual and the Jewish people strayed in the desert of immorality?

The angry and shocking addresses of the prophets served as bold arguments, and they blended with the weekday shadows that fell weirdly on our group and added even more wrinkles to the worried and parchment-yellow face of Hillel Zeitlin. We quoted verse after verse from Amos and Isaiah: "Oh, you sinning people, overladen with transgressions; oh, you bad, spoiled children!"

But the character traits of our people were the focus of my attention on other occasions. Once, at a lecture, Dr. Zalman Bichovsky, a well-known and honored figure among Polish Jews, sought to persuade us that from the very beginning the makeup of our nerves has been decisive in the formation of our Jewish character. And we Jews have been nervous and restless and even neurasthenic since the days of Abraham. Such is our nervous system, and so we were formed biologically, and so shall we remain until the days of the Messiah. As a former Talmud student, Dr. Bichovsky quoted the Talmud to support his medical theory. The term "a hasty people," which is found in Tractate *Shabbat* 87, meant a nervous, bustling people who run about a full speed and don't even always know what prompts their momentum. That sort of Jew, whom we well know and whom we perhaps typify, did not make his first appearance in the works of Sholom Aleichem. Our ancestors in Mesopotamia, in Egypt, and in the Land of Israel and Babylonia were this way too.

In the shtiebl, the modest prayer-house, of the Bratzlav Hasidim in Warsaw, the poet Israel Stern once shared with me his deep anguish at the assimilationist trends which had inundated the Jewish street. At that time Israel Stern lived in the spiritual world of Reb Nachman of Bratzlav, about whom he wrote a series of profound essays. And the false, harsh sounds of assimilation also pained him because, as he said, it did not let the true *niggun,* or melody, of generations vibrate in the Jewish soul. And the remarkable Reb Nachman of Bratzlav himself held that the Jewish soul was an exalted and mysterious *niggun.*

The problem of the Jewish character and psyche became

increasingly complex with the passing of years. Dr. Fishl Sch-
neersohn attempted to illuminate this theme and explained it
with much professional expertise. And though I possessed in
my library his psychological research written in Yiddish during
his Berlin residence, and his Hebrew works written in Tel Aviv,
I always considered this matter complex.

My encounters with the Jewish community in Britain during
World War Two accented the sharp and decisive differences
that exist among Jews. The phlegmatic and restrained Jew of
Birmingham or Edinburgh barely recalled the voluble and
homely Jew of Lodz or Lublin. Shmuel Zyglboim, who was
active in the Bund, the Jewish Socialist movement, and who
wandered in misery from Poland to England during the war,
could not find a place for himself in these "strange" surroundings in which he suddenly found himself. Half-seriously, half-
ironically he would complain to me that though he was sure
that the British Jews were Jews—and the proof was that they
could even say a few words in Yiddish—he felt estranged from
them. They were "cold" Jews, lacking the "warmth" of East
European Jews. And Zyglboim would always conclude his
remarks with a deep sigh.

But this knot grew even thicker during my visits to Israel or
my contacts with Jewish communities in Latin America, where
side by side with Ashkenazic communities, Jews of European
origin, there exist numerous communities of Jews who came
from Moslem lands. Is there also a psychological bridge in
addition to the religious-national one between all segments of
our people? Is it only the feeling of destiny that we have in
common or are we identical in every way? In other words, are
our feelings the same? Do we all think the same? Do we all
react exactly the same way?

If the psychology of nations is generally a difficult problem in
science, it becomes even more complex when one attempts to
fathom the Jewish psyche. In our living side by side with
various races and peoples and among fundamentally different
cultures, attributes and traits from the external environment
had to penetrate our people. Surely they exaggerate who claim

that the external environment had a crucial influence on the formation of our character. And those who want to wipe away altogether every difference, every psychological difference, between Jews and non-Jews who live in the same geographic, physical, or spiritual climate also undoubtedly overstate their case.

Such an error was made by the profound thinker Hermann Cohen, who racked his brains to come up with the theory which said that Jews and Germans were one and the same: the same psychology, the same outlook, the same mind, the same heart. The same error was made by many of the present generation of American-Jewish writers and scholars who come up with all kinds of acrobatic discoveries to show that the Jews and gentiles in America possess the same psychology and are kneaded from the same dough. Still, even discounting the many errors and exaggerations that have slipped into all these theories, it cannot be denied that outside influences had an impact on the Jewish psyche.

It is interesting to note that a Jewish scholar, Professor Moritz Lazarus, rector of Bern University in Switzerland and a prolific author on Jewish ethics, was one of the first, if not the very first, in the latter part of the nineteenth century to lay the foundation of this branch of knowledge, which was new at the time: the psychology of nations. Moritz Lazarus considered habit, customs, traditions interesting and important not only as a means of learning a people's culture, views, religion, its past and present, but above all as a means of knowing the people itself.

Naturally, the psychology of the individual and the group is worthy of research; but no less worthy is the character analysis of a people. For individuals and masses in all nations are diverse as to their character traits, and one cannot expect all of them to react the same way in the same situations. If one wants to understand a people it is not sufficient to know its history and its land—but indeed its very soul.

I recently came across a work of the famous Spanish scholar Salvador de Madariaga. Nearly ninety years old and rich in life experiences, Salvador de Madariaga discusses the British, the French, and the Spanish peoples in his 300-page work. On the basis of scholarship and his own experiences, the author seeks to show the inner nature of these three European peoples. Reading this interesting book, one is amazed at how far apart these three peoples are from one another despite their geographic proximity and the fact that they began their history at about the same time.

It is not only that the British are nonchalant and reserved, that the Frenchmen are temperamental, and that the Spaniards have a tendency to mysticism; they are different in general. This difference was crucial in the path that each nation took. Madariaga writes that national character is something that people will not readily admit to. But this does not mean that the psychology of nations ceases to be important and crucial. In olden times the value of national psychology was appreciated, but the scientific methods necessary for such an analysis were lacking.

Homer's poems and Julius Caesar's chronicles sensed intuitively that it was impossible to measure all ethnic groups with the same yardstick. We in this century no longer rely upon assumptions. Studies help us unravel the complexity surrounding national character.

But can we indeed plumb the depths of this problem when it pertains to the character traits of our Jewish people?

II

What kind of people are we Jews? I once spoke about this theme in London with Rabbi Joseph Zevi Hertz, the Chief Rabbi of England. During our conversation he shone with his usual brilliance. He divided peoples into two categories: mature and immature. He said that maturity was not necessarily an attribute that comes with years. One can be an old man and still remain a child; and one can be young and yet possess maturity. This can happen with an individual and also with an entire people. We Jews are undoubtedly the most mature nation on earth.

As a proof of his thesis, Rabbi Hertz introduced the fact that Jews accept criticism. In Judaism, in contrast to other cultures, discussions and arguments about fundamental principles of belief are permitted. The Talmud testifies to the maturity of the Jew, for it contains discussions and debates; opinions are refuted, and in the majority of cases no conclusions are arrived at; there the young pupil has the right to dispute with his teacher and to say simply: "I don't agree with you!"

Throughout the generations we actually have always been in disagreement with one another. In the generation of Maimonides, Rabbi Abraham ben David dared to criticize sharply this giant of Jewish law; within a short while sides formed that defended the differing schools of thought. Finally, even in this instance, the maturity of the people predominated. Recognition was given to both, to the master of Halakhah and also to his merciless critic. Editions of Maimonides were even printed with the critical annotations of Abraham ben David, known as "Critical Remarks." On the very same page you have one view and its exact opposite!

"We have no need to utilize Hegel's philosophical method that thesis and antithesis create synthesis. With Jews thesis and antithesis go hand in hand. And perhaps also because of this," Rabbi Hertz added with a bright, clever smile, "Karl Marx is actually not Jewish in his thinking, because instead of relying on Maimonides and Rabbi Abraham ben David, Marx—the grandson of rabbis—relied on systems that were formulated by Hegel."

However, it should be added that not all of us have been so sure that we are a mature people. A story is told about the Zionist leader Shmaryahu Levin, whose cleverness was equal to that of the Chief Rabbi of England, that he would make bitterly ironic comments about our supposed wisdom and maturity: "Oh, if only this wise and understanding nation would also have a little bit of *sechel*, intelligence."

Apparently even Heinrich Heine could not come to any clear conclusions about the maturity of the Jews, even though he used all his discernment to penetrate to the essence of our thinking and feeling. Some passages in Heine brim with amazement at the maturity of the Jew and the Jewish people; the nations of the world, even the ancient Greeks with all their poets and philosophers, are described as undeveloped children in comparison with Judaism. But there are also places where the skeptic in Heine predominates and the maturity of the Jew is severely questioned.

The astute eye of Isaac Leib Peretz was also incapable of seeing a unified picture. The three Jewish figures represented in his famous short story "The Three Gifts" are undoubtedly an example of sons and daughters of a people that is mature in its thought and deeds, knows precisely the border between life and death, and understands that life is meaningless if the most fundamental human principle becomes weakened and compromised. But not all the characters that Peretz depicted possess the attributes of those who appear before us in "The Three Gifts." *At Night in the Old Marketplace* shows that the perceptive Peretz was not always skillful in all his works in probing the Jewish soul, and that he too found it a great puzzle. And indeed it is a fact that the theme which intrigues me and the reader has constantly sparked great curiosity. For generations people wanted to tear away the veil of Jewish character by force. They sought the answer by comparing us to other living creatures, for instance the dove. Just as the dove stretches out its neck for slaughter, so does the people of Israel. Just as the dove never changes its mate once it becomes acquainted with him, so too the people of Israel. Once the Jews recognized their God, they did not wish to change him (*Song of Songs Rabbah* 1). We were compared to fruits and plants and nuts. If you remove one nut from a pile, all the others start moving; so too the people of Israel. When one Jew is beaten, all Jews feel the pain at once (*Song of Songs Rabbah* 6).

We were compared to liquids. We are like olive oil. All liquids are mixable except oil. The Jewish people too do not let themselves blend with other nations. When liquids are mixed one cannot be differentiated from the other, except oil: no matter how much you mix it, it always stays on top. So too the people of Israel *(Exodus Rabbah* 33). The nineteenth-century Hungarian sage known as the Chasam Sofer was said to have remarked that we are like an egg. The longer we are cooked the harder we become and the more durable.

And when no conclusions could be reached about one attribute which is characteristic of our people, it was said that three traits are actually characteristic of Jews: we are merciful, shy, and benevolent (Babylonian Talmud, *Yebamot* 79). And despite all the parables and comparisons and contentions, when no one trait could be found acceptable to all, they began to accent the contradiction and the contrast. They said that in the nature of the Jew and the Jewish people the contrast was crucial: "Jews are like the sand on the ground and the stars of the sky. When they fall, they fall to the sand; and when they rise, they ascend to the stars" (Babylonian Talmud, *Megillah* 17).

But contrast, too, did not prove to be the most important trait in the Jewish soul. One of the talmudic sages, who distinguished himself with his clear and logical approach to people and events, gave up on attempting to be precise when the Jewish character was discussed, and said only: "Jews, they are strange in their deeds" (Babylonian Talmud, *Moed Katan* 16).

Two thousand years ago, in his history of the Jewish war with Rome, Josephus Flavius wrote that Jews, more than any other people, worry about their children, and that Jewish parents are more capable than the Greeks or the Romans of sacrificing themselves for the good of their children. One thousand years later, Saadia Gaon noted that the fundamental attribute of the Jewish people is revealed in their thirst for learning and in their immersion in the spheres of spirituality and thought. Albert Einstein expressed himself in similar fashion; he thought that the mark of a Jew is to appreciate the importance of Torah and culture and to strive for education.

However, in our prayers during the Days of Awe it is obvious that we are optimists above all. We believe in man. We believe in the triumph of justice. We believe that evil will vanish like smoke and that the power of wickedness and rage will no longer dominate the earth. According to the Rosh

Hashanah and Yom Kippur prayer book, we not only have faith in the Divine, but we have believing natures altogether. We believe in man and in the system of justice that will be created in the relationships between people. Even in the death camps of Auschwitz and Treblinka, Jews expressed their confidence that man was basically good and that he can and would become better.

Four thousand years of Jewish creativity have surely amassed an enormous literature about the Jewish psyche and Jewish character. Aaron Kaminka, a great connoisseur of Judaism and Hellenism, held that the will to live is characteristic of the Jew. He noted that it is a false contention that the Hellenes, the builders of Greek civilization, bore within themselves the thirst for life. It was the Jews who truly thirsted for life and enjoyed and enriched themselves with the blessings of life. We love life, we close our eyes to negative attributes, and even at the brink of decline our striving to live and survive remains. Max Nordau, who probed the psyche of man, thought that the Jews were a mixture of realists and idealists, of sober reckoners and romantic dreamers. He said that our thirst for life is coupled with misty illusions that actually remove us from the natural, primordial strength pulsating within us.

The difficult circumstances in which the Jewish people find themselves today in the State of Israel bring to mind a remark made by Balaam, the magician from Midian and also an inspired poet. When he and the king of Moab looked down from a mountaintop at the Jewish encampment, he said of the Jews: "A nation that dwells alone"—a people that remains lonely and forlorn among the nations. And when one recalls with amazement the Israeli army's heroic freeing of the captives in Uganda in 1976, the talmudic phrase "Jews are the boldest and most daring of all nations" (Babylonian Talmud, *Beitzah* 25) becomes vibrantly relevant.

And so the question posed at the beginning of our essay, and now repeated at its conclusion, remains unanswered. What are we? What kind of people are we? But perhaps *asking* is the most fundamental trait of the Jewish character. Our first steps in history were made with questions. According to Genesis, the dialogue between God and man began with the question: Where are you? In Abraham's first lengthy conversation with God, he asked Him one question after another and turned to him in amazement: "Will the Judge of the entire world not deal justly?"

One huge and shocking question mark is the Book of Job. And even in the Book of Psalms, whose tender lyrical prayers would presumably contain all answers, one finds difficult, anguished questions. "Why, O God, have you forsaken me? Why?" asks the psalmist at the dawning of the day. The prophet Amos specifically demanded of us that we ask: "Seek me and live!" Seek and ask, and you find a motive and a sense in life. And Jeremiah outlined the most bizarre and sharpest conundrums: "Why do the wicked prosper, and why are all those who deal treacherously secure?"

Generations of Jews have constantly asked questions. They ask, they refute, they inquire, they probe. The concept of questioning has penetrated the Jewish psyche. But for some questions the answer is postponed for the messianic era, when Elijah the prophet will respond. We have taken the talmudic word *teyku*, which stands for an unsolved problem, and have made a Hebrew anagram out of its letters, stating that Elijah will answer all our questions and problems.

Our task is to ask. Even those who never studied Talmud and commentaries and never absorbed the melody of the famous talmudic question "What does this imply?" or "What can we learn from this?" were captivated by this melody and mode and let themselves be led by it. The poet and short-story writer Abraham Reisin took this question and introduced it into a folksong. And even though there is a great gap between the simple folk poetry of Abraham Reisin and the sophisticated symbolic tales of Franz Kafka, they are both thoroughly Jewish. Characteristic of both is a sense of wonder, of questioning. And since time immemorial the great and deeply human question, "What does this teach us?" has been incised into the Jew.

13

Sukkos: An Insight into the Jewish Psyche

I

MUCH HAS BEEN written about the Jewish holidays. Their meaning, their development throughout the ages, the various forms they have assumed in the lands of Jewish dispersion, and their place in Jewish thought have all been discussed. The religious, national, social, and ethical values which they embody have been described. People have frequently expressed amazement at the fact that the Jewish holidays have maintained their intrinsic character throughout thousands of years and have accompanied the Jew under the most diverse circumstances. But very little attention has been paid to the psychology of the Jew as it is reflected in the holidays.

Treatments of this aspect of the theme are few. We have Chaim Greenberg's profound essays whose theme is Sabbath and holiday; Berl Katzenelson's perceptive remark in his book *At the Test* about the folk character that emerges in our days of joy and sadness; and Isaac Leib Peretz's classic Hasidic folktales that deal with holidays. Aside from these, I cannot think of any attempts made in our modern Hebrew or Yiddish literature to find a portrait of the Jew himself in the Jewish days of celebration.

The truth is that the Jewish holidays were carefully pre-

served in our folk memory. They became a component of the
Jewish tradition, and of the Jewish essence and being, mostly
because the Jew saw himself in them, and through them was
able to look into his own heart and analyze his inner world.
Thus, when dealing with the theme of a Jewish holiday or fast-
day, we should also stress, in addition to the holiday's religious
or national intent and the historical event that gave birth to it,
the psychological traits of the Jew that engraved themselves
into each of his days of joy and sorrow, giving them substance,
form, and expression.

In one of his essays Chaim Greenberg writes: "Had the Jew
not felt Sabbathly festive to his core, he could not have produced the Sabbath and would not have been capable of receiv-
ing the Sabbath as a divine gift. . . A symbol is not a concocted
or overly clever sign, and a ceremony is not a calculated
procedure. . . A symbol is a sign which represents a truth that
lives in us."

Berl Katzenelson comes to the same conclusion when he
states that a deep instinct for freedom surely lies deep in the
heart of the people who at the dawn of their history could
create a masterwork like Passover and transmit it from generation to generation. For instance, Tisha B'Av, the Fast of the
Ninth of Av, was doubtless able to maintain its specific character of mourning and folk pain because in it the Jew saw the
destruction not merely of the Holy Temple but of his own
surrounding world.

Actually, this is the leitmotif that threads its way through the
holiday tales of Peretz. If we take the familiar story "If Not
Higher" and ask ourselves whether the Penitential Days inspired the rebbe of Nemirov to assume the role of Vasil the
woodchopper, who lights the oven in the cold room of the poor
ill widow, or whether it is the zaddik of Nemirov who gives
such a lofty human character to the Penitential Days because
every day of the year is actually a penitential day—the response to this question would be rather complex.

We are left with the impression that the Litvak in Peretz's
story is amazed and shocked at the end not only because he

has discovered what the rebbe does during the night of the penitential prayers but also, and perhaps primarily, because the rebbe's tender and moving deed makes it transparently clear why the Jewish spirit and the days of penitential prayers have become so inextricably bound up during the generations and how the Jew seeks the path to heaven.

The Aggadah literature—that is, the Midrash created during the talmudic period, or those passages in the Talmud which do not deal with law but are exalted with the gentle charm of tender poetry—long ago called attention to the identicality of the Jew and his days of joy and sadness. In the Midrash and Aggadah, the Jew and his Sabbath and holidays are represented as a destined couple in love, as a bride and groom. The Jew and his holidays yearn for each other, make demands and converse with each other, complain occasionally, and even create scenes of reciprocal envy, but finally reconciliate and weave hopes and dreams in common.

The community of Israel acts and lives, laughs and cries during its holy days. And the religious or national days of remembrance that appear in the Halakhah as an institution imposed upon the Jew emerge in the Aggadah literature from the depths of the Jewish soul and Jewish feeling. The holiday does not come from the outside but from within.

The Aggadah also raises the question that even earlier in biblical times perturbed the prophet Zechariah: would the Jewish holidays perpetually remain in the Jewish calendar as part of the Jewish way of life, or would they disappear from our folk memory with the march of generations and changes in our circumstances? If in biblical times this question already sparked differences of opinion and debates, then here in the Aggadah the decision comes clearly and distinctly: how can a Yom Kippur or even a Purim be rescinded and torn out of the folk tradition, if Jewish holidays are not only an expression of history or of law entrenched among the people, but they *are* the people themselves?

The mystical poem we sing today to welcome the Sabbath, the famous *Lecha Dodi* by Rabbi Solomon Alkabetz, states:

Come, my friend, to meet the bride;
Let us welcome the Sabbath.

The author, a sixteenth-century mystic poet from Safed, actually repeats the refrain used fifteen hundred years earlier in talmudic times by Rabbi Yannai: "Come in Sabbath bride, enter bride."

That is why I am so attracted to the brief, brilliant, and seemingly offhand remarks scattered in Hasidic literature and Hasidic folklore that pertain to our days of joy and sorrow. As a movement that blossomed out of the heart of the Jewish folk masses, Hasidism intuitively penetrated into the most hidden chapters of the Jewish psyche. A remark of Reb Nachman of Bratzlav or Reb Bunim of Pshishkhe plumbs the essence of Passover or Shavuos more than thick volumes of historical research.

The Baal Shem Tov considered Rosh Hashanah a mirroring of the state of the spirit of Chaikl, the town water carrier, who dragged heavy barrels of water up high steps. The full impact of the sanctity of Yom Kippur, in all its scope and depth, was first felt by Reb Levi Yitzchok of Berditchev when he could not find one Jew in the synagogue who had become drunk during the meal just before the onset of the fast. For Hasidism and its teachers, the holiday and the fast-day are not so much a window of the *Shulchan Aruch* as a window from which Berl the tailor gazes.

Note, if you will, the ideological differences between Maimonides and Judah Halevi, not only in their dissimilar interpretations of divinity or the Jewish spiritual drama, but also in their special approaches to the Jewish holidays. For Maimonides, the master of philosophic thought and teacher of law, the holidays are a component of Jewish thought; they are building blocks in the structure of Jewish Halakhah. But for Judah Halevi, the poet of subtle feelings, the singer of Jewish longings of the heart, the holidays are principally "signs and symbols" in which the inner world of the Jew is revealed. It was Judah Halevi who said that the Jews are like the heart of the world. Following his thought pattern one might add: and the holidays are the heart of the Jewish people.

II

We shall now focus on the festival of Sukkos. Naturally, we realize that this holiday has a national-historic motif. It reminds us of the *sukkos,* or booths, which our ancestors erected many years ago in the desert, where they wandered after their Exodus from Egypt. We also know that the festival has an agricultural character. It reminds us of those times long past when an overwhelming majority of our people, then living in the Land of Israel, was connected with agriculture. At this time of the year, with the onset of autumn, the farmers would gather up the grain from the fields and the fruits from the orchards and take them into the house or into granaries. Therefrom stems the other name of Sukkos—the Harvest Festival. But is this *all* that Sukkos signifies and represents?

The truth is that even in times past Sukkos achieved the highest rung among the sacred festivals and holy days that our people were bidden to celebrate and observe. One might assume that Passover, the holiday of spring and freedom, or Shavuos, when the first fruits ripened and the folk memory returned to the divine revelation at Sinai, would be first and foremost among the festivals. One might also assume that the Jew's attention would be dominated by a serious and lofty day like Yom Kippur.

But this is not what happened. Our classic sources testify that Sukkos was the primary festival. The word "holiday" or "the holiday" in our ancient religious texts, the Bible and the Talmud, refers most often to the familiar festival of Sukkos. And furthermore, Sukkos is also described as "the festival of the Lord." Even if historical studies attest to the popularity of Sukkos among all strata of the people and describe its place in our religious literature with various scholarly motifs, and even if certain books argue about why Sukkos has so deeply penetrated the consciousness of the individual and the community, they still do not reveal the entire profound truth about the Sukkos phenomenon.

More light is shed on this festival by a prophetic vision in which Sukkos takes on an extraordinary meaning. More than the other traditional days of the Jewish year, Sukkos—as seen by the prophets—emerges as an event of universal import. In Zechariah's vision, which portrays the spiritual mountain which humanity will ascend in the future, Sukkos also captivates the non-Jewish peoples. In days to come, according to this prophecy, the nations of the world will come up to Jerusalem, where they will celebrate Sukkos along with the Jews.

The attempt by several commentators to explain the presence of the nations in Jerusalem at Sukkos on the basis of climate (because on Sukkos we pray for rain), or because of the special Sukkos sacrifices, robs the vision of Zechariah of its lofty humanitarian fervor and of its heavenly Jerusalem concept. Therefore, it is not very convincing. The person who comes closest to the prophetic idea is the author of a liturgical poem found in the Sukkos prayer book. He states that Sukkos by itself is as important as all other Jewish laws, ideas, and institutions combined.

This view was expressed even earlier by the ancient thinkers and poets who wrote the Midrashim. They held that the Messiah would come for the sole purpose of making the nations of the world worthy of fulfilling the *mitzvah* of *sukkah*— a rather bizarre-sounding idea. Even if we remove from this midrashic phrase its poetic hyperbole and folkloristic style, it still means that our ancient thinkers and poets did not consider Sukkos only an agricultural festival and a commemoration of a distant event, but regarded it quite explicitly as the highest ideal of Jew and man's redemption. And here we come to what Sukkos actually represents: the belief in the unseen values of the spirit.

When we as a people stepped into the arena of history, mighty and glorious civilizations were already in existence. Mesopotamia and Egypt were primary cultural centers in ancient times; and during the era when Jewish culture was active, other significant civilizations were also developing. It would be superfluous to note here the Greek and Roman imprint upon history. One trait, however, was common to all the other ancient civilizations: the belief in that which could be seen and touched. The belief in gods who possess bodies and form. The veneration for everything that is substantive and material. And this glorification of materiality naturally led to all kinds of consequences: to the adulation of the fist and of raw physical strength.

In sharp contrast to all other ancient civilizations, Judaism aspired to lift men up to spiritual heights. Judaism teaches that even though one's eyes cannot behold everything, the invisible world of ideas is nonetheless real. God, who cannot be touched by hands, is no less real than the idols. The unseen redeemer who is destined to change the face of humanity must become part of our striving and sensibility more than the false, materialistic messiahs to whom people bowed. And the just world that will emerge at the end of days, in the distant or perhaps even the near future, is no less possible and attainable than actual reality.

"For man shall not see Me and live" states the biblical teaching. Man cannot see everything with his eyes. Seeing must not be the criterion with which he judges values and phenomena. Indeed, the words which God addressed to Abraham, the first bearer of Jewish thought, were "Lift up your eyes and see." In order to see things, one must look up. This remark contains the essence of Jewish teaching. An apt comment appears in "On Two Thresholds"—which is, perhaps, Ahad Ha'am's best and most incisive essay. Had someone come to him wanting to learn about Judaism while standing on one leg (in other words, to discover the crux of Jewishness in one phrase), Ahad Ha'am would have replied: "Make unto thee no statue or image." All of Judaism's teachings are contained in this stringent prohibition against serving idols and images and believing in material things.

Sukkos embodies this trait, which became essential for Judaism and for the Jew at the very beginning of Jewish history, and which, during millennia of experiences, became increasingly bound up with the Jewish psyche.

III

Sholom Aleichem has an unforgettable description of Sukkos. And we must remember that Sholom Aleichem plumbed the depths of the Jewish soul as few other modern Yiddish artists had done. He describes what a magnificent experience Sukkos was in his childhood. Indeed, what was the sukkah? A little hut of hammered boards whose thin walls the wind blew and whose sparse roofing of branches and leaves kept falling down. Here the lit candles sputtered and fluttered precariously under imminent threat of being extinguished and leaving the sukkah in darkness. It was a frail, hunched sukkah of Jewish poverty. But the child Sholom Aleichem did not see it this way; and it was not seen as such by the shtetl. For him it was a palace, a wonderful, magnificent palace. And within it sat no mere human beings, but princes, members of the royal household.

Oh, you'll say, this is just Sholom Aleichem's fantasy of Kasrilevke, a little story for children! But consider for a moment: Have not generations of adult, sober, intelligent Jews looked at the sukkah with the same ardent eyes? From generation to generation went the saying that during the week of Sukkos one must move into this temporary dwelling. And let no one be concerned, it was emphasized, that the sukkah is fragile and unstable, open to rain and wind which penetrate it, bend it, and cast it to all sides, and that occasionally stones are cast into it, for external weakness is often a sign of inner strength.

Throughout the generations the sukkah was always decorated, adorned with greenery, flowers, and carpets, and decorated with inscriptions. The mighty Jewish past and the wonderful vision of the future were spread in the sukkah. The sukkah developed as a symbol of Jewish life, of Jewish joy and pain, of Jewish hope and struggle. It became a sign of the Jew. The most variegated meanings, secrets, and significations were read into it. Our books never grew weary of repeating that the sukkah was not as plain and simple as one might assume. It was the sukkah of King David. It was the tabernacle of peace, the sukkah of freedom. The sukkah represented the clouds of glory, the clouds of God's Divine Presence. It is the shield of belief. It is the skin of the Leviathan, the sukkah of messianic times.

We should and we must invite guests into the sukkah—the finest and most important guests. They are the great figures in Jewish history, but they belong to the sukkah panorama, and they will willingly accept the extended invitation. Just like you and me, they were able to lift themselves out of the gray reality that existed in their times and live in a concocted world of ideal and fantasy. The long-established tradition of inviting guests to the sukkah tells us more about the Jewish spirit than numerous scholarly studies written about our people. Day after day, as soon as we cross the threshold of the sukkah we invite these important guests. We greet them with: "Come in dear guests; noble and holy guests, please be seated. You're invited to the meal." Who are they exactly? The ancient fathers of our people, its teachers, its king: Abraham, Isaac, Jacob, Joseph, Moses, Aaron, David.

A children's game? Religious naiveté? No. A wonderful expression of the folk's ability to lift itself up on the wings of spirit. A rare talent of looking with the soul's eyes and perceiving the sense of its phenomena. When Reb Mendel of Kotzk was once told of a Hasid who said that he always saw all seven invited guests in his sukkah, Reb Mendel replied: "If he believes that these guests come to visit him in the sukkah, then he *does* see them, for one sees more with faith than with eyes."

Among all the answers offered to the age-old question as to how we were able to survive the horror and pain of long, dark, and terrible eras, there is much truth to the assertion that we survived difficult times because we were capable of lifting ourselves above the bitter present to live with a dream of the future. Beyond the dark clouds we saw the clear, blue sky.

When stark brutality surrounded us we sustained ourselves with our belief in man. Even when waves of wild hatred raged, we were confident that in the end wickedness would vanish like smoke. The sanctity that hovers in our parchments was more persuasive for us than the rule of tyranny which held us in its vise. Even our obstinate observance of the agricultural character of our holidays during the many centuries when we were completely separated from the land, even our stubborn carrying of the *lulav* and *etrog*, the palm branch and the citron, at times when we were forbidden to plant a tree or sow a seed—even this was a part of our sukkah psyche.

Despite their physical proximity to us, our neighbors who embittered our days and nights remained distant from our concepts. The ruler in whose land we lived and wept was not the sort of power figure with whom our imagination could identify. Our type of folk leader was Moses, a modest, shy stammerer, who pursued justice throughout all his life. The king under whose rod we sighed was not our ideal ruler. Our ideal king was always David, who with a small stone defended himself against the giant Goliath, and who in his moving Psalms sang of human loneliness and of his thirst for spiritual and ethical exaltation.

I would say that from the sukkah of Jewish dreams so many figures have emerged to give our history impulse and direction. Here is the straying shepherd Amos, who dares to deliver his message to the rich and mighty of his generation who would dishonor the principles of justice and morality. And here is Hillel, who with his idea of brotherly love attempted to demolish the brutal civilizations of his time. And here is Rabbi Yochanan ben Zakkai, who believed that with the spirituality emanating from the modest seat of learning in Yavneh, the people would outlive the Roman Empire. And here is the Baal Shem Tov, who in a village lad's fife heard the highest expression of prayer which can split the heavens asunder.

And in the Jewish drama of recent generations this sukkah family—seemingly spun out of dreams but nevertheless real—has grown even more.

Wasn't Theodor Herzl such a sukkah figure? He requested audiences with princes. He ran to state ministers. He spoke in the name of a nonexistent state which was in the process of becoming and which lived only in his fantasy and in the will and the imagination of the people.

Perhaps because my last meeting with Shmuel Zyglboim took place on Sukkos in the sukkah of a mutual friend in London, this representative of Polish Jewry during the years of German Nazi terror is even more firmly bound up in my mind with the sukkah psyche I am discussing. This took place in the horrible times of World War Two. In our conversation, we touched upon various questions relevant at the time for the world and for our people. And no matter which topic we discussed, Shmuel Zyglboim constantly returned to the funda-mental theme which obsessed him and which a couple of months later saddened his soul: the anguished fate of Polish Jewry.

Actually Shmuel Zyglboim was not with us during that conversation. Before his eyes stood the masses of Jews from Warsaw and Lodz, from Lublin and Vilna, who at that time were treading their last path. In our talk we mentioned the sukkahs that Jews in Poland would erect in the courtyards of their Jewish poverty. Episodes that had engraved themselves into our memory were recalled, when I told Zyglboim what I considered lofty and symbolic in the sukkah tradition: the decision to lift oneself beyond the painful reality; and the talent to construct wondrous ideals and to spin hopes, despite ad-verse circumstances, that a new man would arise out of the ruins. Shmuel Zyglboim liked this interpretation. Above all this seemed to him to be the psychological trait of Polish Jewry throughout all periods of its history. The little sukkah hut, he added, evidently helped Polish Jews to construct their magnifi-cent castles of belief and hope.

Many of our sacred books call us the sukkah of the world. We are a people that, from its beginnings, has ascribed importance to the substance of spirituality, in the belief that it is longer-lasting than concrete and tangible values. Now, when from all

sides the axe rises above us against the sukkah elements which
we have brought into human culture, and calls are heard that
only raw reality and power are decisive, surely it is worthwhile
to renew what is essential for our psyche. The most fitting
reading material for the Jewish spirit at this time is perhaps
chapter 14 of the prophet Zechariah, which uplifts and inspires
with its heavenly Jerusalem fervor: "And the nations that will
remain in those days will come up to Jerusalem in order to
celebrate the holiday of Sukkos."

14

Karl Marx's Jewish Problem

I

It may be just a curiosity—or perhaps a tragedy; but it is undoubtedly a phenomenon that deserves consideration. The thinkers who placed their stamp upon our era were in the main either Jews or descendants of Jews, and they introduced ideas that were influenced by Judaism and by Jewish tradition. But instead of stressing that these ideas were inspired in considerable measure by Jewish tradition and to a great extent flow from Jewish sources, these thinkers disdained the spiritual treasure which enriched them; moreover, they falsely interpreted Jewish teachings and distorted the image of Judaism and of the Jewish character.

The thesis developed by Henri Bergson is repeated with different variations in many modern schools of thought. And this French-Jewish philosopher's contribution is certainly very significant. He stressed the meaning of creative intuition in man's dynamic progress. He showed in his philosophic essays, whose prose is actually intoxicating poetry, that by means of stunning creative intuition man is able to escape the confines of dull and narrow mundaneness and open the gates to godliness and higher humanity.

At a time of superficial enthusiasm for anything pragmatic and average, Bergson brought new enthusiasm into religious thought, which was considered petrified by the people of the twentieth century. He called attention to the fact that miracles did not happen only in the far-off time of Creation and that man himself was one unceasing and constant wonder. For revelation is a process that is constantly in our midst, and we alone, no matter who we are, are a part of this revelation.

Henri Bergson came from a fine Polish-Jewish family that had emigrated to France. One of his grandfathers, Reb Shmuel Zbitkover, played a significant role among Polish Jews in the twilight of the eighteenth century. His grandmother was the famed Temerl, who devotedly and enthusiastically supported Hasidism when the budding movement had to defend itself against critics and opponents. One does not have to rummage too deeply in Bergson's philosophy to find the influence of the Jewish heritage, which came to him from different sources.

In our kabbalistic books, and even earlier in the Aggadah scattered in talmudic literature, man's partnership with God at the very beginning of Creation is indicated. Naturally, this powerful mystical structure is based upon the short, thought-filled Eighth Psalm, which expresses amazement at the divine inspiration inherent in man. The sacred book of the Kabbalah, the *Zohar*, is not only a product of creative intuition, its task and goal are to bring us all into a sphere of profound wonder which began in the distant past with Adam and Eve and with which we are willy-nilly continually involved.

Rabbi Moses ben Nachman (Nachmanides)—in a generation that had become drunk with the illusion that one can proceed through life with rationality—never grew weary of warning that when a person assumes that he has torn away the veil of the great secret with which man was created, he stumbles into an endless maze in the fearsome desert of thought.

Needless to say, the mystical poetry that flourished in the sixteenth century under the clear blue skies of Safed is a moving expression of the gnawing longing for infinite secrecy that hovers around us and within us. The Sabbath *zemiros*, or table hymns, composed by the Safed kabbalist Rabbi Isaac Luria, even lifted up the static Sabbath table from its place and transformed it into a dynamic ethereal experience in the garden of mysticism. "Static" and "dynamic" are Bergsonian terms, of course, and Rabbi Isaac Luria used different concepts to bring the world of the *Zohar* to life. But basically their essence is one and the same: the man of flesh and blood, whose powers of thought are limited, and who is bound to time and place, carries within himself the hovering spirit of infinity.

One century before Bergson, indeed at the time when his grandmother, the aforementioned Temerl, was alive, Reb Nachman of Bratzlav was telling tales to his congregation of Hasidim. In his own fashion he showed that in our world the border between fantasy and reality is effaced; that the depths of mysticism pulsate even in the gray mundaneness of our daily toiling; and that even when we stride from border to border, from imagination to reality, we find ourselves constantly in the sphere of incomprehensible mystery.

Curiously, however, Henri Bergson held that Judaism is "dry," "cold," "sober," and that even if the prophets of old had ascended to the mystery of God and man, they found no followers among Jews in later periods. According to Bergson, it was the Catholic faith that ascended the high rungs of mysticism. The Catholic thinkers probe into the depths of mystery.

Whether Henri Bergson converted or remained officially a Jew is unimportant. Concerning this, too, there are various theories. What is crucial, however, is the theme which we are treating—the thoroughly false interpretation which he gave to Jewish spirituality. With just a little effort, Bergson could have perceived that Judaism was at all times deeply involved in the mystery of heaven on earth and that the mysticism he so glorified in the Catholic Church actually penetrated there via Jewish sources.

The ever unsatisfied soul-longing which Bergson considered essential in man's personality did not cease in our creativity with the close of the Bible. One can say that it fills the entire Jewish book of generations. Even the rationalism of Saadia Gaon and of Maimonides is somewhat exaggerated. Surprisingly, when they encountered problems and questions for which they had no solution, they unhesitatingly depicted the great role which intuition assumes in the process of life.

Ezekiel's vision of the heavenly chariot gazes out from every page of our past. It is also a component of our present, and, very likely, of our future too. This is the chariot that is harnessed to four thousand years of Jewish history. It is strange, then, that Bergson noticed the fluttering wings of mystery in Catholicism and did not even feel that the mysticism that had captivated him was in essence but a fragment of Jewish Kabbalah.

The elements of Jewish thought to be found in Freud's theories are a subject for discussion. Does the sharp light with which Freud penetrated man's subconscious, the complex world of dreams he attempted to make familiar and explain, have any connection to the teachings of Jewish spirituality?

A Jewish scholar, David Bakon, in a book which appeared about twenty years ago in Princeton, attempted to show that Freud's theories were greatly influenced by the teachings of Judaism. Even if such a view is somewhat exaggerated, still it cannot be denied that analysis, the inner world of man, the struggle between the conscious and the subconscious, the drive to know oneself, and the gnawing dissatisfaction with oneself, had already found their magnificent expression in the ancient sources of Judaism and draw their inspiration from it.

In a chilling dialogue that took place five hundred years prior to Socrates, the prophet Nathan has a dramatic encounter with King David. He forces him to cut his conscience with a sharp knife and expose his inner, secretive experiences. Three hundred years prior to Plato, Isaiah and Hosea probed deeply into the human psyche. The attempt to interpret in an allegorical fashion the sentiments and emotions that pulsate within us and to look for a symbolic explanation for the ancient chronicles of history which have been passed on from generation to generation—a method which Freud utilized with so much subtle sophistication in his research—has to be ascribed to the Jewish thinker of Alexandria at the time when that Egyptian city was the capital of Hellenism. It was Philo who introduced into philosophy the symbolic interpretation of religious experience. Symbol, he argued, is basically realistic, and it bears witness to reality even more than reality itself.

One must admit that Freud brought the symbol out of the mythological or religious framework and fit it into the all-encompassing human psyche. But Philo also deals with the human soul, its striving and longing, its restlessness and anguish, its song and tears. It is hard to believe that Freud, who in his youth moved in circles that were involved with Jewish tradition, should not have known anything about the enormous influence of Jewish thought upon world culture. The very attempt to place man in the center of all investigation was thoroughly Jewish.

The Bible is not a scholarly study about God. The Bible is in no way similar to the ancient Greek works, which are full of descriptions of gods and demigods who multiply in the mountains, in the forest, and in the seas. Nor is the Bible comparable with Christian theology, which to this very day has not yet reached a conclusion about the nature of God. The Bible is dedicated to man, his struggles and achievements, his wanderings and return, his descents and ascents. Even the dialogue between body and spirit—and it is such a dialogue that Freud's psychoanalysis strives to achieve—was introduced into European literature by the medieval Spanish-Jewish poet Solomon ibn Gabriol. In a moment of self-analysis, Freud indeed admitted that the challenge to probe into the abyss of man's psyche came to him from Judaism. It was perhaps the Nazis, who forced him to flee Vienna in the years of the raging anti-Jewish bacchanale, who prompted Freud to make this introspective statement. Not only did the Nazis consider the creator of the theory of psychoanalysis a Jew, but they considered the entire system a "product of the Jewish spirit."

And yet—and in this case we once again encounter the bizarre oddity—Sigmund Freud, who uncovered the subtlest nuances of man's soul, was at the same time the author of a labored and clumsy theory that monotheism—which for thousands of years had been considered originally Jewish—was born among the Egyptian people.

According to Freud, when the Jewish slaves were building Pithom and Raamses in Egypt for the Pharaohs, along with the clay and bricks they also kneaded out the faith in an unseen god, which was an Egyptian product. Moses was not the son of Amram and Jocheved, but an Egyptian prince whose personality and education were shaped by the Egyptians. It was Pharaoh's people who were capable of formulating the vision of a one and only God, but not the children of Abraham, Isaac, and Jacob. Freud's work *Moses and Monotheism* is full of absurdities that are controverted by history and psychology. It must be regarded as one of the dark shadows cast upon the Jewish soul of the founder of psychoanalysis.

If one has the choice of being a firm opponent of the materialistic theory upon which Karl Marx builds his revolutionary ideas, one also has the choice of believing that Marx overstressed the significance of economic factors in society's historical processes. But one dare not deny that many of Marx's intentions, especially his passionate call to create a new and just social order, are rooted in the historic Jewish storm and stress against wickedness and oppression. The demand to implant justice in man's dealings with his fellow man has, in the words of Heinrich Heine, a ringingly Jewish accent.

The Five Books of Moses long ago proclaimed the principle of human equality, and that text trumpets forth the protest against injustice and demands just treatment of the poor and defenseless. All men have the right to enjoy the blessings of life; this fundamental truth, which prompted Marx to take up his battle on behalf of the abused working masses, had already, at the dawn of Jewish history, been engraved into the tablets of the Ten Commandments at Sinai. So was the Fouth Commandment, which states clearly that the weekly day of rest was introduced so that everyone—the slave, the servingmaid, the native resident, and the stranger—could refresh themselves after their labors.

This truth is proclaimed in the clearest possible fashion in many Torah verses stating that the worker must be paid promptly and that wages must be allocated justly.

"The wages of a laborer shall not remain with you until morning" (Leviticus 19:13).

"You shall not abuse a needy and destitute laborer, whether a fellow countryman or a resident alien, in your communities. You must pay him his wages on the same day, before the sun sets, for he is needy and urgently depends on it; or else he will cry to the Lord against you, and you will incur guilt" (Deuteronomy 24:14–15).

For all intents and purposes, the laws pertaining to the *shemittah* year—the sabbatical year, the seventh year when the land was to lie fallow and debts were remitted—abolished private ownership. The grain grown in a landowner's field had to be left for the poor (Exodus 23:11). The *shemittah* law even forbade the collection of debts (Deuteronomy 15:2). The jubilee year firmly implanted in the consciousness of landowners that their land was not their possession at all (Leviticus 25:23).

These and many other commandments recorded in our ancient Scriptures can serve as an example of progressive social legislation to our own day. The introduction of a just order in human society is the leitmotif of the entire Bible. No socialist expressed his rage or pain at seeing workers and farmers unjustly treated with greater fervor than the prophets. No one used sharper language. Isaiah rebuked the rich "who rob and grind the poor as though with millstones" (Isaiah 3:14–15). The prophet Micah hurled his bitter accusation against those who mercilessly exploited the forlorn man. The rich, he openly stated, are full of thievery (Micah 6:12). Ezekiel compared the avaricious to angry wolves who devour and spill blood (Ezekiel 23:27).

Upon Karl Marx's tombstone in London are engraved the words he had written in *The Thesis Concerning Feuerbach*: "Philosophers merely interpreted the world in the most diverse fashions: the problem is to change the world." With this phrase, characteristic of Marx and of his revolutionary zeal, the builder of socialism expressed his repugnance toward those who thresh empty hyperbole and do not actively enter into the struggle for a better tomorrow for mankind, especially when it involves personal sacrifice.

But in their daily and untiring struggle, the Jewish prophets indeed remained true to the message they brought to the people. Fearlessly, they jumped into the flames of the dissatisfaction they kindled, and strove earnestly to change society, man, system. Amos, the shepherd from Tekoa, was accused by the royal court of organizing a coup against the reigning order; he did not deny this accusation. With stirring courage he called: "Oh, you who satiate yourselves with the toil of the poor. Oh, you who exploit the forsaken man. Will not the earth shudder on account of your crimes?"

The story is told that Jeremiah (chap. 22) stood at the doorway of the king's palace in Jerusalem and warned the king and his ministers about the flagrant social wrongs they were committing: "Woe unto those who build magnificent palaces for themselves—but their foundation is injustice because they don't pay the worker his wages. They exploit their fellow man; their eyes and heart look only to gather up wealth; and they spill innocent blood while committing acts of robbery and murder."

Indeed, because of his daring stance Jeremiah was incarcerated. From Moses to Malachi, the last of the prophets, the Bible proclaimed this fearless and resolute demand to change the world. The central teaching of Malachi too is the concern for the reshaping of society, where the worker will no longer be abused, his rights will not be abrogated, and the values of man will be respected (Malachi 3:5).

If Ralph Waldo Emerson's contention that dissatisfaction is testimony to the authentic man is correct, then the prophets were those who showed the way to conscious, stirring dissatisfaction.

Karl Marx's enormous erudition still amazes us today. He must have read the Bible attentively and known all the details proclaimed by the Jews in connection with the call for a just society that flows from the Holy Scriptures. One can accept that Marx knew little of the Talmud or its content; but he surely studied the Bible in the German evangelical high school where he was educated.

Without a doubt he was well acquainted with the writings of

his predecessors, the dreamers of a utopian socialism, where verses of the Bible are quoted endlessly and where the vision of the Jewish prophets serves as the foundation for the ideal of the new man. Only recently did the French writer Ionesco state that it is impossible to comprehend Marx without the Bible. And Zalman Shazar, the late President of Israel, in an essay about Marx published in the 1920's in Yiddish, wrote that one would be thoroughly mistaken not to take into consideration the decisive influence which the zeal of the prophets against tyrants and their raging anger against injustice left in Marx's ideology.

Shazar believes that the age-old Jewish messianic ideal, the unquenchable longing for redemption, the steel-strong faith in the triumph of justice, resounds with a strong echo in the life and works of the father of the modern socialist movement; and from this Jewish awaiting of redemption, there comes a mysterious path to his source of dreams.

And yet—and once again we come face to face with an amazing oddity—despite the clearly conspicuous thread which leads from the ancient commandments in the Five Books of Moses to the ideal which stirred Marx's passion, not only did Karl Marx *not* recognize that the call for social justice developed and matured among Jews and Jewish teachings, but he also falsely portrayed Judaism and Jewish culture. Karl Marx painted the people from which he himself stemmed in black and repugnant colors.

II

The tendentious historians of Soviet Russia are no longer permitted to mention the Jewish ancestry of Karl Marx; nevertheless the fact is undeniable; the creator of modern socialism, as his close friend and co-worker in the world of socialist ideas, Frederick Engels, said: "was of pure Jewish blood." In fact he stemmed from fine Jewish lineage. In the family tree of his father, a lawyer named Hershl Halevi, appear famous rabbis and heads of yeshivas who were among the foremost representatives of Jewish spirituality in Padua, Mainz, and Cracow.

In the family of his mother, Henrietta Pressburg, there were also rabbis from Hungary and Holland.

The father of Hershl Halevi was a rabbi in Trier, in the Rhine region of Germany, where Karl Marx was born. Henrietta's father occupied the rabbinic post in Nijmegen, Holland. However, because of a Prussian anti-Semitic law that liquidated the liberal movement, which had penetrated Germany under the influence of the Napoleonic victories, and forbade Jews to be in the legal profession, Hershl Halevi could no longer practice as an attorney. As a result of this he converted to the Protestant faith and changed his name to Heinrich Marx. He also had his wife and children baptized. Karl Marx was then six years old. This was a conversion "out of convenience," according to the famous cynical remark of the apostate from Russia, Professor Daniel Chwolsohn. It was he who said of himself that he had converted to Christianity because he had persuaded himself that it was more comfortable to be a professor in the University of Petersburg than a Hebrew teacher in Aishishok.

Understandably, the apostasy of Hershl Halevi caused gloom among members of this fine and tradition-bound family. Hershl's brother too was a rabbi in Trier. From the beginning of the seventeenth century members of the Marx family had been spiritual leaders of the Jewish community.

Regrettably, one hundred and fifty years ago conversion was a popular phenomenon among German Jewry. Assimilation was enticing. The foundations of Judaism were crumbling. People were ready to pay any price for entry into German society. But the first price to pay was conversion to Christianity. Many talented sons of our people took this path of desertion. But there were those whose consciences tormented them after they had acquired the baptismal certificate.

In order to redeem himself in small measure from this transgression, Ludwig Börne entered into a passionate struggle for Jewish equality. Heinrich Heine bared the wounds of his regret and, by outbursts of confession in which he assured himself that despite all he remained in his soul faithful to the God of Israel, hoped to free himself of the burning reproach that robbed him of his tranquility. Heinrich Heine and Karl

Marx were close friends. In a letter that Heine wrote to Marx he accented the commonality of ideas that surfaces in their work. But they were at cross-purposes in their thinking concerning Jewry and Jewishness.

Even Karl Marx's occasional remarks show his disdain for Judaism. He had many prejudices toward the belief and life-style of his grandfathers. His repugnance is expressed often in his correspondence. In a letter to Engels describing his visit to Ramsgate in England, he states, "Ramsgate is full of Jews and flies." When he wants to poke fun at the path to socialism that Ferdinand Lassalle had chosen, Marx considers it important to add "the Jew, Lassalle," and to draw attention to the color of his hair and the shape of his head. Marx spoke sarcastically of the Jewish religion. He considered it a negative aspect that it had penetrated all corners of life and also embraced the physical needs of man.

This sort of monotheism, Marx declared, takes on a polytheistic character. In the articles he published in the *New York Daily Tribune* when he was its European correspondent, he never missed an opportunity to stress that the Jewish bankers, the Rothschilds, were the main stronghold of European reaction. Here and there one can find other negative remarks concerning Jews in his articles. But one searches in vain for a compassionate word about the Jewish masses in Eastern Europe who were then suffering from persecutions and edicts and lived in a state of poverty. At the beginning of the 1880's Jewish refugees streamed to England from Czarist Russia, victims of the wave of pogroms. Marx was then living in London. Many British Christians raised their voices in solidarity with the persecuted and tormented. But in the face of this Jewish tragedy Karl Marx did not react.

Even more shocking is Marx's essay on the Jewish question, published in 1844 in the German-French yearbooks he edited in Paris. I was shaken by this treatment when I read it years ago for the first time. But when I reread it recently after the terrible events our people suffered during the Nazi German horror, Marx's article grieved and depressed me.

Even assuming that Robert Payne exaggerates in his biogra-

phy of Marx when he writes that "Marx's solution for the
Jewish question is not much different than that of Adolph
Hitler, for both wanted to destroy Judaism"—still, I must
recognize that many arguments used in the German anti-
Jewish propaganda to "justify" the extermination of the Jewish
people are to be found in that essay by Karl Marx, entitled "On
the Jewish Question."

The thesis begins by asking if it is indeed necessary to free
the Jews from the state of injustice in which they find themselves, according to official theories. The essay was supposed
to be a polemic with the German theologian and historian
Bruno Bauer, who held that the one condition for equality was
conversion.

Marx opposed Bauer's position. For him the Jews were not a
religious grouping anyway. Religious values, according to
Marx, played no role and were never crucial in maintaining
Jewish existence. Jews survived pain and persecution not because they remained loyal to spiritual and moral principles, as
they themselves claim, but because of their active involvement
in commerce.

In any case, if we treat the theme of Jewish equality, attention should not be paid to the Jews' religious convictions but to
the Jews themselves: their character, their behavior, their
actions. The truth is, Karl Marx assures us, that in essence the
Jews have already achieved emancipation, and it is not worthwhile worrying about it. They won emancipation in their own
Jewish fashion. Of course, this refers to their material resources. Marx notes: "The illusory nationality of the Jew is the
nationality of a merchant and money man." Jews honor
money, wealth, possessions.

It is no wonder then, Marx declares, that in the nineteenth
century, the century of capitalistic commerce, Jews are the ones
who represent the capitalist class. Judaism is identical with
capitalism. Jews are the enemy of the new social order. They
oppose economic change.

"Not only in the Pentateuch and in the Talmud," Marx
writes, "but also in modern society we see the nature of the

Jew as it truly is. . . . What is the secular basis of Judaism? Practical needs, egoism. What is the worldly cult of the Jew? Underhanded dealings. Who is the Jew's secular god? Money. . . . Judaism has an anti-social foundation. . . . Money is the jealous god of Israel, and he doesn't let any other gods come near. . . . The true god of the Jew is the promissory note."

These arguments, which Marx considers so sound that he doesn't even bother to substantiate them, bring him to the conclusion that the most important thing is not the emancipation of Jews but the emancipation of Christians. The Jews' superstitious belief in money does not suffice them; they also cast their Jewish "belief" upon the Christians and upon European society. The "practical spirit of Judaism" has penetrated into the Christian world and appears everywhere as the practical spirit of the European peoples.

"The god of the Jews has become secularized and has developed into the god of the world," Marx accents. Because of Judaism money has become a world power. Jewish strivings and deeds determine the fate of nations. "The Jew has become intolerable," Marx cries out. The time has come for Christian society to free itself, in the name of social progress, from Jewish influence and from all its revelations. Only this will lead to the full emancipation from the era which must end with capitalism, a system which is no more than "practical, basic Judaism." Marx concludes with the words: "The social emancipation of the Jew is the emancipation of society from Judaism."

These few brief excerpts from Marx's essay bear testimony that he is speaking here not about a larger or smaller group of wealthy Jews whom perhaps he had encountered in his native city or other European towns where he lived. The subject here is not certain Jews who have accumulated wealth. Here Marx is discussing Jews in general, Judaism, the Jewish spirit.

Here Karl Marx is not merely speaking of nineteenth-century Jewish society; here he speaks of the Pentateuch, the Talmud.

Marx's essay "On the Jewish Question" states that the world must free itself of Jews and of Jewish influence. He contends that "the Jews have attained emancipation to the degree that the Christians have become Jews," and Christian society is summoned to fight this condition.

I do not know whether Nazi German propagandists indeed utilized Marx's essay as part of the anti-Jewish poison they concocted. But there is no doubt that Marx's position against Judaism helps Soviet Russia to "legalize" the anti-Semitic incitements occurring there. Marx places the stamp of "authority," so to speak, upon a hate movement which is definitely not in conformity with the socialistic ideal.

III

We have to deal with the painful phenomenon that Karl Marx hated the people from which he stemmed. He looked with disdain at the wellsprings from which he had drunk. He cast insulting, disparaging remarks against the culture which gave birth to the idea that encompasses all his works—that justice is the driving force in man's history. How can one explain this distorted interpretation of Jewish history and spirituality by the founder of modern socialism?

The virulent anti-Semitism of Marx's teachers and masters evidently played a bizarre role in his anti-Jewish manifestations. Of all the German philosophers who contributed to Marx's spiritual development, Hegel stands in the forefront. And Hegel was an anti-Semite. He entangled himself in strange theories which contradicted one another, and all of which were full of misunderstanding concerning Jewish values. Hegel remained blind to the merits of Judaism for the progress of humanity. He argued that the Jewish faith was a religion of enslavement. He said this even though Jews were the first to proclaim opposition to slavery, and even though the slaves struggling for freedom in many corners of the world were not inspired by Homer's poetry—the product of the Greek civilization that Hegel so greatly admired—but indeed by the verses of the Book of Leviticus.

Hegel considers the Bible a monument of passivity, even though each book is permeated with a fully positive attitude toward life, and each verse brims with turbulent activity. Hegel argued that Judaism did not contribute any idea which deserves to be called great and creative, despite the fact that human history would remain devoid of sense and significance without the extraordinary manifestation of Jewish creativity.

Hegel felt that Judaism is an institution of "dead dogmas," although the truth is that of all the civilizations born in antiquity it is the Jewish one that excels with its dynamism and its continuous history. In Hegel's eyes, even the biblical story of the *Akedah*, the Binding of Isaac, a moving drama of father and son that stands so sharply in contrast to the idol-worshipping cult of Molech, where children were sacrificed to the god, and that was recounted with the explicit purpose of stopping such barbaric rites and raising the worth of man and the sanctity of human life, was a sign of Abraham's severe character and his lack of fatherly sentiments.

Hegel condemned the Jewish people to decline, even though, despite his collected potpourri of misinformation, he should have known that he was not the first to offer such a "destructive" judgment, and that history (which was for him the court of last resort) had placed itself in opposition to this judgment.

The Danish philosopher Kierkegaard quite simply announced that Hegel did not know what he was blathering about. Marx considered Hegel the master of philosophic thought and seems to have taken his anti-Jewish doctrine out of the Hegelian school. A no less inimical evaluation of Judaism was given by the German thinker Ludwig Feuerbach, with whom Marx occasionally polemicized, but who influenced him greatly.

In Feuerbach's thought process, the Jewish faith is only a mirroring of general Jewish aspirations. Both the people and the faith are thoroughly egocentric. Neither possesses a spark of altruism, and both are "focused solely on self-interest."

The philosopher Fichte, who was the rector of the Berlin University at the time when Marx studied there, considered the Jews the guilty ones in the social and economic problems that had arisen within the capitalistic system. Fichte looked upon the Jews as a "negative mercantile power." He declared his opposition to giving Jews citizenship by saying that they were "a nation within a nation."

No little antagonism toward the Jews was felt in the radical circles in which Marx moved. In a narrow-minded and one-sided fashion, they exaggerated the role of Jews in the rise and development of capitalism. Of all the bankers, the finger was wagged at Rothschild. And Engels chimed in by proclaiming Rothschild "the King of the Jews."

Even in a short analysis of the reasons that led to Karl Marx's anti-Jewish outlook, it is impossible to avoid seeing that hand in hand with the great echo of Jewish ideals that emerges from his demand to build a just new society there are also profound differences. Marx took note of the distance that separated him from Jewish concepts. The idea structure erected by the creator of dialectical materialism lacks the ethical fervor that appears with such overwhelming force in the words of the prophets.

No stress is placed on the active effort that man himself must make in order to better himself—that effort which would prompt a new and just society. Marx's theory skips over the meaning and effect of moral aspirations. Economic conditions are crucial. When the economic structure is changed, says Marx, man too will change.

Judaism teaches that along with a concern for the material well-being of the poor and the oppressed comes the conviction that human behavior is ultimately dependent upon man himself and not upon the distribution of wealth.

Evil and injustice will not disappear only because private ownership has ceased to exist. The Jewish teachers forbade making superficial the problem of good and evil. They probed into the depths and warned that if someone strives to uproot oppression and wickedness he must begin with himself, listen to the voice of God in his conscience, and build in himself "a new heart and a new spirit." A new man will not be created by a changed economic system, but a new man will create a just social and economic order.

From the opposing concept of Karl Marx concerning man

and the economy there sprouts forth a great abundance of negative attitudes toward the people who in their culture, Torah and Talmud, developed entirely different principles from those which Marx expressed in his thesis of dialectical materialism. And if indeed it is true that Marx cannot be understood without the Bible, then it is no less correct that the great and mighty component of Marxist teaching is none other than the Bible.

But of all the reasons that could have led to Marx's hatred of Jews and Judaism, it seems that the most crucial is a tormenting inferiority complex because of his Jewish ancestry. Marx did not feel comfortable that he was born a Jew. He did not protest the lack of Jewish rights and did not react against those who humiliated the Jew and spread malevolent canards about them.

Marx began to consider the Jewish people inferior and was ashamed of his rabbinic grandfathers. With his publicly proclaimed anti-Jewish position, Marx wanted to cover up his Jewish ancestry and persuade himself and others that he had thoroughly freed himself of his Jewishness.

Assimilation is not only a social and cultural process. It is also a psychological one. It is responsible for the development of Jews, half-Jews, or converts with a split psyche who are tormented by their Jewish heritage and driven to base self-hatred. If those who have not let themselves be drawn into the net of assimilation are proud of their Jewishness even when cast into the abyss of suffering, then Jewishness is an insoluble problem for those whose happiness is measured by their acceptance into non-Jewish society.

Otto Weininger was an Austrian-Jewish philosopher, the author of *Sex and Character*, a work which sparkles with extraordinary wit and absurdity as well. At the beginning of the twentieth century he was oppressed by the burden of his Jewishness, which he considered unbearable, and committed suicide. For the German-Jewish intellectuals who were carried along in the stream of assimilation in the last one hundred and fifty years, Judaism was a tragic struggle. Frederick Julius Stahl appeared as the ideologue of the ultra-reactionary "Christian German State"—that is, of the theory that Germany, as indeed all of Europe, must assume a purely Christian character and forbid the Jews to live within its boundaries. Walter Rathenau attempted to justify his Jewishness with the explanation that a fusion of Jewish and German values was possible; and that if Judaism and the "Prussian character" could find common ground, then perhaps it was not such a terrible sin to be a Jew.

Alfred Doeblin was truly at loggerheads with Jewishness: first he drew near, then retreated, and finally cast himself into the arms of the Church. Franz Werfel sought to cover up his Jewishness with his pious enthusiasm for the Catholic saints.

Those of us who lived in Poland before the Second World War vividly remember the tone of cheap mockery which the poet Antoni Slonimsky, grandson of the scholar Chaim Zelig Slonimsky, used when writing about Jewish tradition and the Jewish way of life. Moreover, a leading Polish literary journal attacked Jewish spiritual values because by so doing its editor, M. Gridzevsky, sought to show that he was no longer connected with his Jewish roots.

So many Jewish intellectuals and writers are beset with an inferiority complex. They are dying to open the doors to gentile society for themselves; in their desire to be accepted as "equals" they make the comitragic assumption that they have been freed of "the Jewish remnants" or of "Jewish separatism." They spit on their own parents, they cast filth on the Jewish home, they change beautiful Jewish attributes for abominable traits, they vulgarly caricature the Jewish character, and they perform all kinds of acrobatic tricks to show how far removed they are from the Jewishness into which they were born. But what they really succeed in showing is that they have lost the feeling of self-respect and that Judaism has remained a difficult problem for them.

Marx's anti-Jewish position, his indifference to the Jewish fate, his superficial and malevolent treatment of the Jewish question—all of these testify that Jewishness was a difficult problem for him. His hostile attitude toward the people he came from was supposed to persuade everyone, and reassure himself too, that no shadow of "suspicion" should fall on him; that he was far removed from those "Halevis" with whom he associated in his childhood; that nothing bound him any longer to his grandfathers and uncles, the rabbis; and that he was on an equal footing with everyone else in European Christian circles; equal to Hegel, to Feuerbach, and to his father-in-law, the Prussian counselor, Ludwig von Westfalen.

Otto Rulle states in his biography of Karl Marx that Marx's remarks about the Jews seem to be an attempt to shout into the ears of the world: "Know that I, Karl Marx, am not a Jew!" But ironically enough, he convinced no one. He did not convince his friends. His associate, Frederick Engels, considered him "a Jew of the purest blood." He did not convince his opponents. The anarchist Bakunin assaulted him on account of his Jewishness and held that Marx acted in tandem with the Jewish people because that is the way Jews are: even when political divisions separate them, they are in fact united among themselves.

The ideologue of racial theory, Eugen Dühring, saw in Marx a typical representative of the Jewish race who wanted to pass himself off as one of the elect. In reactionary propaganda, Marxism is constantly labeled as a "product of the Jewish spirit," and many enemies of the Jews go out of their way to stress that the founder of the Marxist school of thought was "the Jew Karl Marx." He did not even convince his own children. His beloved daughter Eleanor even showed a warm interest in the Jewish community. She shared the joys and sorrows of Jewish workers in the East End of London and wanted to be considered a Jew.

The bitter irony lies in the fact that Karl Marx, who attempted to "change the world," as he himself expressed it, was not even successful in solving his own "Jewish problem." With all the genius of his intellect and all the zest of a revolutionary, Marx remained a psychologically split and bitter apostate, consumed by his Jewish inferiority complex.

15

Jewish Influences on West European Culture

IT IS COMMON KNOWLEDGE that the Greeks contributed to the shaping of Western culture. Moreover, academic circles also emphasize Roman contributions to the development of the civilization and culture of which we are a part.

But it must be established that not everyone takes note that Jewish culture also made an extraordinary contribution to the development and growth of our civilization and culture. The term "classic" was developed in connection with Greek and Latin culture. But rarely is the Hebraic culture referred to as part of this "classical" tradition. That is why I think that the time has finally come for a revision in our manner of thinking.

What is the meaning of "classic," and why do I stress that Hebraic culture too should be labeled "classic"?

The term *classicus* was first used to designate the highest and most important category of Roman citizenship, as created by King Servius Tullius. Later, people began to use "classic" in referring to the finest, most noteworthy, and most respected literary works.

With the passing of centuries, when people wanted to enhance the significance of Greek and Latin culture in the development of the Western World, they began using the word "classic" in connection with the two cultures. Naturally, we have no intention of denying that our aesthetic values are sourced in ancient Greece—from thence stems poetry, literature, art. Likewise, there is no gainsaying the fact that from ancient Rome stems our concept of law, our political institutions, and our organization of society.

However, isn't Jewish culture in the same niche, and isn't it on the same level—if not higher? Don't we in our Western civilization breathe the air that was brought over by Jewish thought?

The foundation of Jewish thought is the Bible. It was the Bible that presented mankind with the idea of a universal God, of a one and only God. The Bible stresses the protest against idolatry, deification of material goods, and human sacrifice. But I will not confine myself to the theological contribution of Jewish culture. Rather, I would prefer dealing with other Jewish contributions, no less extraordinary and no less current.

Everything that humanity possesses in reference to ethical achievement, social accomplishment, and political progress is a heritage of Jewish culture. The Ten Commandments, the foundation of our civilization, were given in Hebrew. The First Commandment begins with the proclamation of divine might in the universe, in mankind, and in history; but the laws deal principally with elements of human decency and ethicality. The Ten Commandments aspired to implant the divine in man and demand that even society should possess something of the divine influence.

It is not even sufficiently clear to us that everything we achieve or hope to achieve in society comes to us from the Bible and from Jewish thought. The love for fellow man, social justice, the rights of the poor and of workers, the protest against the inequitable distribution of wealth, the demand for agrarian reform—all these modern concepts, which sound so familiar in today's social terminology, have their roots in the Jewish ideational world. The Bible was the first code to be concerned with the welfare of the worker, his wages, and his legal status. It was the first code to oppose the exploitation of the needy.

Furthermore, for the first time in history Jewish culture stressed the dignity of man, the value of life, the value of the human being. Man is not a number, not a member of a mass, but a creation in and of himself, whose significance stems from the fact that he was created in the divine image.

In those far-off times, when rulers regarded themselves as privileged to impose only duties upon the oppressed masses, Jewish culture stated clearly and sharply that rulers too are duty bound. A thousand years before the common era, the prophet Samuel protested against the institution of monarchy—he disliked the very fact of having a king who would rule over the people. And five hundred years earlier, in the Book of Deuteronomy, when Moses speaks about monarchy, he adds the monumental phrase: "The heart of the king must not exalt with pride over his brethren."

This meant that the king should not consider himself higher than his subjects and fellow citizens. These words are apropos to our present era as well as to periods closer to the time of the giving of the Torah. When the Israelites wanted to anoint a king, Samuel exclaimed: "Why do you need a king? He will only want to take material goods for himself alone."

In all the pages of the Bible, our ancient monument of Jewish culture, we learn about teachers and leaders whose courage and truth-seeking surpassed man's normal capabilities. When the prophet Nathan learned that King David—a king beloved and honored by the people—had committed an enormous sin against one of his officers, Uriah, the husband of Bathsheba, Nathan appeared before David and sharply rebuked him. Nowadays no one would dare address an absolute ruler in such a manner.

"Thou art the man who has committed a great crime!" were the accusatory and bitter words of Nathan to the king.

Two centuries later, about eight hundred years before the common era, a king of Israel, Ahab, unjustly arrogated his neighbor's vineyard; then he concocted a false accusation against him, which led to the death of that innocent citizen. In the face of this heinous crime, Elijah the prophet comes before the king. In a burst of anger he cries out: "Shall you murder and also inherit? How dare you remain a king in the land of Israel?"

I am just offering a few examples to show that the desire to create a human society upon the foundations of justice and human equality—based upon the rights of the citizen—penetrated humanity not through the influence of Greek or Roman culture, but via Jewish thought. In biblical times, Jewish society already attempted to abolish slavery, the earth was proclaimed as the land of God, the citizen had the benefits of social legislation which is still a dream in the twentieth century. Jewish culture, said Thomas Huxley, is actually the constitution of the poor and of the workers.

Now to the basic concept of freedom. Where did the leaders of the American Revolution—and following them the leaders of the great French Revolution—get their enthusiasm to achieve the ideals of freedom? From whence came the slogans proclaimed on the banners raised in the American uprising, and later on the barricades in Paris?

Upon reading the chronicles of the American Revolution one frequently gets the impression that its pages are taken from the Bible. The fighters for American independence utilized biblical symbols. They compared their destiny to the destiny of the Jews who suffered in Egypt under the yoke of Pharaoh. They stressed that their determination to achieve freedom was forged in the chapters of the Bible. Heinrich Heine, the famous German-Jewish poet, declared that ever since the Exodus from Egypt, all of mankind, when struggling for democratic ideals, spoke with a Hebrew accent. For it is the Hebraic heritage which inspired men with the will and the hope to break the chains of oppression.

Of course, we must recognize that the ideals herewith mentioned—equality, justice, and human dignity—are also found in the teachings of Buddha, Confucius, and the Greek philosophers. But we dare not forget that the prophets Nathan, Elijah, and other masters of Jewish culture lived and worked hundreds of years prior to Buddha, Confucius, and the Greek thinkers who arrived at the same conclusions.

So now we ask the question: If the term "classic" is ascribed to those who first promulgated certain ideas, isn't Jewish culture more deserving of being labeled "classic" than Greek or Roman culture? Moreover, there is a big difference between Jewish culture and other ancient civilizations and their approach to the concept of the rights of man. In the ancient civilizations, theories were indeed formulated and ideas expressed. But the teachers of Judaism sacrificed their lives in order to realize their aspirations here on earth.

With rare exceptions the Greek philosophers were unable to awaken enthusiasm in their followers. They developed theories which bore fruit with the passing of time, but they kindled no flame of boundless devotion in the souls of men. The Jewish masters were not satisfied with mere words. They set themselves at the head of the masses. And they led the masses to the battle. The Jewish men of the spirit declared that an idea that remains in a book is not worthy of being considered a living idea. An idea is valuable when it goes beyond theory and assumes skin, flesh and bones.

Jewish culture excelled from the very beginning with its active, optimistic attitude toward life; with its belief in the progress of mankind; with its faith in the spiritual and moral ascendancy of man, and in his ability and strength to renew himself.

There is another important difference between the Greek and Roman civilizations and Jewish culture. The former made their contributions and then vanished from the pages of history. Jewish culture lives constantly. The words of prophets such as Nathan and Elijah, Amos and Isaiah, not only serve as a theme for research in universities—and they should, of course, serve as themes for historical scholarship—but they continually have disciples among the people from whence they sprang. The Jewish people, the people of the prophets, constantly extends the golden chain of the past. It attempts to weave together the vibrant present with the heritage of generations; it does so in the language of the Bible, the sacred tongue.

Jewish culture pulsates with vitality in the twentieth century. Isaiah's vision of freedom is not only in the Bible but is inscribed at the entrance to the United Nations building in New York. The wall of the institution that expresses the will of nations to live in peace is engraved with the verses of Isaiah that radiate the ideal of beating swords into plowshares.

How did Jewish ideas penetrate into Western European culture? How did Jewish concepts become a component of our civilization? The Bible was translated into Greek three hundred years before the common era by seventy Jewish scholars in Alexandria. The translation they made—later called the Septuagint—caused a deep spiritual upheaval in the Greek-speaking world of that time. Scholars of the Hellenistic era note the strong change in the literature written prior to and after the third century B.C.E.

A new spirit developed among Hellenistic thinkers; the world of the Bible was revealed to them, a new world of ethical ideals, social laws, and drama of God and man. The Septuagint was the first translation of the Bible. After the rise of Christianity, others followed in increasing numbers. The Latin Vulgate translation was accepted in the world of culture during the Middle Ages. Jewish ideas were translated into every language. In our time, the Bible has been translated into every language known by man.

Bible translations inculcated people with ideas, concepts, and hopes. Moreover, these translations taught people to write, to create verses and to transform words into poetry. There is not one literature in Europe that was not first—and profoundly— influenced by the Bible. The Hebrew Bible prompted the rise of Spanish literature; English literature grew out of the English translations of the Bible. The same thing happened with other literatures. In short: because of Bible translations Jewish ideas penetrated world culture.

But there were also other ways. The second point I want to accent is the cooperation that developed among Jewish thinkers and masters of Hellenism. Our studies of the ancient periods are still quite modest. Consequently, we still do not know precisely all the details about the great bridge which stood in that distant past between Judaism and Hellenism. It is a fact that during the first and second centuries B.C.E. an important center of Jewish thought was formed in Alexandria which utilized Greek as its linguistic instrument.

One thinker of the philosophic school of Alexandria should be mentioned: Philo. This Jewish thinker introduced Neoplatonic concepts into the idea world of the Christian teachers who came two or three hundred years later. In his important studies, Professor Harry Wolfson of Harvard University shows that an understanding of Philo's thought places the works of Augustine, Thomas Aquinas, and other masters and builders of the Christian philosophic system into clearer perspective.

The third path by which Jewish thought penetrated into Western European culture, Christianity, should also be mentioned. We know that the creators of the Christian religion were Jews. We know that Jesus, Paul, and Peter were Jews. Here it is not only a question of their ancestry. Here the fundamental question concerns their mentality, their doctrine, their outlook, which—despite all its deviations—was influenced by Judaism. They spread their doctrine at the very time when the Talmud was being formed in the Jewish world. And here we have to note the other classic monument of Jewish culture, the Talmud.

Hillel, who said that the Torah's entire essence is contained in the concept of human love, is the leading personality in that period of God-seeking and God-wrestling. The latest scrolls discovered by the shores of the Dead Sea show how deeply Jewish thought had influenced the first Christian sects.

The Essenes, a Jewish sect active about two thousand years ago, placed their stamp upon changing the usual Jewish way of life, an approach reflected in the newly formed groups. The Talmud served as the foundation for Christian legislation in the Middle Ages and for the Code of Justinian, upon which European law is based.

This is not the place for a delineation of details. I would just like to add that in order to recognize this classic culture one must become familiar with the source, with Hebrew. Non-Jewish intellectuals in all periods wanted to learn Hebrew and immerse themselves in the roots of human culture. All Christian humanists had this desire, including several famous figures of the Renaissance: Dante, Petrarch, Reuchlin, and Erasmus. The leading figures of Spanish culture, Luis de León, Lope de Vega, Arias Montano, all delved into the Hebraic roots. Lope de Vega, when speaking of the three languages that characterized the cultured person, cites Latin, Hebrew and Greek.

Every language has its soul, its character, Latin excels in majesty, in inner force; Greek, in its beauty and charm; Hebrew, in its plasticity, harmony, and expressiveness. Hebrew has another attribute which neither Latin nor Greek possesses. Hebrew has vitality.

Efforts have been made to revive ancient Greek, ancient Latin, Sanskrit, Gaelic. All these attempts failed. The only language used in ancient times which continues with renewed life and fresh strength in modern times and in modern civilization is Hebrew. The Hebrew language is the language of the revivified State of Israel.

With the course of generations, Jewish culture, which first made itself known in Hebrew, radiated out into other languages wherein Jewish poets and thinkers expressed their ideas. This fact helps to add more allure, more universal character, and more multifacetedness to Jewish culture.

In speaking of the Jewish influence on Western culture the monument of ancient periods hardly suffices. Those who deal with the Jewish contribution to human thought cannot omit the twelfth-century philosopher Maimonides, of whom Thomas Aquinas speaks with great admiration. Referring to him as Rabbi Moses, Aquinas stresses that it was Maimonides who taught him how to harmoniously resolve reason and divine revelation.

And speaking of modern culture, we cannot forget Baruch Spinoza, the father of the pantheistic theory of philosophy. We cannot skip over Henri Bergson, the French-Jewish thinker who developed the doctrine that the inextinguishable creative spark of intuition glows deep in man. We also cannot leave out

Martin Buber, from whom we learn the term "I and Thou," which points to the continuous dialogue of man with God, and of man with his fellow man.

Jewish culture is a chain that began with Moses, the teacher and fighter for justice, and which counts four thousands years of uninterrupted contributions to permanent thought. This cannot be said of either Greek or Latin culture. In Jewish culture there is continuity. The State of Israel was reborn on the soil where Abraham, Amos, and Isaiah lived and were active, the land of the prophets, which manifests its intervention in the course of modern history with great spiritual strength.

16

Simon Rawidowicz, Lonely Philosopher

I FIRST MET Dr. Simon Rawidowicz one wintry morning in 1941, at the beginning of World War II, in Leeds, an industrial city in England. At the time I was serving as rabbi of the Polish Army in Exile, which had been incorporated into the British armed forces. I had come to Leeds to visit the Jewish servicemen who were at bases in the area. Along with the services I arranged for the soldiers, I was also supposed to make contact with the rabbis in Leeds.

It was in the synagogue of the Chapelton district, where Rabbi Isaac Cohen officiated, that I chanced upon Dr. Simon Rawidowicz. He was then a professor at the University of Leeds and happened to come that morning to the Chapelton shul on an errand. I had already previously read some of Rawidowicz's works and I knew who he was. At our first meeting he impressed me with his friendly glance, his clever smile, and the love for his fellow man that emanated from him. I was also taken by his simple, touching modesty and by his morale-boosting warmth.

We immediately found a common language, buttressed by the fact that we both spoke Hebrew. Not only was Simon Rawidowicz's writing laden with thousands of quotations from

Torah and Torah learning, but so was his daily conversation. Rich with the poetic diction of the prophets, it also contained the vast linguistic treasures of the Mishnah and medieval Jewish philosophy. Yet his language was not labored and dense. It had the grace and charm of olden times which possess the magic and secret of eternal youth. The Hebrew of Dr. Rawidowicz that rang out that gray morning in Leeds reminded me of Nachum Sokolow's rich and wide-ranging Hebrew.

But this comparison was not entirely exact. Rawidowicz's language was not as entangled and muddled. It breathed freely. It rather reminded me of a symphony. As Dr. Rawidowicz spoke I heard Beethoven's Ninth Symphony. The same celestial melody, the same music which takes you by the hand and leads you to the heights; the same wave of joy that emanates from the sound itself; the same music which is continual ascent.

Our theme brought us closer together too. Dr. Rawidowicz came from the Polish town of Grayeve (Grajewo) in the Lomza district. During my childhood I studied in Shtzutzin (Szczuczyn), which is near Grayeve, the town where my grandfather, Reb Heschel Shapiro, and my uncle, Reb Yossele Kohn, served as rabbis. He knew Shtzutzin quite well and remembered Reb Heschel and Reb Yossele. He told me stories about Reb Yossele's saintliness that had become engraved in his memory. Above all, he told me, he was full of rapture and admiration at Reb Heschel's strength of character. When Reb Heschel was already quite ill, Dr. Rawidowicz said, during his last moments of consciousness before death, he was devotedly reviewing the laws of expiration; the laws pertaining to how a Jew must conduct himself when his soul is departing.

Rawidowicz's eyes sparkled with a secretive little fire when he told me this. For a while he was deeply immersed in thought, as though transported to that rabbinic courtroom in Shtzutzin where the dying rabbi, Reb Heschel, was studying the laws of how a Jew departs from the world. And when Rawidowicz returned from his flight of introspection he told me: "Don't say that your grandfather died. Jews like him lived even when they passed away; they live even after their death."

We enlarged the topic of our discussion to the war, Polish Jews, the East European cultural heritage, English Jewry. Strands of spiritual kinship formed between us. Throughout the course of the war years we frequently met during my visits to Leeds. Not only did Dr. Rawidowicz write passionately, but he also put temperament and soul into his learned oral discourses. And the question to which we would constantly return whenever we met was: Jewishness.

During the war Dr. Simon Rawidowicz issued a journal called *Mezuda* wherein he published his articles and essays. Financial support for this venture was provided by our common friend, Ben Zion Margoliot. He was a Polish Jew who had emigrated and settled in London, where he became very wealthy and contributed munificently to Jewish cultural causes.

Incidentally, it should be mentioned here that Ben Zion Margoliot was extraordinarily charitable, too, to the Yiddish writers and cultural figures who had been cast into London during the war years—among them the poet Itzik Manger. Dr. Rawidowicz would prepare his articles for the journal, and it was often my task to look over the manuscripts.

During this period he was developing the idea which he brought to fruition in his book *Babylonia and Jerusalem*. Its basic concept was that Judaism cannot be divided and parceled up into historical or even geographical fragments. Beside the many thousands of years of Jewish history, and despite the profuse Jewish geography, in essence there were no parts and distances in Judaism. Just as the God of Israel is One, so the people of Israel are one and Jewish culture is one. The leitmotiv of Jewish faith is one, and the leitmotiv of Jewish existence and Jewish culture is one.

It is true that Judaism has two faces: Babylonia and Jerusalem. Such is the face of Jewish culture throughout the course of history. For Rawidowicz, Jerusalem means the Land of Israel and all that was created in it: the Bible, the ideas and ideals that developed in the Land of Israel. In Rawidowicz's view, Babylonia is not just a piece of land by that name. He holds that Babylonia is Jewish creativity outside the borders of Palestine, or Eretz Yisrael: Jewish culture that developed in the Diaspora. In one of his essays, Rawidowicz states that Babylonia is every place outside of the Land of Israel where Jewish spirituality flourished.

Babylonia refers to the Babylonia of Ezra and Nehemiah, of Hillel and Rabbi Hiya. It is also the Babylonia of the Geonim, the great rabbinic sages of the Babylonian period. But Babylonia also includes the Alexandria of Philo; the Spain of Hasdai ibn Shaprut, Solomon ibn Gabirol, and Judah Halevi; the Africa of Rabbi Isaac Alfasi; the France and Germany of Rashi and the Tosafists, the post-Rashi generation of commentators of the Talmud; and the Germany of Moses Mendelssohn and Moses Hess. Babylonia means—the Poland of the Baal Shem Tov, the Lithuania of the Vilna Gaon and of the Haskalah.

Babylonia—in its broadest concept—existed historically before Jerusalem. The Torah was given to the Jews even before they entered the Land of Israel. It is true that Jerusalem was exalted with sanctity in Jewish tradition and that the Land of Israel is the Holy Land for the Jew. But the waters of the Jordan River also flow into the Rhine, the Thames, the Vistula, and the Hudson.

Babylonia and Jerusalem are the generations-long Jewish bond. This is also the Jewish path in the twentieth century and will continue to be our path throughout the coming ages. The two faces of Jewish culture are actually one face. But those who deny the characteristic and magnificent aspects of the Jewish path through history divest the Jewish people of that quality which transforms them into a nation beyond compare. Dr. Rawidowicz sharply disputed the theory of Ahad Ha'am about there being one Jewish center in the Land of Israel. The Diaspora too is a spiritual center. Babylonia too is a center of Jewish creativity. In the Diaspora too the Jewish people manifested their will to develop an original national life and to maintain Jewish singularity.

Simon Rawidowicz's ideas triggered virulent opposition in

some circles. In the heat of the polemic he was almost reputed
to be an anti-Zionist. Several times I found this lonesome
philosopher disappointed and embittered. He took stock of his
loneliness and knew that this was his fate. He would speak to
me about the courage that the teacher and the thinker displayed in all periods of Jewish history. And if courage is the
attribute in which every thinker must excel, then a Jewish
thinker must have this attribute in plenitude, Rawidowicz once
told me. Very rarely did the Jewish kings bow down before
philosophers, he added with mild irony.

I cannot think of one conversation with Rawidowicz that
didn't refer to Nachman Krochmal, the nineteenth-century
Jewish philosopher from Galicia. Simon Rawidowicz reissued
Krochmal's *A Guide to the Perplexed of Our Time,* appending a
precise and carefully thought out commentary to the book.
What brought Rawidowicz close to Nachman Krochmal was
the latter's firm belief in *Sar Ha-Uma,* the Guardian of the
Nation, the eternal folk-spirit which hovers over Judaism.

Simon Rawidowicz found himself fused into the circle of age-
old Jewish thought; and it seemed to me that he did not
consider Maimonides, Moses Mendelssohn, or Moses Hess
distant figures but personalities with whom he lived, breathed,
argued; personalities with whom he frequently agreed and
with whom he occasionally debated.

But Nachman Krochmal, it seems to me, never left him.
Once, I remember, as we were walking through the streets of
Leeds, Simon Rawidowicz was explaining one of Krochmal's
thoughts. Gesticulating, he attempted to explain Krochmal's
idea just as the Galician philosopher might have explained it to
his friends and pupils in the fields of Zhulkiev where he lived
more than one hundred years ago. At that moment I had the
impression that Rawidowicz and I were not strolling by ourselves in the streets of Leeds but that the author of *A Guide to
the Perplexed of Our Time* was accompanying us. When I mentioned this to Rawidowicz he replied: "I once told you that
great teachers live eternally. Believe me, Reb Nachman Krochmal is walking with us now."

Despite the disappointment occasionally visible in Simon

Rawidowicz's clever eyes, I always left him with my belief in the Jewish people and Jewish culture strengthened. He refuted every doubt about Jewish will and strength to survive the persecutions and difficulties. And one should remember that he maintained his firm belief even during the dark period of the Nazi German terror when the horrible news reached us in England about the destruction of our brothers and sisters in the gas chambers and torture chambers. "The destruction is enormous," he once told me, "but even more enormous is the Jewish will to live and the Jewish strength to continue the chain of creativity."

I must admit that I did not possess his iron-clad faith; I was depressed during those years when the Job-tidings concerning the destruction of the Jewish people in Poland reached us. I explained this to him too. But his faith did not waver. With wonderful mastery he opened up for me the vision of our people's history.

"Surely," he remarked, "we are a nation that has shed tears; indeed, there is much to bewail and bemoan. The destruction is awful, but no destruction, no matter how painful it may be, signifies the downfall of our people and our creativity. Even the first Jew, our forefather Abraham, trembled during a moment of fear when he thought he might be the last Jew, God forbid. Moses felt this horrible dread. The prophets were worried about the continued existence of Judaism. The sages of the Talmud, Maimonides, the great deciders of Jewish law, the kabbalists—all carried within themselves fear for the future of the Jewish people.

"Our modern writers are not free of this fear either," Rawidowicz continued. "The poet Judah Leib Gordon uttered the painful question which consumed him: Was he not perhaps the last person to sing of Zion? Standing at his old bookcase, the poet Chaim Nachman Bialik was overcome by bizarre thoughts that perhaps he was the 'last of the last' who were browsing through the old sacred texts. Brenner and Berditchevsky were overcome with a feeling of doubt and despair. Klatzkin saw only decline in the Diaspora. But not destruction, not apostasy, not assimilation can annihilate the Jewish people and Judaism. In Babylonia and Jerusalem there is continual beginning. Jewishness is constant ascent. Jewishness is permanent vigor. Jewishness is unceasing beginning."

During that period of pain and despair the words of Simon Rawidowicz rang in my heart with special force. And it reached a point that with the passing of time I went to Leeds not so much to fuifill my obligation as a chaplain but more to be warmed by the fire of Simon Rawidowicz's faith and be strengthened by his indestructible wonder-vision.

In 1955, when I was living in San José, Costa Rica, I received a letter from my friend Dr. Y. N. Steinberg. He preached ethical socialism and was one of the most gentle of the Jewish figures of our generation—Zalman Shazar, late President of Israel, termed him "the saint of the Russian Revolution." Dr. Y. N. Steinberg lived in New York, but he spent several weeks in Boston with Dr. Simon Rawidowicz, who was then professor of Judaic studies at Brandeis University. In a letter from Boston, Dr. Steinberg wrote that Simon Rawidowicz and he wanted me to spend the Intermediate Days of Passover in Boston so that we could be together at least for a few days.

For various reasons I could not undertake the journey. And I deeply regret the fact that I never again had the opportunity to meet our generation's remarkable and lonely Jewish thinker. Dr. Simon Rawidowicz died in 1957 at the age of sixty-three.

17

Zhirardov, a Jewish Shtetl in Central Poland

IT IS NOT EASY for me now to turn my thoughts back to the shtetl, the small town, where I was born and where I spent my childhood. Not only does the holy community, the Jewish shtetl, lie in ruins. Obliterated too is the lifestyle that developed along with the shtetl. And furthermore, gone is the special atmosphere characteristic of this destroyed Jewish center. Since those far-off childhood years, I have lived in different places and been active in spiritual and educational work in various Jewish communities; but in no place have I found the lifestyle and the aura that were representative of Jewish Zhirardov.

Zhirardov, a provincial town, can serve as a paradigm for all the annihilated Jewish shtetls in the part of Poland that was called Congress Poland. It possessed the singular traits of the Jewish provincial town in Poland in the 1920's and 1930's, the time period with which this memoir deals. Here one could have heard the whisper of generations. Here too one formed the impression that Jewishness had been inrooted in the shtetl since the six days of Creation, and that the most powerful windstorm would not have been able to eradicate the Jewish community. Here too one could have felt what was felt in other

252

provincial towns of that now-destroyed world: not only that
the Jew had been Jewish for generations, but that nature, the
landscape, the waters, and the trees were also Jewish, and
certainly that the streets and the houses were Jewish. Here too
one could have encountered the social differences that
emerged sharply in Jewish society; but here too, over all the
contrasts, there rose a mighty, invincible general consciousness. Here too one shared joy and pain, pleasure and sorrow.

But still Zhirardov was different. After the great destruction
that befell us, we are inclined to embrace with one common
tear the entire rich and colorful world which was laid waste.
We speak of the destroyed Jewish communities collectively as if
they were all of a piece, but the truth is that in Congress Poland
the Jewish shtetl had a completely different and special character. In Congress Poland the Jewish shtetl was a full world unto
itself.

These small towns were close to Warsaw and Lodz. And
these quiet provinces were inundated by the vigor of the
tumultuous metropolitan centers.

The Jews of Zhirardov cannot be portrayed in the same
fashion as the Jews who lived back in the hinterland of Poland—of them it cannot be said that they were cut off from real
life and had little contact, with real problems, that they webbed
themselves into the cobwebs of illusion, and were consumed
by passive impotence, and became wilted into helplessness.
The fresh breezes of its neighboring cities blew into Zhirardov.
People would often travel from here to Warsaw and Lodz.
People went on business and to work and visit relatives.
Salesmen would even travel every morning to Warsaw and
return home in the evening. The provincial way of life was
coupled with the restlessness, the activity, the movement of a
large city.

Moreover, Zhirardov was a factory town. Sources of livelihood were connected with the factory. The Jews of Zhirardov
were not strangled by the horrible economic want which so
many Jewish residents of many other towns had suffered. The
nearby turbulent centers on the outside and the smoking

chimneys of the factories within the town brought zest and energy into Jewish life and into the Jewish psyche, and opened windows to the world.

But proximity to the big centers and their ideas did not weaken the inner, spiritually Jewish, drama in the town. The hard reality of life did not stand in opposition to the great romantic Jewishness. And the sobriety that developed in contact with the harsh day-to-day life did not imperil the dreams of generations.

When I travel via thoughts to those half-misty years of childhood, I still sense the strong wind of the Jewish folksiness in the shtetl. In the long millennia of our dispersion, Jewish communities developed in various corners of the world. Nahardea and Pumbeditha are well-known towns of the Jewish past in Babylonia, but surely they were not the first provincial towns beyond the borders of the Land of Israel. There is no need to enumerate all the smaller and larger stopping points of our wanderings where a rich Jewish life flourished. Worms and Granada still shine forth with the impact they made on our spirit; and Liady and Radin have inscribed pages of creativity in our culture.

But no Jewish shtetl in our long past and in the all-embracing universal Jewish geography had the mighty, dramatic element that was apparent in the central Polish province. Toledo is perhaps the magnificent garden in our poetry. Mainz may have been the locus of Jewish learning. And in Mezhibuzh the sources of Jewish feeling could have welled up. Navaredok may have cut into our consciousness with its deep ethical struggle. But these communities as well as others lacked something which was unique to the shtetl in Congress Poland: a shimmering rainbow of diverse worlds and antithetical ideas, which nevertheless fused into the one solitary color of Jewish folksiness.

Zhirardov had no yeshiva. Generally speaking, its Jews did not excel in keen learning. Zhirardov was not a center of Jewish knowledge; neither did its Jews climb to the highest rungs of thought. The town had Misnagdim, Hasidim, and enlightened people, but Zhirardov was not a leading Misnagdic center or a prominent Hasidic one; and it was not a significant seat of the Haskalah.

It was characteristic, however, that here one did not have to make strenuous efforts to be a Jew. In essence, here one did not have to study to become Jewish. Here they had no fear of foreign influences. Jewishness was natural. As natural as nature itself. Like the course of the river. The sounds of the forest. The Jewish community could inhale the air from the outside and still not lose its Jewish life spirit. The youth could sing foreign melodies, but they were transformed into Jewish tunes and enhanced with a Jewish ideal. The border was actually erased between the modern books that were read in the newly established library and the ancient holy texts studied in the Hasidic shtiebl.

Deeply etched into my memory is the figure of one of the most eloquent representatives of the old generation in the shtetl, Reb Joseph, the son-in-law of the Zhirardov rabbi. (Later, Rabbi Menachem Mendel Albeck came to the town.) He was a teacher and a decider of law, a *dayan*, a man of profound integrity and piety. He was the embodiment of pure saintliness and moving, childlike innocence. He never worried about himself. He needed nothing for himself and his family. The great concern that throbbed in him was to uphold and preserve traditional Jewishness in the community.

During the hot summer days, he would stop us little Talmud Torah youngsters in the street and inspect us to see if, God forbid, we had been too lazy to put on the *tzizis*, the fringed garment. Obviously, sharp words were exchanged between Reb Joseph and the founders of the Zionist organization and the founders of the socialistic library. But in the new secular organization, Jewishness truly assumed a new form. Jewish content was also vibrating beneath the new look. And the revolutionaries too were busy laying bricks for the Jewish future.

No. It was not only a common fate that bound together the diverse sections of the shtetl's Jewish community.

Jewish values implanted throughout the generations and long-established life patterns watched over Jewish uniqueness like a synagogue's eternal light. A discussion I once took part in at the Zionist club in Zhirardov still resounds in my ears today like a distant echo. The subject, in which the leading maskilim participated, was Jewish faith. My father—may God revenge his martyr's death—participated that evening too.

My father gave voice to a thought (albeit in a popular vein) which later was a beam of light for me along the paths and byways of my spiritual wanderings. (This thought too was lucidly formulated in one of Chaim Greenberg's essays.) All our cultural achievements, he said, have found articulation in Jewish belief. Throughout history Jewish culture expressed itself principally in religious creativity. The dawn of our people, its historic ascent, its struggle and heroism, took on the form of a religious *Kiddush Hashem*. And tearing the religious page out of our history means leaving Jewish history naked and desolate.

The Jewish shtetl, which seemed to be part and parcel of the factory and counted its hours by the factory clock, gave the impression that in essence it lived quite removed from the factory. Frequently the Jewish masses seemed to move in a different sphere that hovered *above* the place and lived within its own time zone. The sirens of the factory were first heard at seven in the morning, but already at gray dawn businessmen and artisans were striding to the early morning service in the *beis medresh*.

In the territory of time, the shtetl celebrated its Sabbaths and holidays, its religious and national days of commemoration. In the territory of time these practical Jews constructed their hovering air towers of Yiddishkeit.

Jews then were a minority. But only from a statistical point of view. Spiritually and psychologically, these Jews, who were far from being idlers and were not alienated from the surrounding world, lived in a world where they were the majority; where the God of Israel is the God of the world, and where the Jewish Torah is the Torah of humanity.

During my childhood political sovereignty over the shtetl was passed from power to power. This happened during the First World War. Regimes changed as if in a delirium. The Russians left; the Germans came in, followed by the Poles. Even expulsion did not rob the Jews of the feeling of belonging to the shtetl and the consciousness of continuity. Nothing could deprive the Jews of the confidence that the edict was only temporary.

And in reality, as soon as circumstances changed, the people returned to their homely, close streets and courtyards, they built up the ruins, and Jewishness was spread again where no one had the power to drive it away. People adapted themselves to the changed circumstances and energetically sought new sources of livelihood. Their souls were not shaken. The dynamic events did not break their Jewish outlook and did not crack their faith. For everything is bound to crumble in a time of madness and chaos, of war and unrest, but not the feeling of Jewish eternality, which was immured in the Jews of the shtetl.

A young person in the shtetl was drawn into the struggle for existence quite early. Rarely did anyone go to study abroad. When quite young one began to help father at the store or at the workshop; one was apprenticed to a craftsman or began to do business and work independently. But the reality of life did not rob the youth of their ideals. Impelled to become mature and sober at an early age, the youth did not cease to nurture the tender belief in the possibility of reshaping the world under the kingship of God, the belief in a bright future that would come for man and Jew. They stood with both feet on the ground and yet raised themselves up to a higher reality.

I still see before me my pupils in the shtetl. I was eleven or twelve at the time and they were already grown youths absorbed in daily affairs. But they had the desire to study the prophets. Exhausted and overworked, they would come to me, shaking off the dust of the week, and thirstily drink in the teachings of Judaism.

In the many years that have passed since I left the shtetl, I have prayed in various places during the night of *Kol Nidrei;*

but I was never permeated with the holy shudder of great expectation as I was in that half-dark ecstatic Ger shtiebl in Zhirardov with its many wax-dripping candles that gaze down at me from a misty Yom Kippur of my childhood. In yellow prayer-shawls moist with tears, the worshippers stood bent over, while above them fluttered the Divine Presence, above them hovered the mystical proclamation that the day would come when rage would vanish, when wickedness and hatred would be wiped away, and the sins of those who had never stopped praying and hoping would be forgiven with mercy and lovingkindness.

The same trembling of deep expectation emanated from the *Hatikvah* anthem which was sung with pious ecstasy at the Zionist meetings in the shetetl. It was not a song; it was a search for expression, a gathering up of the collected national identity and fervor of one's ancestors. The same fervor of generations-long tension was felt at the socialistic gatherings in the shtetl, which were saturated with so much romanticism and filled with belief in freedom and in the coming betterment of mankind. No matter how far apart these camps stood, they were still unusually close to one another. They all dreamed the great Jewish dream.

In these diverse forms, the sons and daughters of the Jewish shtetl in central Poland—busy, overworked, deeply immersed in the practical world—repeated the call of the old prophet who had once stood in the holy city of Jerusalem: "For lo, the day shall come, the great and awesome day of God."

The character of the Jews in the shtetl was built upon the sharpest contrasts: furious activity and gentle dreams, hard realism and fantasy, stormy vigor and quiet hope, ardent vigilance for contemporary problems woven into the magic circle of yesterday and of tomorrow.

This could have taken place only because of the strength of the Jewish folksiness present in Zhirardov. The Jewish folksiness that pulsated in the shtetl contained within itself the pristine force of Genesis. It could thrust aside all the stones in its path and dislodge all obstacles. It was imbibed together with one's mother's milk. This was a Jewish folksiness which, it seems to me, had never appeared before in any other part of the world in our history with such a natural, overwhelming strength.

And, despite the deep contrasts that existed, it is in this magnificent, internal harmony in the people's character that we see the essential trait of Jewish Zhirardov, the Jewish shtetl in Congress Poland, which, alas, was destroyed in our generation.

18

My Father

MY FATHER AND TEACHER, Reb Zalman Klepfisz, was one of the most notable people in Jewish Zhirardov in the years before and after the First World War. He represented the transition from the old lifestyle to the new mode and ideas that slowly began to crystallize in town; and his rich, colorful personality affected the community's development.

My father was born in 1884, in Shtzutzin (Szczuczyn), in the Lomza district, where his maternal grandfather, Reb Heschel Shapiro, served as rabbi. Stemming from a noble familial lineage, Reb Zalman was a descendant of the famous Warsaw rabbi, Reb Samuel Zeinvil Klepfisz. From his earliest youth he displayed brilliance in learning, and after studying in the great yeshivas of Poland and Lithuania, he was ordained as a rabbi. He was also drawn to the Haskalah and secular education, and to the Love of Zion movement.

At the beginning of the twentieth century, my father moved to Zhirardov, for he had met and married a native girl, Bracha Friedman. My beloved mother came from one of the finest Hasidic families in town. Her grandfather Shmelke was one of the first Jewish residents of Zhirardov in the nineteenth century, and was therefore nicknamed "Adam" by the townspeople. My maternal grandfather, Hillel Friedman, a patriarchal figure in town, was a sugar merchant and a very important businessman. He was one of the builders of the community and the beloved prayer leader during the Days of Awe. His wife, Hannah, was known in the entire region for her open hand and good heart.

Immediately after his arrival in Zhirardov, the house of Reb Zalman Klepfisz became a center of Torah and Haskalah. Scholars would come to him to talk about holy texts. Hasidim from the shtiebl knew that no one could surpass his proficiency in the teachings and the mysteries of Hasidism. Young *maskilim*, the enlightened, would discuss with him the latest works of Hebrew and Yiddish literature. In addition to his expertise in all branches of Jewish knowledge and his extraordinary acumen was his rare talent as a conversationalist. His conversations excelled with great wisdom and sparkled with the brilliance of his thought. A wonderful synthesis of all streams of the Jewish spirit glowed in his soul.

The outbreak of the First World War and the expulsion of the Jews from Zhirardov broke the economic foundation of the Friedman family. Their sugar business was ruined. My father spent the years of homelessness in Warsaw with his family. After the defeat of the Russian army, when Jews were permitted to return to Zhirardov, my father began to build his life anew upon the ruins.

And here begins his blessed activity for the community.

First, he founded a Hebrew school. This was the first modern cheder in the history of Jewish Zhirardov. A divinely-graced pedagogue, thoroughly imbued with a sense of responsibility for the future of the people and with a deep love for Torah, my father threw himself heart and soul into educational work for the young generation. He understood that the old-fashioned cheders were no longer suitable for the young people in the modern era. New winds began to blow through the little towns. The old, established way of life had begun to crumble. And to prevent the generations-long structure of Jewish tradition from disintegrating, the youth had to be addressed in a new, readily understandable language and approached with modern methods.

Lacking sufficient financial resources, but believing strongly in the nobility of his idea, Reb Zalman took up the call of the hour.

Even the physical appearance of the school showed that this institution differed from all the other cheders in town. The furnishings were modern; in addition to blackboards on the wall there were desks and chairs. No longer did the students sit around long tables as in the old-fashioned Talmud Torahs.

Spiritually, the school was on a high level, and it could have been included among the exemplary Jewish educational institutions of that period. The subjects were prayers, Pentateuch, Rashi, and Talmud. But much attention was also given to Bible and the Hebrew language.

My father was one of the wonderful Jewish educators that Polish Jewry produced during the breakup period in its history. He developed the character of his pupils; he strengthened their Jewish consciousness and pride, and inculcated them with the spark of sacrifice, of *Kiddush Hashem*, a spark that glowed in them with so much ecstasy later during the Holocaust.

In addition to serving the Hebrew school, my father also offered evening courses for young adults, which attracted many young men and women and gave them the opportunity to learn Jewish history and the works of the Jewish spirit in Hebrew and in Yiddish. For Yiddish too, my father would say, has become sanctified with Jewish tears. At this school the students soaked up love for all aspects of Jewish culture. Spreading Torah learning was Reb Zalman's ideal. And his students' affection gave him great satisfaction and joy.

The Hebrew school, which educated hundreds of children, existed for nearly seven years. Many of those who studied with this great Jew and idealistic educator live today in various corners of the world. They doubtless carry in their hearts a feeling of gratitude to their teacher for enriching their inner life.

Naturally, my father had many devoted friends in town; he had a close friendship with the rabbi, Reb Menachem Mendel Albeck. He had followers and admirers in all circles of Jewish society—among the Talmud scholars, the intelligentsia, as well as among the artisans and workingmen, whom he attracted with his *ahavas yisroel,* love for all Jews, and his warmth for all human beings. Regrettably, however, my father was not understood or appreciated by everyone in the community. There were Jews of the older generation who looked askance at his activities and at his new directions in Jewish education. Looking back, his fate was like that of many great men of his generation. But this small-minded criticism did not deter him or diminish his activism. With courage and endless devotion he continually performed his great work for Torah and Jewish culture.

The Balfour Declaration and the increased efforts for the rebuilding of the Land of Israel gave new content to my father's life. Reb Zalman's heart, which anguished over every Jewish trouble, was encouraged by the great national hope. And in the souls of his students were surely engraved the lessons he taught about the mysterious love which the Jewish people have always felt for their holy land. He also lectured at open meetings and called for the most far-reaching help for the reconstruction of Eretz Yisrael.

Everything my father said came from the bottom of his heart. That is why his Torah reading was so impressive and unforgettable. Those who heard him reading the Book of Lamentations on Tisha B'Av always remembered his plaintive and stirring melody as he chanted about the destruction of the Holy Temple. And those who heard the melody he used when chanting the Song of Songs at Passover always recalled the joy of Jewry's magnificent past on its own soil.

My father published articles in the Hebrew and Yiddish press of Warsaw, in *Hatsefirah,* in the *Warsaw Tageblatt,* in *Moment,* and in other periodicals. In his articles he discussed various issues concerning Jewish life; they appeared under the pseudonyms S. Yitzchaki, S. Zalman, and other names. Great rabbinic authorities of the generation and famous writers exchanged letters with him. Among his admirers in the rabbinic world were Reb Shlomo David Kahana, Reb Chaim Leib Yudkovsky, Reb Moshe Soloveichik, and other great scholars.

Among his friends in writers circles were H. D. Nomberg, B.

Yeushzon, S. Pyetrushka, and many others. The Hebrew philologist Aaron Jacob Shapiro, author of the *Book of Grammar*,
would consult my father about philological problems; he sent
him his *Book of Grammar* in manuscript, requesting his opinion
of the work. In the leading circles of the Jewish spirit in Poland,
Reb Zalman Klepfisz was considered a man of comprehensive
erudition, with encyclopedic knowledge and a phenomenal
memory.

My mother, Bracha, an intelligent and sensitive woman,
helped her husband in his difficult, thorny path in life. Her
husband's educational activities brought her no great material
wealth. And with her quiet poise and the prayers she would
whisper on Sabbath night before Havdalah, my mother
brought a soft spirit and purity into the house, which was
always bustling with people.

In the 1920's, after the death of my father's father, Isaac
Mordecai, who had been a *shochet* (ritual slaughterer), Reb
Zalman and his family moved to Warsaw. There he assumed
his father's post of ritual slaughterer. Although his activity in
Zhirardov had ended, his spiritual influence remained there
for many years. Even much later the youth recalled his name
with longing and appreciation. And in various places even
today one can meet former students who express a feeling of
reverence for their great teacher.

My father and mother perished during the dark Nazi German years along with all the other holy martyrs. Martyred too
with them, in the bloom of their youth, were my sister Breyndl,
a gifted Beth Yakov teacher, a graduate of Cracow's Beth Yakov
seminary, and my brother, Rabbi Isaac Mordecai, a young
genius who had received rabbinic ordination at seventeen.
Both were born in Zhirardov. My brother took part in the
battles of the Warsaw Ghetto, and his radiant name is num-
bered among the holy martyrs and heroes who fell in Polish
Jewry's last tragic armed struggle. Earth, cover not their blood.

Besides the writer of these lines, the other of Reb Zalman's
children who has survived is his daughter Sara-Gitl, who lives
in Miami Beach with her husband, Joshua Yachsen. The Jerusa-

lem Talmud states: "It is not necessary to erect monuments for the righteous—their teachings are their memorial." The memorial for my father, Reb Zalman Klepfisz, is the Torah which he spread and the love for Jewish spirituality which he sowed in others' hearts.

His name deserves to be eternalized among the spiritual heroes that Polish Jewry brought forth on the eve of the Destruction.